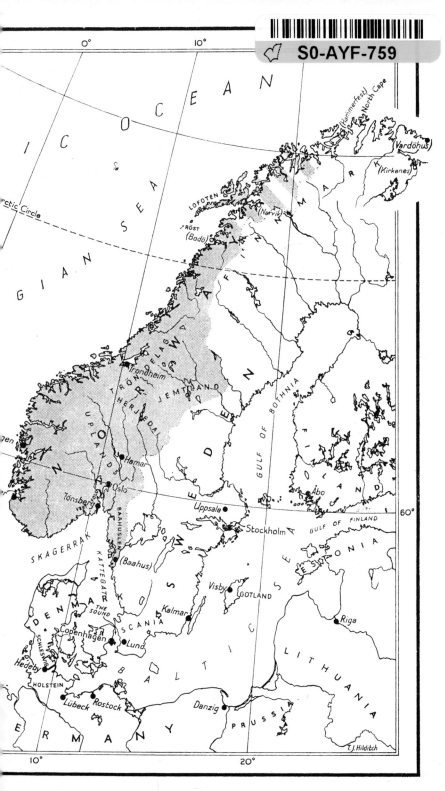

T. J. Hilditch

A SHORT HISTORY OF
NORWAY

A SHORT HISTORY
OF
NORWAY

by

T. K. DERRY

D.PHIL.(OXON)

GREENWOOD PRESS, PUBLISHERS
WESTPORT, CONNECTICUT

Library of Congress Cataloging in Publication Data

Derry, Thomas Kingston, 1905-
  A short history of Norway.

    Reprint of the ed. published by Allen & Unwin, London.
    Bibliography: p.
    Includes index.
    1. Norway--History. I. Title.
DL448.D4 1979   948.1   79-10688
ISBN 0-313-21467-0

First published in 1957
Second Impression 1960
Second Edition 1968

Reprinted with the permission of George Allen & Unwin Ltd.

Reprinted in 1979 by Greenwood Press, Inc.
51 Riverside Avenue, Westport, CT 06880

Printed in the United States of America

10 9 8 7 6 5 4 3 2 1

PREFACE

❀

WHEN Andreas Andersen Feldborg, a Dane who had resided much in London, put together from Danish sources in 1817 the first modern *History of Norway* to appear in English, he remarked in his preface, 'The history of few countries has undergone less deep research than that of Norway, arising from the difficulty of obtaining authentic materials'. The same complaint could not be made today. On the contrary, the foreigner is liable to find himself overwhelmed by the quantity of minute study which is embodied, for example, in the two standard multi-volume national histories or in the shorter and more recent *Norges Historie* by Andreas Holmsen and Magnus Jensen. But the task of presenting the story of Norway to English-speaking people as Norwegian scholars have revealed it has been left almost entirely to a succession of distinguished Norwegian-American writers, while British historians have concentrated upon particular periods, districts, or aspects, such as the civilization of the Vikings.

It is therefore hoped that a short survey of the whole course of Norwegian history may serve a useful purpose. For Norway has from of old had close ties with Britain, of which we ought to be aware, and there is a mounting interest in her contribution to the contemporary world — a contribution which is rooted in her past. The book accordingly lays emphasis on our mutual relations and on the more recent periods of history. The presumed interests of non-specialist British and American readers have also dictated the character of the bibliography, and are held to justify some departures from Norwegian practice in the spelling and use of proper names.

The author has been encouraged to embark upon the study of Norwegian historical literature by generous help from the

British-Norwegian North Sea Foundation 1953 and by the expert advice of the Office of Cultural Relations (Royal Norwegian Ministry of Foreign Affairs) and of the Oslo University Library. To the staff of these institutions, and to many other Norwegian friends and critics, he would like to express his most grateful thanks.

The second edition incorporates a number of corrections in points of detail, for which the author is indebted to a Norwegian correspondent. The story has also been continued very briefly to 1968, and a relatively full chronological summary of the most recent years is added for the convenience of students.

CONTENTS

❋

FREFACE   *page*

   I *Introductory: Land and People*   9

  II *The Viking Age*   22

 III *The Realm of St Olaf*   44

 IV *Decline and Fall*   68

  V *A Nation in Eclipse*   89

 VI *Revival*   109

VII *A New Norway*   130

VIII *Sentiment and Achievement (1844-64)*   151

 IX *The Democratic Programme (1864-89)*   173

  X *A New Monarchy*   194

 XI *The Impact of World Affairs, 1914-39*   216

XII *The War of 1940-45 and Some Consequences*   237

Chronological Table of Main Events   260

Bibliography of Modern Works in English   266

Maps: Norway in 1263, its Dependencies and Neighbours,
    Central and Southern Norway since 1660   on end-papers

INDEX   273

CHAPTER I

INTRODUCTORY: LAND AND PEOPLE

NORWAY strikes the most casual visitor as a land where nature still reigns supreme. This fact, which is the secret of its attraction for the tourist, is also the secret of its history. The country has an area larger than the British Isles, but since modern civilization began its population has always been at least ten times sparser. Moreover, at most periods of history even that sparsely settled population has had a harder struggle for existence than at any rate the English and the Lowland Scots—a poorer diet, inferior housing, fewer reserves to meet a period of drought or deluge. This is least true of the two periods we know best, that in which the Vikings explored and exploited and our own century, which has seen Norway transformed by the earnings of a huge merchant fleet and the development of hydro-electric power. But the Norwegian people of today still live in a country where man's foothold is precarious, since the fleet earns its money in all the seven seas and even the electric smelting industries are almost entirely dependent upon imported metals. They need look no further back than the Napoleonic wars for a period when Norwegians, forced to live almost entirely from their own resources, starved as the English have never done. In the west and north there are plenty of hillside farms and clusters of fishermen's cottages, still in use, where it takes the whole of a man's courage, ingenuity, and waking hours to win a livelihood from Norway's natural resources. It is against this background that we must see the political and social progress of the people.

Norway is a land of ancient mountains, shaped and scraped during the ice ages, when some of the soil in which it is now so sadly deficient was carried as far away as Britain. The summits are much lower than in the Alps, but the whole country is virtually a single high plateau, seamed by deep valleys, whose bottoms, when drowned in sea-water, constitute the famous fiords. Nearly four-fifths of the whole lies above the 500-foot contour line; on an average, Norway lies nearly twice as high as the rest of Europe. It is also the farthest outpost of Europe, and indeed of the civilized world, towards the north. One-third of the west coast is north of the Arctic Circle, and although this, the tourist's Land of the Midnight Sun, plays a relatively small part in the Norwegian economy, it is an important fact that even the southernmost point in Norway is well north of our own Highland Line, beyond which cultivation has always been found difficult and unrewarding. What soil there is in Norway is above average in fertility; but except at the edge of the fiord it is nearly always difficult of access, wooded, and bestrewn with huge boulders, which — in the days before bulldozers — had to be laboriously split by the application of fire and water and then manhandled to the edge of the clearing. It is not therefore surprising that the cultivated area is, even now, less than three per cent — about one-half of what is actually cultivable. Forests cover another quarter. The rest of Norway is a lofty wilderness, crossed by a few very expensive and skilfully engineered modern roads and railways and dotted with *seters* or mountain chalets to which from time immemorial the cattle have been brought up from neighbouring valleys to graze in sheltered spots during the brief summer season.

It was long supposed that a country so rich in mountains must be rich in minerals. But primitive man found a disappointingly small supply of flint and, at a later stage of development, was entirely dependent on such quantities of bronze as could be procured from its makers overseas. In the early iron age (as we shall see) Norway flourished on the manufacture of bog iron. But in modern times the superiority of the iron ore mined on the other side of the Scandinavian peninsula was one of the decisive advantages enjoyed by the Swedes. A fair quantity of copper and small and intermittent amounts of silver have been mined since the 17th century, and modern aircraft manufacture has given importance to Norwegian supplies of one or two rarer metals, such as molybdenite. Norway's only coalmines are in the Spitsbergen archipelago, of which she acquired the sovereignty after the first world war.

But what the land withholds is partly compensated by the sea. Ever since the first human beings established their lairs along the Norwegian coast, the harvest of the sea has made up for many deficiencies in the harvest of the land. From a very early period, too, the long fiords and the continuous coastal channels or Leads, which chains of islands and skerries protect from the risks of open sea navigation, have been used by men as a system of water communications which modern canal engineering could not hope to rival. But even more important is the influence of the sea upon the climate, for apart from this much of the country could never have been inhabited at all. The east of Norway, even in the latitude of Oslo, has such cold in winter that before the days of steamships the port was almost annually frozen up. To the west of the mountains, however, the genial influence of the Gulf Stream warms the entire coastal region. The fiords are not frost-bound in winter, even in the vicinity of the North Cape, and in Finnmark, which is the northernmost county, farmers developing new ground dig up the tools of Stone Age man. The most ancient—and artistically the finest—Norwegian rock-carvings are those in the far north, and there is some reason to think that the coast of Finnmark, facing the Arctic Ocean, was both habitable and inhabited during the last Ice Age.

The climate of course changes quickly as the traveller climbs out of the mild, wet, coastal strip into the mountains, which have their crests so near to the west coast that at least two-thirds of central and southern Norway shares the cold, dry, 'continental' climate of Oslo. This made it hard for man in the early days to penetrate inland, and still makes it virtually impossible to live all the year round on the highest ground, which includes more than 1,000 square miles of glacier. But once he was established, man found the frost and snow his ally for travel and transportation by ski and sledge; and the rivers, which flood in the spring but never run shallow (because of the snow and ice at their sources), provided the essential basis for the ancient timber-floating and for the modern hydro-electrical industry.

Topography and climate have combined to make Norway throughout its history a country of rather sharply defined regions. Towns have always been few and by English reckoning unimportant. Villages in our sense of the word hardly exist: the nearest equivalent is the *bygd*—a 'settled district'[1], which may have neither church nor shop and will certainly lack both publican and squire. In Norway the natural unit is the single farm, linked with other farms by its de-

[1] T. Gleditsch's translation (Olsen: *Farms and Fanes*, p. 98).

pendence upon the valley or the fiord, which in turn is most commonly thought of as part of a region or *land*. Thus the 'East Land' means essentially the half-dozen great valleys of the Uplands, the convergence of which lent prosperity to Oslo and the Oslofiord. It was the district of Vestfold on the west side of that fiord which nourished the first civilization, the earliest kings of all Norway, and the oldest of the existing towns.

Two other regions, however, joined in a long contest for supremacy: even today many of their inhabitants would strongly resent any imputation of provincialism in their way of life as compared with that lived in the environs of the modern capital. The 'West Land', from which the Norwegian Vikings mostly sailed, contains the longest and loveliest fiords, reaching as much as 100 miles inland; but neither the fiord sides nor the steep valleys at their heads provide as good agricultural or forest land as the east. The poverty of the hinterland, however, was in marked contrast to the wealth of Bergen, for centuries the largest town in northern Europe. Stavanger and some smaller fishing ports also to some extent relieve the picture of austerity, physical and spiritual, commonly associated with the life of the west. The Tröndelag, on the other hand, though a west coast region and farther north, has the larger farms and more fertile land characteristic of the east of the country. Trondheim, though it did not provide the first king, provided the first capital of Norway; the Trondheimsfiord bound the region securely together; and there was an additional source of wealth in direct trade through the valleys eastwards into Sweden.

North Norway and the 'South Land' have, at most periods of history, played a much smaller part. The former begins with the county of Nordland (i.e. North Land), which adjoins the Tröndelag on the north but was cut off from it—until the trunk road and the railway were built quite recently—by a 40-mile break in the Leads. For Norway at this point becomes closely hemmed in between the sea and the Swedish frontier, a narrowness which continues up to the approaches of the Arctic Ocean. There the counties of Troms and Finnmark have been constituted in modern times from the vast frontier district at the extremity of the original 'North Land'. Finnmark by itself is as big as Denmark, and together the three counties make up rather more than a third of Norway's total area: but the struggle for existence in this region, lying mainly beyond the Arctic Circle, has always been terribly severe. Before the completion of the railway linking the Swedish ironfield to Narvik in 1902 and the discovery of the native iron ore resources near Kirkenes in the following year, North Norway's one considerable industry was fishing—chiefly the seasonal cod fishery of the Lofoten Islands. Inland the Lapps and their reindeer roamed the Finnmark plateau, as they had done from time immemorial, passing freely to and fro over frontiers which it hardly seemed worth while to define.[1]

'South Land', on the other hand, is a name invented by a modern poet for a chain of idyllic small towns and their immediate hinterland, stretching along the south coast on the indefinite frontier between east and west. It is sufficiently distinct to have its own speech characteristics; but the golden age, in which this stood out as the richest and busiest part of the country, is long past. Its most important centre nowadays is the garrison town of Kristiansand, while Arendal, which once had the largest fleet of sailing-ships in Norway, and a host of other little ports lie dreaming of the wealth that came and departed with their timber trade.

It is perhaps ten thousand years since the first men entered Norway. There is some reason to think that, unlike most later migrants, they came from the north-east, into Finnmark, and (as we have already seen) their arrival may have occurred before the end of the last Ice Age. As land and sea became more productive, the easy passage up the Leads attracted an increasing population of fishers and hunters and harvesters of wild berries, who lived on all the produce which bountiful nature placed within their reach. They kept close to the coastline, where piles of refuse—fifty kinds of animal bones have been counted on one spot—show their catholic tastes, and impressionistic drawings of animals their artistic skill and, probably, the magic which was supposed to help the chase. Flint for axeheads being scarce in Norway, these early inhabitants made great use of implements of carefully fashioned bone. But gradually we may trace the influx into Norway of better techniques for working stone, and while the huge battle axes were brought in (and no doubt used) by a

---

[1] In early days, 'Finnmark', meaning thereby the Lapp country, was thought of as stretching to the Kola peninsula at the entrance of the White Sea (*Norges historie fremstillet for det norske folk*, 6 vols., 11 parts, Oslo, 1909-17, Vol. I, Part 2, pp. 142-3).

tribe of newcomers from east-central Europe, the native product is shown by experiment to have been capable of felling trees. But, though the domestication of animals was now common, the first beginnings of agriculture consisted of mere spading-up of chance open spaces. Throughout the millennia of the Stone Ages new ideas made their way slowly from south to north, through trade, through casual adventure and accident, or through migration of peoples. It is significant that their crowning glory, the megalithic tomb, is found in Norway only scantily and at the extreme south-eastern verge.

Towards the end of the period when only stone was used—perhaps about 2,000 years before the birth of Christ—the tribes entering Norway could have been identified as speakers of a distinctive Nordic language, the branch of the Teutonic language group from which modern Swedish, Danish, and Norwegian are all derived. It would be wrong, however, to picture this as a single, precise event: some tribes came into the country well after the beginning of the Christian era. It would be still more wrong to picture it as the coming into the land which has been their unchallenged possession ever since of a single, well-defined racial type. The Nordic stock was probably already a mixed one before it began to make its way into Norway from the south (across Denmark and Sweden), from the east (into Tröndelag), and by the natural passage up the west coast through the Leads. Moreover, the last of these routes was in use by other tribes of immigrants, who contributed a strain of darker, shorter people, who still give the west coast population in many places an appearance quite different from the Nordic blonde. Nevertheless, it is a striking fact that the very tall, very fair, blue-eyed Norwegian of today was already the predominant type on the other side of the North Sea at a time when the Celts were tentatively establishing the first and least important of the four main layers in our own island population.

It is almost a misnomer to speak of a Bronze Age in Norway, a country which lacked the necessary metals and was therefore still fashioning its implements mainly of stone throughout the millenium when bronze was characteristic of the rich civilization of the Mediterranean and central Europe. But the amber trade brought bronze to Denmark, whence it penetrated in small quantities into Norway, both as finished articles and as raw material, which the Norwegians cast for themselves in soapstone moulds. Works of rare beauty were produced which, taken together with the many symbolic rock-tracings of ship-men and sun-worshippers, enable the imagination to reconstruct some fragments of the life of men long dead. Norway at this time enjoyed a better climate than she has ever known since: from the whole of southern and central Norway what we think of as the eternal ice and snow had disappeared, the trees grew a thousand feet higher up the mountains, and the dry, warm ,valleys invited mankind to forsake the hunter's life on the coast for that of the more civilized settler inland. Consequently, in that part of the people which seized the favourable opportunity for the first serious attempt to subdue the wild we have the first real link with modern Norway. Agriculture was developed in new areas with the help of the horse, which had not yet lost its protective winter coat of white. Its growth was accompanied by a flourishing overseas trade, not only to the south but westwards to the British Isles. But it is the massive stone tombs, the labour they represent, and the richness of their contents which chiefly indicate the nature of society at this era—there was evidently a class of leaders at the apex of the settler community, regarded probably as both priest and god, and serving the purpose of an aristocracy in cherishing each new cultural impulse from abroad. But the old life of the Stone Age hunter continued side by side with all that was new. In the far north, indeed, there are practically no traces of bronze, and it may have been in these centuries that the Lapps established themselves there, with a way of life which is still akin to that of the primitive hunter and as remote as their race from the agriculture increasingly practised by 'Nordic' man.

The last centuries before Christ were for Norway a period of regression. The rise of classical civilization, it is true, brought the country for the first time within the orbit of written records, when Pytheas of Marseilles about the year 300 BC made his way across via the Scottish islands to 'Thule' and the midnight sun. But there was little to record. A deterioration of the climate checked the hopeful progress in agriculture, as it became necessary to keep the flocks under cover in winter (as it still is) and the long-lying snow restricted tillage. The old legend of a 'fog winter' probably represents a dim racial memory of this time; but it needs no more than some additional cold and rain in summer to cause a disastrous alteration in the treeline—the pine requires three extra-warm summers in succession to become established, a combination which *normally* occurs only once in a hundred years! At the same time the advance of the Celts into central and western Europe blocked the trade routes of the past and, as the Celts had little interest in the north, their proficiency in the use of iron did not spread to Norway. Even when the Celts were subdued by the rising power of Rome, and Roman trade reaching far beyond the Rhine frontier brought iron and textiles and cheap pottery to south Norway in considerable profusion, what Norway received from Rome was not at first comparable with the civilization which she imprinted upon her own subject provinces.

But from the second century of the Christian era Norway began slowly to develop the formidable strength which she revealed to the world in the age of the Vikings. The Roman influence was partly cultural. The imitation of imports led to the creation of beautiful native work in pottery and metals. The runic alphabet was received, probably from some Germanic people more closely affected by Rome; but Norwegians, as they laboriously cut the first magic inscriptions in runes, no doubt felt that they were invoking a power of which Rome had long possessed the secret. But Rome's greatest gift lay in the fact that the iron tools and weapons from Roman and Romanized sources encouraged the Norwegians to advance from the making-up of imported raw iron to the exploitation of the bog iron which could be had for the digging in many of the inland valleys. That profusion of iron was later to present obvious temptations. In the meantime it helped the labour of clearing the country, as the frontier of settlement moved inland up the valleys, generation after generation. It was not a job which could be quickly completed; in the far north there are whole valleys where cultivation began as late as the 18th century. But the impetus of this period gave Norway the necessary minimum basis of food production and settled life.

The age of the great migration of peoples, in which the Roman Empire disappeared from the west, caused fewer convulsions in Norway than in lands farther south. The west coast tribes used the bigger and better boats, which the iron axe had now enabled them to build, to develop trade with the Frisians at the mouth of the Rhine and with our own ancestors, newly arrived in England. This was also the period of the settlement of two new tribes dislodged from Germany upon the west coast, the Ryger and Horder, and by about 550 the whole of that region was sufficiently stabilized for its tribes to be enumerated in the correct geographical order by the far-off

Cassiodorus, the first historian of the Goths[1]. Other new settlers came in from the east to the wooded valleys of eastern Norway near the modern Swedish frontier, remote from the sea and therefore previously almost unoccupied. Finally, the mustering of the tribes which inhabit Norway to this day and have made the whole of its recorded history was completed by the immigration of the Trönders into Tröndelag. When and how they came we do not know. But the 12th-century *Historia Norvegiae* says that Tröndelag was populated by a movement from Sweden, which geography makes likely and the attitude of the Trönders in later periods confirms.

Up to this time development in Norway had been purely local and regional. The unit which mattered most was the large farm — large, that is, in the area of land which its first settler took for his tilth and meadow, rough grazing and timber-cutting, with rights of hunting and summer pasture more vaguely defined on the mountain above. A cluster of wooden barns and store-houses, then, as now, surrounded the dwelling-house. The great problem was that of warmth in the long winter, so the byre was usually built on to one end of the living-room, which was of course windowless, with its door-opening on the south side and a hole in the roof to emit the smoke from the central hearth. The life lived on such a farm, which might contain three generations of the same family, was patriarchal and self-sufficient. It was directed by a single effective head, the eldest man in full vigour, and passed without division to his heir, but it was thought of as a property in which the whole family shared an interest. Not only did the farm provide food, clothing, and shelter, but wood carving and coloured embroidery gave scope for the arts, and piety found expression in acts of devotion to the divine beings who haunted its lands and governed the mysterious succession of the seasons. A considerable proportion of the oldest farms were centres of a formal religious worship, in which the landholder figured as high priest. Such is the origin of the *bonde*, the peasant owner of a substantial odal freehold, who has been regarded as the representative Norwegian, even in periods when his numbers have been smaller than patriots care to admit. It is clear that from the earliest times, wherever (as in the west) there was a scarcity of usable land, smaller and less dignified freeholds must have come into existence,

[1] *De Rebus Geticis*, as summarized by Jordanes.

B

as also a class of people who paid by work for parcels of land rented from a peasant owner.

Conglomerations of farms grew into the petty states, which were being organized in Norway at about the time of the great migrations, through the operation of at least three forces. Man is a political animal, as Aristotle had long ago pointed out; he has social instincts, which cause him to unite with his fellows; and in the idea of greater worship of a greater god we find a definite reason for union, which in historical times helped to bring into existence a kind of fellowship among the at one time wholly independent Norwegian settlers in Iceland. The second force is that of human depravity. Norway produced a whole class of so-called 'naze kings', lords of a single headland who played the tyrant over ships and people. The third and probably most powerful force was the desire for mutual insurance of property against raiders and invaders. The object being the maintenance of peace, which in all ages requires a definition of aggression, this leads on to a system of law-making—or at least to agreement about what has been 'law from time immemorial'—and to some system for judging disputes.

There is some evidence that small kingdoms with councils and sanctuaries existed in the districts of early settlement just north of Oslo soon after the beginning of the Christian era. But the Trönders provide the first example of an elaborate combination of small states, based no doubt upon a close racial connection as well as upon the exceptionally good water communications of the long Trondheimsfiord. *Fylke*, which is our word 'folk' and the modern Norwegian term for a county, was the name given to each of eight small districts, having a chieftain (who was also a high priest), a place of sacrifice, and an assembly of independent peasants known as a *ting*. The four districts on the northern, and the four on the southern, arm of the fiord maintained their separate principal temples at Maere and Lade, where the worship of Odin, the god of war and wisdom, was significantly combined with that of Frey, the Swedish god of fruitfulness. All eight were further combined in the Öreting, an assembly which met at a convenient river-mouth, where the city of Trondheim now stands, as a legislative and judicial body for the whole area. This ancient close relationship between heathen rites and political unity may help to explain the obduracy with which the Trönders were later to resist the introduction of Christianity. But it was from Vestfold on the west side of the Oslofiord—in modern times the home of the Norwegian whaling fleet, but owing its earlier prosperity largely to the proximity of Denmark—that a line of kings exiled from Sweden set out to achieve the unity of Norway.

Nevertheless, it is already possible to see the interplay of the three factors which run through Norwegian history and create much of its interest—the local, the national, and the international. For, although we are now approaching the end of what might be called the period of local development, local interests have never ceased to sway the fortunes of the country. An example has just been given of the independence of the Trönders; it is scarcely more marked than the diff rence of outlook which separates the well-to-do peasant of the rich eastern valley from his struggling counterpart in the bleaker west. The towns, too, have always had a particularized outlook, whether it be Trondheim and Bergen struggling for control of northern fisheries, or Oslo and Bergen opposed in national politics, or smaller centres competing bitterly in the parliament for steamer routes and railways. Local loyalties are even carried overseas, so that the Norwegian-American finds himself tied most strongly to the old country by a club which keeps fresh the contact with his own or his father's original neighbourhood. This concentration of interest upon local affairs was a cause as well as an effect of the long period of Danish ascendancy. In recent years, too, it lies at the root of the language controversies which have often distracted attention from urgent national needs.

At the point which we have reached in this survey, however, it would be an anachronism to speak of a national feeling about Norway. The name itself, meaning 'the way to the north', came into existence before strong kings established any unity of the peoples who followed that way through the Leads; and, as we shall see, the fact of unity in turn preceded the creation of a true national feeling about that unity. But it is already possible to forsee some of the forms which national sentiment in Norway must eventually take— the bond of seamanship and the sense of dependence upon the sea; a tradition of self-reliance, adaptability, and hardihood that resulted from living in the least tillable land in Europe; the pride of autochthonous possession of a land which, if poor, continued to be handed down from father to son for fifty generations. The culture which had so far been developed was a very small thing by comparison with the

classical glories of warmer climes, and no one could have guessed at
the distinction of the shortly coming age of the sagas, which the
Norwegian national anthem envisages as still 'sending its visions
over our earth'. But for modern Norway it is an article of faith that
a nation lives by virtue of the continuity of its history, and that a
small nation can only rival the great powers by the greatness of its
culture. Therefore the pious skill of the archaeologist and the place-
name expert has been exerted to the full to give these small beginnings a significant share in a nationalist reconstruction of the
precious past.

The international or foreign relation shows itself more clearly.
The people who came to inhabit Norway are largely identical with
the mixture of races, predominantly Nordic, which populated
Sweden and most of Denmark; up to the period of their history
which we have so far reached, their language was the same. New
materials, new techniques, new art forms entered Norway from
Denmark or Sweden. More rarely as yet, they came eastwards from
overseas: only in the imagination of ultra-nationalist Norwegian historians of the 19th century did a 'pure Nordic' culture move down-
wards from the far north of Norway along its coast into less
favoured lands. Uppsala in Sweden was the chief centre of religion,
Hedeby (the modern town of Schleswig) the chief centre of trade,
and the most important area in Norway was Vestfold, where Danish
and Swedish influences met. Norway had the smallest economic resources and, in all probability, by far the smallest population of the
three; but everywhere except in the extreme south-east she enjoyed
the protection of a strong natural frontier of desolate mountains or
the sea. Norway was perhaps unlikely to be swallowed up by her
more powerful neighbours, but down to the 20th century there were
few periods of her history when the possibility was altogether remote. The attitude towards Sweden and Denmark from the very
dawn of nationality was fated to be compounded of contrary
elements — sympathy, because they were blood-relations, neighbours, and easily understood as regards speech and culture; an-
tipathy, because for either of them Norway was the natural object
of an expansionist policy.

To redress the balance, Norway must herself expand — overseas.
Trade had been conducted across the southern parts of the North Sea
for centuries, and there is a tradition that Norwegian ships by the

year 600 had even made the perilous voyage round the North Cape in search of the furs of the White Sea hinterland. It is quite possible that the first scattered colonization of the Shetland Isles, which seems to have been but thinly peopled before, may be not much later in date. If so, it was an unrecorded and probably peaceful process, very different from the uproar that filled Europe from the time of Charles the Great to that of Canute the Great—two centuries which culminate in the short-lived Danish North Sea empire. Norway's great age of expansion was thus part of a wider movement, in which the three Scandinavian peoples, actuated by simultaneous impulses, made their first and greatest impact on the outside world.

CHAPTER II

THE VIKING AGE

THE record of the Viking raids on England, which fills many pages of the Anglo-Saxon Chronicle, opens with a reference to men from three ships of the Horder, who landed at Portland in Dorset and killed the royal reeve. This was in the reign of Beorhtric, king of Wessex from 786 to 802. An apparently isolated outrage, it is not the true beginning of the movement, even if it preceded—a fact which we cannot determine—the first of the attacks upon the Celtic monasteries, located in pious seclusion on islands and lonely headlands of the North and Irish Seas. Discovered perhaps by accident, they were a prey to whet the barbarian appetite—rich, religious, accessible, and defenceless. Thus Lindisfarne, the holy island of St Aidan and St Cuthbert, and Iona, the home of St Columba and burial-place of Christian kings, were sacked in 793 and 802, not without stabbings and drownings of monks and nuns. 'On June 8,' writes the Chronicle, 'Heathen men cruelly destroyed God's church on Lindisfarne with plunder and manslaughter': a gravestone is still to be seen on the island which displays on one side the Cross, the Hand of God, and two religious kneeling at their prayers, and on the other side the Northmen swinging their great war-axes for the attack.

But, in any attempt to trace the activities of the Norwegian Vikings or sea-rovers, it is important to bear in mind that their voyages, which most commonly followed a course somewhat north of the latitude of the Scottish mainland, were part of a movement in which the Danes also went out, chiefly by the southern part of the North Sea and the English Channel, and the Swedes traced a river route from the Baltic to the Black Sea and the Caspian. This fact partly explains their overwhelming success, since Christendom was exposed to simultaneous attack from so many quarters. It also complicates the story, for England, France, and Ireland were all ravaged by both Norwegian and Danish Vikings, operating in alliance or in rivalry or in a mixed force under leaders from either country. Monastic chroniclers were naturally more interested in describing the overpowering numbers and devastating cruelties of these heathen peoples, whom they regarded as a scourge sent from God for the punishment of sin, than in distinguishing between the almost unknown lands overseas from which the successive expeditions had emerged.

Our records are also misleading in another way. They give a picture of three main stages in the Viking assault on a country—the first casual coastal raids lead on to a later penetration inland, ship-borne up the big rivers and horse-borne over the shocked country-side; and this in turn leads to the dreadful year when the native chronicler tells for the first time of the Northmen having wintered in their midst, the prelude to systematic conquest and exploitation. In reality it was a much more opportunistic affair than this suggests, in which one of the biggest factors was the mobility of the single ship's crew, able almost at a moment's notice to give or withdraw support as it pleased. Cruelty and the spirit of aggression were only one part of the Viking stock-in-trade. He settled, as we shall see, in many lands which required no conquering because they were virtually without inhabitants. In others, his primary interest was the establishment of markets where he could buy and sell. In western Europe the Vikings figured as mighty conquerors, and left a great imprint on the history of many states, chiefly because the opposition to their first sporadic efforts was weak and divided, which lured them on. Constantinople, on the other hand, though six times attacked, was never captured, so that in the history of the Eastern Empire the part the Vikings played was that of mercenaries, the Varangians of the Imperial Guard. And if we look still farther east, it was only as traders that they ever attempted to lay their hands on the fairy-tale wealth of the strong Caliphs of Baghdad.

Norway at the dawn of the Viking age lay far behind Anglo-Saxon England in some important aspects of civilized life. It was untouched as yet by the Christian religion. At the major sanctuaries great feasts of horse flesh, accompanied sometimes by human sacrifice, were held on fixed dates in autumn, at mid-winter, and on April 14—at the outset of the campaigning season. But the worship of such gods as Odin and Thor the thunderer was increasingly enriched by the stories forming the Asa mythology. These led men on from thoughts of Valhalla and the Valkyries bearing thither the spirits of the brave to profounder speculations about Creation and human destiny and a whole world order doomed to perish at Ragnarok, when the wolf slays Odin in the twilight of the gods. Norway had no written literature, however, for all the magic runes which survive could be printed on a single half-page, though we know that poetry was being composed and that there was a numerous class of skalds or bards, who sang the warriors' praises in an intricate verseform, with plentiful allusions to the popular religious myths. It was also a country completely lacking in town life, where trade was conducted at seasonal markets which sprang to life during the sailing months or when snow and ice made transport possible down through the mountains. In comparison with the England of the Heptarchy Norway was slow, too, in its approach towards political unification, having perhaps as many as thirty different states, if we count those chieftains who exacted tolls from shipping round a single headland.

But the mention of ships is a reminder that in some of the arts of practical life the Norwegians must have lain ahead of the Anglo-Saxon and other contemporary peoples: mere ferocity by itself could never have enabled them to proceed so rapidly from tip-and-run raids to the exploitation of wide territories. They were remarkably skilful, as we have already noticed, in iron-working, which the difficulties of transport encouraged them to develop in every district and even in every farm where a supply of bog-iron could be located. Thus in the matter of iron equipment it is claimed that a quite small and poor Norwegian farm would compare favourably with the position as shown by inventory on a large Frankish manor in the centralized empire of Charlemagne. The comparison is borne out by the quality and quantity of the iron weapons—axe and sword and spear —commonly found in Norwegian graves from this period. In particular, they contain the well-made axeheads, which—long before their cruel use on tonsured skulls—had shaped the timbers for those ventures overseas which became at last both practicable and urgently necessary. It was their skill with the axe and familiarity with timber-working which had enabled the Norwegians by about AD 600 to set a deep keel and an efficient side-rudder in a clinker-built craft of oak, as much as 50 feet in length and about 9 feet wide amidships. There they hoisted the square striped sail of which all Europe was soon to live in dread, and stood prepared to test the practical qualities of their ships by the first voluntary open-sea voyages ever undertaken, so far as we know, by western races.

As for urgent necessity, it must be admitted that the chronicles of the period shed very little light on the causation of what they obviously regarded as a mass movement, when for example 'The ocean poured torrents of foreigners over Erin'. But the wealth of the south had been familiar to the Norwegians long before the break-up of the Roman Empire; and up to the time of their conquest by Charlemagne the Frisians are known to have carried on a trade in superior weapons, glass, and textiles from the Continent as far north as the Tröndelag. One type of Viking expedition therefore seems easily explicable in terms, not of necessity but of greed. Their actual timing may possibly be related to some special *élan vital* in the spirit of the age; but it is at least equally plausible to suppose that the first few casual forays resulted from the tempting isolation and defencelessness of the Celtic monasteries, or when a ship was blown off course and its crew made a more or less innocent landing in search of necessary food. The news of these chance successes would spread fast, the start of a plunder-rush not very different in atmosphere from a 19th-century gold rush. At a later stage, when plunder would be becoming harder to unearth, the weakness of their enemies gave them a further incentive, because it proved feasible to exact the payments of 'protection money' which we dignify by the name of Danegeld. It is hard to say which suggests the more abject picture of misery—the Irish bronzes, lovingly executed by pious hands for church use or as ornaments of bookcases, of which more are now to be found in Norwegian Viking graves than in the whole of Ireland; or the hoards of English coins from the reign of Ethelred the Unready, scattered as far afield as Russia to show how widely the prospect of getting something for nothing made its appeal. But there was of course no compelling need behind the demand for riches and luxury; they ministered to a love of finery and ornament which the envious foreigner already described as a national weakness. There was, no doubt, a certain stimulus to native handicrafts. But the main effect was to generate rivalry among chieftains, and quarrels over the spoil led to the phenomenon of Viking raids in reverse, which (as we shall see) tended to frustrate the work of the nascent Norwegian monarchy.

But there were also necessary voyages, which native historians do not hesitate to compare in character and importance with the emigration from their country to the American Middle West a millenium later. The iron axe felled the woods, built the farmsteads, and helped to make a wide variety of wooden structures and implements, ranging from hay-lofts to split fences, from hand-ploughs (the Celtic *caschrom*) to irrigation troughs, on which Norwegian agriculture depended — and still to some extent depends. The inroads it made into the wild can be fairly accurately ascertained by the study of farm names, which shows the 6th and 7th centuries to have been a period of rapid clearance and growth in population and prosperity. Indeed, the evidence of the graves suggests that there was even an increase in average height — to the discomfiture of our own ancestors, when they were confronted with the Viking shield-wall. But towards the close of the 8th century the development of the land reached a stage at which west Norway — the narrow fiord valleys pent in by high mountains and opening on to a bleak and barren coastline — had nothing more to offer. Prosperity, and perhaps some hypothetical improvement of climate, had bred a generation of men resolute enough to experiment. In leaving west Norway, they had four ways to choose from. Some went eastwards over the mountain passes or northwards up the coast, to look for new homes among their own people in districts where there might still be possible farming land to reward the pioneer. Others turned south along the old Frisian trade routes, to compete with Vikings from Denmark. But those who made history were the men who went to the west. They led a movement overseas which eventually reached such dimensions that the least profitable of the old West Norway farms were left deserted.

The first stage was the easy move to the Shetlands, where the power of the Picts, who had once built the famous and today still formidable *brochs*, was by this time in decay. We do not know what population the newcomers found in the islands or what became of it, but their territory now developed instead a small fishing and pastoral community completely Norwegian in character. Much the same is true of the Faeroes or 'sheep islands' farther north in the Atlantic, though in their case the greater distance from the mother-country gave greater independence to the leading families and the local council or *ting*. Even easier than the journey onward to the Faeroes was that to the Orkneys, where the Norwegians again found a Pictish power in decline and effectively replaced it by their own. The Orkneys, like the Shetlands, were islands whose inhabitants depended on the use of boats for their living, yet they possessed no supply of timber. This made a very precarious basis on which to build up a community which in both cases amounted to some 20,000 souls: nevertheless, the Orkneys came to form a semi-independent state, which for several centuries played a distinctive part in Norwegian history.

Orkney was a corn-growing region, valuable in itself and well situated for an advance to the Scottish mainland, to the Hebrides, or to Ireland. It would make a natural appeal to an ambitious chieftain, anxious to establish his own local maritime ascendancy or 'pirate's nest'. It is therefore likely that the earls of Orkney had made themselves masters of the peasant settlers in the islands for a generation or so before the first king of Norway, in the course of a punitive expedition to these western waters, officially conferred the earldom in his capacity as overlord. In any case, the earls of Orkney sprang from an illustrious family of west Norway chieftains which, according to Norwegian sources, also contained Rolf the Ganger, who founded the dukedom of Normandy. Before the end of the 9th century they had crossed the Pentland (i.e. Pictland) Firth and seized Caithness, where the severed head of a Pictish leader, dangled in triumph from his saddle-bow, killed one earl by a posthumous graze with a poisoned tooth. This kind of warfare, full of macabre incident, continued with varying fortune, and at one time the earls held Sutherland (the 'southern land') as well as Caithness and controlled the Scottish coast as far as Dingwall, seat of a *ting*. But the *Orkneyinga Saga*, which told the story of this dynasty of predatory princes as they still lived on in 13th-century tradition, has little space to spare for the affairs of ordinary men. Yet two of the saga episodes are revealing.[1] One of these explains that an earl who died about the year 940 acquired the nickname of 'Turf' Einar because he introduced from the Scottish mainland the practice—meaning perhaps an improved method—of cutting peat for fuel. Before this, life in winter in these wind-swept, treeless islands, when they had no regular means of heating their hovels of earth and stone, must have

[1] *Orkneyinga Saga*, Chapters VII and VIII.

been hard indeed! The other story concerns the odal rights of the freeholders, which they surrendered to this same Einar when he paid a collective fine imposed by the Norwegian Crown, but which were received back as a glorious gift from one of his successors. This confirms the view that the earldom was in fact imposed upon an original community of free settlers, who carried their ancestral rights with them from their earlier homes in Norway.

The second stage in Norwegian expansion is the attempt, which for a time came very near to being successful, to convert the whole Irish Sea from a Celtic to a Norwegian lake. In the Hebrides, as on the islands lying closer to west Norway, there had been some quiet unrecorded settlement made before the historic period of Norse predominance in these waters opened with a raid on Skye in 795, followed by four desecrations of Iona. Colonization in the Hebrides then attracted the attention of some famous chieftains from Norway, but so far as we can tell it took the form of a peaceful sharing of the soil with the existing Celtic population. The culture continued to be mainly Celtic; but the Norwegians introduced their own political forms, and supremacy over the islands was disputed between the Orkney earls and the kings of Man. Man was important for its strategic position rather than as a place of settlement, and it was only the northern half of the island which was actually colonized by the Norwegians. But for several centuries they were the undisputed rulers of the whole, and at the present day the House of Keys, the Deemsters, and the Tynwald (where new laws are proclaimed with solemn ceremonial each midsummer) survive to show the kind of institutions of self-government they brought with them a thousand years ago. On the other hand, the evidence of sculptured stones, for which Man is also famous among archaeologists, shows that the religion of the Vikings had a much smaller capacity for survival on new soil. Emblems of the heathen Valhalla are to be seen inscribed upon the Cross, marking the transition to the worship of the 'White Christ'; and the heathen mode of burial appears to have fallen into desuetude within two generations of settlement among Christian neighbours.

But in the proud heyday of paganism it was the descent on Ireland — 'the southward trek most renowned' — which had most to offer. The spoliation of the Celtic Church there, which had been the light of western christendom in the darkest of the Dark Ages, is perhaps the saddest and grimmest part of the whole Viking story. But the soft, low-lying Irish countryside, accessible from the sea in every quarter, with harbours on which it was easy to base further expeditions for conquest or commerce in lands beyond, appealed also as a place of settlement. After the raids had persisted for a generation the raiders started to winter in Ireland, and about the year 839 Torgils, a chieftain of royal blood, began a systematic conquest. He founded Dublin and took possession of the ecclesiastical capital, Armagh, where he installed himself as abbot. By the time he fell into the hands of the Celtic High King, who duly had him drowned, the whole island was becoming the prey of the 'white strangers' and their rivals, the 'black strangers' or Danes, while mysterious forces of 'foreign Irish' (renegade Christians and persons of mixed race) intervened for or against the High King as booty offered. The newly arrived Danes made a temporary alliance with the Irish·against the Norwegians, to which fact we owe the unusually clear distinction between the two Viking peoples in the Irish chronicles and some objective pictures of their savagery, more satisfying to the historical judgment than many pages of conventional monkish lamentations.

> After the battle [of Carlingford] messengers from Maelsechlainn, the High King of Ireland, came to the Danes. They found the army encamped on the very battlefield, engaged in cooking their meat. The cauldrons were placed on top of heaps of fallen Norwegians, with spits stuck in among the bodies, and the fires burning them so that their bellies burst, revealing the welter of meat and pork eaten the night before. The messengers reproached them with such conduct, but they answered that their enemies would have wished to do the same to them.[1]

The central figure in a confused and brutal struggle was a Norwegian chieftain, who may perhaps be identified as Olaf the White, a descendant of the ancient kings of Vestfold. His arrival in 853, when he established a Norwegian kingdom based on Dublin, looks indeed like the continuation of an enterprise which had been planned in Norway and interrupted by the overthrow of Torgils. Olaf went back home finally in 871, but he left a dynasty which maintained its position in the numerous wars of the following thirty years. How many settlers came to Ireland in this period is unknown.

[1] H. Shetelig: *Viking Antiquities*, Part 1, p. 53.

The quantity of Irish relics to be found in graves in Norway from all parts of the 9th century shows that there was much intercourse of one kind or another. But the chief evidence that this intercourse was related to large-scale settlement lies in the commercial stamp which Dublin and other seaports never afterwards lost. When the Norwegian king and army were expelled in 901, enough Norwegian residents—perhaps a christianized element—were left behind to make a rapid reconquest possible two decades later.

Olaf the White had clearly envisaged the use that could be made of the lordship of the Irish Sea. Before his time the impact of the Viking raids on its eastern shores had been comparatively slight. Devon and Somerset had been harried to some extent from Ireland, but with no lasting consequences. In Wales there was a lodgment at points on the coast, where the development of trading ports cannot have been unwelcome, but attempts at inland settlement met with a strong resistance. Farther north, indeed, the Viking ascendancy at sea had a consolidating effect on land, for the separation of the Scots from their kinsmen in Ireland was one cause of the union between Picts and Scots, whereby the kingdom of Scotland was founded in 844. But Olaf fought three campaigns in Scotland, by which the situation was transformed. In alliance with the Norwegian chieftains of the isles, he almost eliminated the nascent kingdom from the control of its own west coast. The British kingdom of Strathclyde, between the Clyde and the Lune, fared even worse. Olaf occupied its capital, Dumbarton; a mixed population of so-called 'Viking-Scots' became established in Galloway; and what we call the English Lake District was opened to penetration. When the Viking army was expelled from Dublin in 901, the last-named area, which bears so much resemblance to their homeland, became an important place of Norwegian settlement. Moreover, the fact that Olaf staked out big claims from the west at the very time when the Danes, advancing up the east side of England, set up their kingdom of York (867) prepared the way for a Norwegian attempt to oust the Danes from the control of Northumbria, which was a cardinal feature of Norwegian Viking policy in the following century.

From Ireland the Norwegians also made their way south into the Mediterranean, on joint expeditions with Danish Vikings. The story may be true that they sacked Pisa and Luna, delightedly supposing the latter city to be Rome. Certainly they visited the coasts of the

Moorish kingdom in the Peninsula as well as its Christian neighbours, with the result that a Moorish embassy to Ireland made the
only reconnaissance of a heathen Viking court on record from this
period. The poet who headed it was much attracted by the beauty
and free manners of the Viking queen, but apparently failed to obtain the release of the prisoners that had been carried off, who remained as 'the blue men in Erin'. An easier advance from their Irish
bases brought the Norwegians into the valleys of Seine and Somme
and Loire, which resulted in their participation with the Danes in
that most momentous of Viking enterprises, the foundation of Normandy. But if we judge, not from a European but from a Norwegian
point of view, there remains another work of settlement, begun in
this same crowded period, which had a much closer influence upon
Norwegian fortunes. This was the discovery and colonization of Iceland by Norwegians from the homeland and from the existing settlements overseas.

Iceland, like the Faeroes, had previously been the sanctuary of a
few Irish monks, intrepid sailors who nevertheless left both countries
when the solitude they sought was seen to be liable to invasion by
what they regarded as mere bands of heathen robbers. It was discovered by Viking voyagers driven off course, and settlement began
about 874, with a leader who cast into the sea the wooden pillars of
his ancestral 'high seat', carved with the figures of the gods. Where
they floated ashore and were found next year, he made his new
home, which became the eventual capital. In the course of the next
two pioneering generations the immigrant population reached a
total of about 20,000 souls. Most of them came from Norway, which
according to Icelandic tradition harboured just at this time a
numerous class of adventurous malcontents, eager to escape from
the firm hand of a newly-established central monarchy. Others came
in organized expeditions from Ireland or the smaller islands, like
Aud the Deepminded, a Christian chieftainess from the Hebrides,
who may have been one of Olaf the White's widows and who certainly travelled north in fitting dignity via the Faeroes, where she
paused to arrange a suitable match for an accompanying grand-
daughter. These expeditions were not purely Norwegian, for there
would be wives and numerous slaves of Irish and Scottish stock, and
it is suggested that the infusion of Celtic blood influenced the flower-
ing of the Icelandic saga—Njal, for instance, is a Celtic name. The

details are better known than those of any earlier oversea settlement in history, having been carefully recorded early in the 12th century, while even before then the Icelanders had a seriously maintained oral tradition of how they came into possession of their several estates. But we must confine our attention to the effects on Norway.

How far it was a specially unruly element which departed to Iceland it would obviously be hard to tell. But it is clear that some western districts were so seriously depleted of their population that a special tax had to be imposed on would-be emigrants, and the west coast region as a whole lost a part of its previous importance. Conversely, it was in many ways an advantage to Norway, long after the spectacular conquests of the Viking Age had faded into the past, that she retained a peculiarly close relationship to one state of her creation overseas. Independent Iceland was always closely tied to Norway by trade needs, and Icelanders were allowed to keep their citizenship rights in the home country. The establishment of their famous parliament, the *Alting*, in 930 was preceded by a three-year enquiry into the legal system maintained by the different Norwegian *tings*. But what in the long run mattered most to Norway — and to the world — was the fact that the isolation and austerity of Icelandic life proved strangely favourable to the growth of a literature in the old Norse language which the settlers took with them. In the so-called *Poetic Edda* they assembled the poems, written in some cases as far afield as Greenland but for the most part probably in Norway itself, to which we owe our best knowledge of Viking religion and earlier tradition. These include the *Voluspaa*, with its haunting vision of Ragnarok — 'time of axes, swords, and splintered shields, time of the wind and the wolf, ere the world dissolve, and no man spares his fellow'[1] — and the promise of a new world to come, and the contrasting *Havamal*, which expresses the proverbial and often prosaic wisdom of Odin. But it was in their native sagas that the Icelanders developed one of the most remarkable art forms in human experience; and some of these prose epics, though not as it happens the very greatest of them, repaid the debt to Norway by the immortality they conferred upon its early kings, who first rose to power in this many-sided Viking age.

The earliest written account of Norway from any Norwegian

[1] *Voluspaa*, stanza 45.

source dates from about the year 890, when a trader from the far north of the country came by design or accident—it is impossible to say which—to the court of Alfred the Great. The king had good personal reasons for an interest in anything to do with the Vikings, who since his wars with Guthrum the Dane had held all England east and north of the Watling Street. He therefore included whatever Ohthere could tell him in his Anglo-Saxon version of world history, based on the Latin work of Orosius. It is perhaps unfortunate that Ohthere lived, as he said, 'the farthest north of all Norwegians in the north part of the country by the western sea', and was a practical man with no apparent interest in history or political institutions. What he does describe from personal experience is the life of a chieftain in about the latitude of modern Tromsö, having his own herd of 600 reindeer, a few other cattle and horses, a little plough land, and an extensive trade in walrus tusks and hide and in the skins and down which came to him as tribute from the Lapps. He had made a Viking voyage of his own round the North Cape and eastwards as far as the White Sea. As for the rest of Norway, he is aware of its general shape, of the vast expanse of mountains, and of the restriction of the cultivated area to the neighbourhood of the coast. He had seen it all from the sea— a month's sail to the south, given following winds and allowing for rest on land at night. This would bring him round the Naze and along the south coast to the harbour of Skiringsal, which was within a few days' travel of the port of Hedeby 'which belongs to the Danes'. Ohthere shows some knowledge also of a land of the Swedes and even of the Finns, but he has not a word to say about the growth of a kingdom of Norway, though Skiringsal lay in Vestfold, where that growth began.

The saga traditions describe the establishment there, on the west side of the Oslofiord, of a line of kings descended from the Swedish family of the Ynglings, who had once held sway at Uppsala in primitive and mysterious grandeur. It is a little like tracing a connection with king Arthur of the Round Table; so we may be content to notice that the saga gives details of five generations of kings who ruled in Vestfold during a period of perhaps one and a half centuries preceding the reign of Harald Fairhair, the first king of all Norway. It would be impossible to guess from the saga accounts of their greatness that these kings were for the most part satellites of Danish rulers. All the same they were great, as the manner of their burial shows. The

C

Oseberg and Gokstad ships, rediscovered a thousand years after the entombments, are not Viking 'longships', designed for the business of war, but graceful vessels of a lighter type, which their thirty-two oarsmen once propelled in stately progresses through the Leads. They are, indeed, marvels of the shipbuilder's art: but what is most revealing is the astonishing richness of their contents, the things of use and beauty piled up on board to accompany their royal owners on the symbolic voyage to a new life. We might perhaps expect to find traces of a holocaust of horses and oxen, but not such an exotic companion as a peacock, which must have been brought all the way from France. Or again, among beds and tents and boats and sledges and domestic implements galore, all evidencing high technical standards in their construction, there stands out a ceremonial cart, 'decorated all over with carvings in most interesting and curious designs'.[1] Yet another significant item is a wooden tub of British workmanship, with hoops of bronze and Buddha-like human figures formed in enamel where the handle is fitted to the rim—the trophy of some long-forgotten foray.

The personages who were honoured with such magnificent grave-furniture can be fairly certainly identified from the saga. The Oseberg ship, which is the more splendid of the two, was probably the last resting-place of queen Aasa, named in the saga as mother of Half-dan the Black, the father of Harald Fairhair; and the Gokstad ship more definitely that of her stepson, who shared the succession to the kingdom with her son. At all events, they enable us to form an impression of the economic strength which was available to support the claims of the Vestfold rulers to exercise a wider sovereignty. It may even be right to regard the Viking expeditions as a movement in which the petty kings of west Norway were originally led to participate by pressure of poverty, but the kings of Vestfold through their wealth, inspiring them to emulate the nearby Danes. Vestfold is specifically named in French records as sharing in an expedition of sixty-seven ships, which came from Norway in 843 to reinforce the Viking stronghold at Noirmoutier, the island at the mouth of the Loire. Meanwhile, at home the kingdom was already beginning to figure as a state with an important hinterland, which had won some measure of control over the east Norway valleys or Uplands and for a time touched the inner reaches of the long Sognefiord. Its frontiers

[1] Brögger and Shetelig: *The Viking Ships*, p. 92.

kept changing, but experience must have suggested that a further advance was not impossible. There were two other considerations. On the one hand, the power of the Danish kings reaching along both sides of the Oslofiord was a direct threat to the Vestfold dynasty, which needed to find a new base if it was permanently to keep its independence. On the other hand, the long coveted wealth which now flowed into the west Norway kingdoms as a result of overseas raids and settlements had made their mutual rivalries more acute. When, for instance, Olaf the White disappears so suddenly in 871 from the records of the Irish wars, it seems reasonable to suppose that he was recalled because the services of a doughty Vestfold prince were urgently needed in unquiet Norway.

Out of the mist of uncertainty there arises the heroic figure of Harald Fairhair, the king of Vestfold who in some sense united Norway. Inheriting his throne in early youth, we first see him suppressing a revolt in the Uplands. He then made a pact of some kind with his most formidable rival, the earl who ruled the coast and taxed the trade of North Norway. This enabled Harald to take what proved to be a decisive step, when he and his men crossed over the mountains from the east into the rich farmlands of the Tröndelag. The eight small districts forming the Öreting were joined with the northern coastal earldom, which already reached to some point south of the mouth of the Trondheimsfiord, and the earl himself moved his seat of power southwards to the great temple at Lade. Haakon earl of Lade clearly accepted Harald as his suzerain, but it is likely that for both of them what mattered most was the further development of their control of the coastal trade, which was the main source of their wealth.

There followed, accordingly, a long and doubtless bloody struggle against the kings of the west coast districts, in which earl Haakon perished but the Lade earldom continued to grow. It ended with a famous and decisive victory won by Harald Fairhair in a seafight at Hafrsfiord, near Stavanger. As in all Viking naval battles, the longships were used simply as fighting-platforms:

> They carried a host of warriors
> With white shields
> And spears from the west lands
> And Frankish swords

The beserk were roaring
When battle was offered,
Warriors in wolfskins howling,
And the irons clattering.[1]

Hafrsfiord made Harald king of Norway. It remained for him to consolidate the position he had won by overawing turbulent elements both at home and in the Norwegian settlements abroad, which (as the verse suggests) had bolstered up the cherished independence of the west coast states from which they originated. The sagas go so far as to make Hafrsfiord the starting-point of the colonization of Iceland by those Vikings who refused to submit. All that is certain is that Harald spared time from his cleaning-up operations at home to make an expedition to the Shetlands and Orkneys, where the earl became his man: British and Irish annals show no trace of his presence farther west. He also showed his general disapproval of Viking activities in Northumbria or elsewhere when he sent his youngest son Haakon to be brought up at the court of king Athelstan. Indeed, at the time when these two North Sea kings exchanged gifts in token of their friendship—a ship with a gilded prow and purple sail, a sword of the much-prized English forging, ornamented with gold on hilt and scabbard—Norway was in theory the more united country of the two.

In practice, however, the geographical factors, if nothing else, made Norway a much harder problem for a unifying monarchy; the rule of Harald, though it was important as creating a tradition, was very superficial. He accumulated power as a great landowner by confiscating the estates of those who resisted him: if lucky, they fled abroad; if unlucky, they were 'burnt in' at home. Like the earls of Lade, the king exacted tolls on the coastal traffic. He also claimed a general right to tax his subjects, but this was a cause of universal discontent and seems never to have been attempted in the remoter inland districts: there it was harder to burn people in, and petty kings were left undisturbed. Law-making and administration in any case remained a local concern except in the late-conquered west coast district, which Harald prudently chose for his chief place of residence and where he seems to have fostered the growth of the first important legislative body, known as the Gulating. The first king of

1 Torbjörn Hornklove in Snorre: *Heimskringla*, III, 18.

Norway died at a ripe old age towards the year 940. There followed a century of disputed succession to the throne, in which the fortunes of the new kingdom were largely shaped by two outside influences — the continuance of Viking enterprise and the growing challenge of Christianity.

❀

In the 10th century the Viking peoples were still the great settlers of the western world as well as its chief plunderers and conquerors. In one sense their achievements culminate with Eric the Red, who voyaged over unknown seas from Iceland to Greenland and in 984 planted his colony on that inhospitable shore, which remained for many hundreds of years the last straggling outpost of our civilization. Its barrenness drove them on almost at once to feel for, and find, the American coast beyond: but the 'Vinland Voyages', which fascinate the modern historian, are really an appendix to the astonishing venture in Greenland. The Englishman's interest, however, is naturally diverted to the Danes and the outright conquest which made London by 1016 the centre of a Danish North Sea empire. But this was also a period of substantial Norwegian settlement on British soil—in the north and west of Scotland; along the west coast of England from Carlisle to Chester; and by a largely unrecorded supplanting of the Danes in some parts of Yorkshire by new immigrants from across the Pennines. For the return of Norwegian kings to Dublin soon after 920 meant that the Norwegians could enter Britain, as it were, by the back door, and for three short periods rulers of this heathen dynasty even established themselves as kings over the christianized Danes of York. Indeed, the threat of a Norwegian empire of the Irish Sea did not wholly vanish until the battle of Clontarf (1014), where Brian Boru slew some 7,000 members of a grand alliance of Norse Vikings. In Ireland they then began to subside into the Hostmen of the ports, whose purely economic privileges survived the later English conquest. In Scotland, too, the death of the earl of Orkney at Clontarf put an end to an accumulation of territories in one man's hand—five Scottish counties, the Orkneys, Shetlands, Hebrides, and Man—which constituted a serious rival to the Scottish kingdom. As for England, it now fell under the memorable rule of Danish Canute.

In the long run, the confusing struggles of this age are chiefly important for what they left behind, namely, a definite Norse strain in the population of Scotland and northern England and a less pronounced one in Ireland and a few coastal districts of Wales. This has had some lasting influence on national temperament and international sympathies. But at the time, what this period of close intercourse with the British Isles signified for Norway itself was a complication of the contest for the throne and, more fortunately, a connection which introduced Christianity as a factor in that contest.

Harald Fairhair left at least nine sons, and he had tried to follow the pattern of Charlemagne's empire by designating one over-king and many under-kings. King Eric Bloodaxe was not apparently of a keenly intellectual type, and it would have required considerable skill to play off his half-brothers against each other, since the prestige which Eric derived from the royal blood of his Danish mother mattered less than their local family connections. The period which opens in this inauspicious way has a natural interest for Norwegians, both on account of this local significance in many of its events and still more because of the dramatic skill with which their sagas recount the careers and characters of its famous men. But for us it is enough to trace the main thread of the story, which opens with the simple fact that Harald Fairhair was a man in advance of his time. The petty inland kings never seriously submitted themselves to his rule, much less to that of his successors. The chieftains of the larger districts, even the earls of Lade, were not free from the sinister calculation that a foreign ruler in the distance was to be preferred to a native ruler on their own doorstep. Thus, at a time when (as England learnt to her cost) the power of Denmark was on the increase, a pro-Danish party grew up almost of itself among the Norwegian chieftains, who were in any case accustomed to mingle without modern 'nationalist' scruples in Danish-Norwegian Viking enterprises.

Eric Bloodaxe married a Danish princess, daughter of the first king of all Denmark, but was driven from the throne within a year or two by his youngest brother, the Haakon who had been brought up at the court of king Athelstan. A would-be Christian, he was forced by the stubborn and rebellious Trönders to inhale the steam of heathen sacrifice and taste the sacred horse-liver at Maere. Thus there were obvious limits to his power, but his name is associated with the growth of two important institutions. Each coastal district was made responsible for the provision of warships of a specified size, complete with crew, armament, and supplies.[1] The three great law districts, Gulating in the west, Frostating in the territories of the earls of Lade, and Eidsivating in the eastern valleys, likewise began to develop definite codes of law and administration for the people of their district, whose representatives formed the *lagting*. In both cases the king built upon the best national tradition: yet Haakon the Good, also styled 'slayer of Danes', was succeeded by his nephews, the sons of the deposed Eric, under Danish influence and with Danish backing. From then onwards each ruler of Norway was either a Danish protégé, such as the earls of Lade for a time became, or was destroyed by Danish influence. It is only after an interval of some seventy years and the death of Olaf II at the battle of Stiklestad (1030) that his translation into a national patron saint enables us to see the emergence of something like a self-conscious nation.

From a mundane as well as a spiritual point of view, therefore, Christianity was England's most important gift to Norway. It had already been spurned once, as we have seen; but meanwhile the exiled Eric had established himself for two brief periods as king of the partly christianized Danish kingdom of York. His sons therefore returned to Norway as Christians, and an optimistic English source speaks of a monk from Glastonbury becoming a bishop there. In point of fact this second attempt to overthrow the heathen temples, though more determined than that of king Haakon, was completely defeated in the Tröndelag by the earl of Lade, though a mission under Danish influence may have survived in the extreme south-east, beyond the reach of that doughty champion of paganism. It was not until the closing years of the 10th century that the Christian faith made its effective entry upon the scene, when it was imposed by the strong hand of Olaf Tryggveson.

This memorable king was a great-grandson of Harald Fairhair. His father having been killed before he was born, he was brought up as a warrior and an athlete among the Vikings of Kiev, and went out on his first expedition at the age of twelve. In 991 he led the fleet of Viking ships which reduced the kingdom of Ethelred to ruin, and

---

[1] The *leidang* was kept up for several centuries, even in Norwegian possessions overseas. Six 26-oared ships was the quota for the Isle of Man as specified in a grant made by king Robert the Bruce in 1313 (*Oxford History of England*, IV, 596). But eventually it was commuted into a tax like Ship Money.

exacted a danegeld of twice the annual revenue. Returning three years later, he besieged London and ravaged the home counties, until Ethelred bought him off for a second time and at a still stiffer price. Like many other Vikings of this later era, Olaf had been christened (in the Scilly Isles) without any notable change appearing in his way of life. But after the second bribe had been paid over, he was confirmed at Andover by the bishop of Winchester, with his principal victim Ethelred as godfather. He then left England for Dublin, where some kind of invitation reached him to come and wrest the control of his native country from the earl of Lade. Perhaps the conversion of Russia by Vladimir of Kiev was his model. At all events, at least three missionaries from England accompanied his little fleet, which had no sooner arrived in the Tröndelag than the way to the throne was cleared through the murder of the hated earl by his own slave in the pigsty where he had sought refuge. In a reign of only five years Olaf I made the mark of his zest and energy. Both the region of the Oslofiord, where he had been born, and the west coast districts facing England, which had had some casual contacts with Christians before, accepted the new faith. The Orkneys and the Hebrides had been christianized by Celtic influences, but now Shetland, the Faeroes, Iceland, and even Greenland began to receive the gospel, as a result of conversions exacted by Olaf when their leading men visited the old Viking in his homeland. Only Tröndelag and the far north remained recalcitrant, though the heathen temples at Maere and Lade were destroyed by the king in person and the more determined votaries of paganism pitilessly mutilated or put to the sword. The king therefore made Tröndelag his place of residence, choosing the site near the river mouth — reminiscent, perhaps, of both London and Dublin — on which the city of Nidaros or Trondheim slowly grew. But this was not enough to hold in check a mutinous opposition, which could rely on Danish and Swedish help. In the year 1000, deserted by subjects and allies alike, the first king Olaf fought a last desperate battle at Svolder, then sprang from his famous flagship The Long Serpent, and disappeared beneath the waters of the Sound, leaving Norway to another period of Danish (and Swedish) suzerainty, rule by the earls of Lade, and full toleration of pagan rites.

Fifteen years later, however, England's extremity again proved to be Norway's opportunity. For when Canute the Great had succeeded to the newly-won English throne and our ancestors made their last forlorn attempt on behalf of Ethelred the Unready, the new earl of Lade—whose father had perished in the pigsty—took part in his Danish master's expedition across the North Sea. Again there was a descendant of Harald Fairhair available to lay claim to Norway, a second Olaf and a future saint, who had had the same Viking training as his predecessor from early youth. He is the reputed hero of a famous exploit in which London bridge was broken down by a water-borne attack against its wooden piers, which would make him the only Viking chief to achieve immortality in nursery rhyme. The details of this Olaf's early career are, however, hopelessly confused; but latterly at least he had been fighting for Ethelred against the Danes, which gives an additional reason for his leaving England in the autumn of 1015, when that unhappy king's fortunes were finally on the wane. Olaf II may have had some contact with Christianity during his early childhood in east Norway, but his Viking career does not confirm this: Church tradition states that he was both baptized and confirmed at Rouen, where he served the Norman duke.

Certainly it was as a Christian having close relations with the English Church that he set out to claim Norway in two merchant vessels, which carried 120 followers, including some priests, and much Viking gold. He was defeated in a first attempt upon the Tröndelag, but quickly gained support in the valleys of the Uplands by his conciliation of a new class of substantial peasants. This had been growing up during the Viking Age, when the pressures which sent some men overseas had led others to pioneer the cultivation of new land at home; it provided the Crown with a far more reliable support than could ever have been obtained from the turbulent Upland chieftains of Harald Fairhair's days. At the end of the winter of 1015-16 a fleet came down from the north to challenge the power which Olaf was evidently building in the south-east, and a single fight at the mouth of the Oslofiord made him effectively king.

The reign of the second Olaf was regarded by the pious tradition of a later age as having been a great era of royal legislation: but in fact legislation was still the localized activity of the *tings*. The fourth of these great quasi-independent institutions, the Borgarting of the extreme south-east, may actually have been established at this time. What the country needed most, however, was the enforcement of law, and this the great king gave it. In the words of his Icelandic skald:

Those who did deeds of rapine oft tendered red gold to the keen-eyed king to buy their liberty, but the king said No. He had their heads struck off with the sword; they received exemplary punishment for their plundering. Such is the way to protect this land. The great king ruined the families of robbers and ravagers; he caused each nimble thief to lose both hand and foot. Thus peace was restored in the prince's realm. What best showed the power that the guardian of the land possessed was that he had full many a Viking put away with sharp weapons.[1]

In such circumstances the priests whom Olaf had brought with him, Englishmen, we may presume, of Norse or Danish ancestry, found a readier hearing and obtained an authority which the earlier missionaries, including doubtless some unremembered martyrs, had largely lacked.

The Church of Norway, which was the chief English daughter-church in medieval Europe, dates its establishment from 1024. In that year the king and his ecclesiastical adviser, bishop Grimkell—perhaps in imitation of the conduct of Church business by the English Witenagemot—held a special *ting* at Moster on the west coast, where Olaf I was supposed to have made his first mass conversions. Here a code was drawn up, which had then to be submitted for modification and approval at the regional *tings*. Due provision was made for churches and church officials and the observance of sacraments and holy days. Severe penalties were enacted for continuing the worship of the old gods or the closely-related practice of witchcraft. But what is most revealing is the attempt to conciliate conservative opinion by keeping up the beer-feasts, which had been held in the temples at the end of each of the three annual solemnities. The beer was now to be blessed, and the first toasts were to be drunk 'in honour of Christ and the Blessed Virgin for good years and peace'.

But peace the great king could not secure. Even his work for the Church was hampered by the hostility of Canute in England, which made it necessary for Grimkell to receive consecration, not from the mother-church of Canterbury but from the newly-established archbishopric of Bremen. Olaf tried in vain to strengthen his position by an alliance with Sweden and the launching of an anticipatory attack on Denmark. But Canute was too strong for him. When he

[1] Sigvat in Snorre: *Heimskringla*, VIII, 181.

came to claim the overlordship of Norway 'with fifty ships of English thegns' and a powerful Danish fleet (the Anglo-Saxon Chronicle ignores the latter), the leading men saw their interest served by siding with a foreign king who controlled the trade routes to the west—and would rule them from a safe distance. For two years Olaf took refuge with his Swedish wife's relations at Kiev. Canute appointed the earl of Lade as his deputy, but when the earl was drowned next winter in the Pentland Firth, his successor in office was a mere boy, Canute's son by his English wife, Aelfgifu of Northampton, who accompanied him to rule in Norway. They had barely arrived when Olaf emerged from the mountain passes into the Tröndelag. He led a forlorn hope of men from his first home in the Uplands and a few Swedes, collected on his way, and as they came in sight of Norway the king was heard to say ruefully that 'many a day he had been happy in that land'. On July 29, 1030, at Stiklestad, he faced a force twice the size of his own, made up of the local peasantry under their chiefs and some disaffected magnates from the far north.

King Olaf lost the day and his life; but the bruised body was rescued by friends and a remorse-stricken foe, and was sent secretly to Trondheim. Only twelve months later, bishop Grimkell was able to place it above the high altar of St Clement's church as the earthly remains of an acknowledged saint. The greatest cathedral of northern Europe was later built in his honour, on the sandbank in which the body had been hidden. But a greater place was that which the image of Saint Olaf *perpetuus rex Norvegiae* built for itself in the hearts of the Norwegian people.

CHAPTER III

THE REALM OF ST OLAF

❄

FEW saints of the middle ages achieved a more suddenly universal renown than the defeated warrior of Stiklestad. Within ten years of his death his name was working miracles in far-off Russia; he was the last western saint accepted by the eastern orthodox church at Constantinople. Six London churches bore the name, and other English dedications were as widespread as Exeter, Chester, and York. Within two generations Trondheim had risen to be a famous city in the eyes of the ecclesiastical historian of the north, who wrote at Bremen:

> The capital of the Norsemen is Trondemnis, which is beautified with churches and visited by a great number of people. There rests the body of the blessed Olaf, king and martyr, at whose grave God to this day performs great wonders of healing, so that many journey thither from distant lands, hoping to receive help through the merits of the saint.[1]

How much of this astonishing transformation should be attributed to the spirit of the age—a northern christianity just ripe to acclaim a martyr-king; how much to the policy of bishop Grimkell, who had remained in Norway after his king's downfall and was the first to assert his claim to sainthood; and how much to the character of the dead king himself, we shall never know. It seems evident that he must have possessed some traits of disposition and achieved some actual deeds consistent with the idea of the saint, on which contemporaries could plausibly begin to base the legends now remaining of him. But Olaf was above all *felix opportunitate mortis*.

The English-born queen Aelfgifu and her son made themselves immediately unpopular by treating Stiklestad as a Danish victory, which it was not, entitling them to rule the Norwegian chieftains

1 Adam of Bremen: *Gesta Hammenburgensis Ecclesiae Pontificum*, IV, 32.

and peasants as a conquered people. The consequence was that, within four years of the battle, the very men who had won it for Canute were on their way to fetch home Olaf's 11-year-old son from Kiev. Aelfgifu and her son fled to Denmark, leaving Magnus— the name echoes the Viking admiration for Charlemagne—to be accepted as king by all the *tings*. The death of Canute himself followed almost immediately, and with the consequent break-up of his empire the Danish threat to Norwegian independence was for a time abated. Magnus (1035-47) in his later years shared the throne with St. Olaf's half-brother, Harald III, who had escaped from the rout at Stiklestad to win fame and fortune in the service of the eastern empire. This illustrious Viking is more familiar to us as the Harald Hardrada whom our own Harold slew at Stamford Bridge in 1066. As he in turn was followed by three generations of direct descendants, the period we have now to consider amounts to nearly a century, throughout which the national life was left free to develop without that curse of medieval Norway—a disputed succession to the throne. In this period, which coincides with the transformation of Edward the Confessor's England by the hammer-blows of the Norman conquest, Norway figures as a partly self-governing kingdom, increasingly civilized, and a force in the international affairs of the day.

The characteristic institution of the age was the *ting*, for the *bönder*, the yeomanry or peasant freeholders, were the dominant class of society. It is true that the class of freemen as a whole was being diluted by the emancipation of the thralls or slaves, who had become a fairly numerous element at one time as a result of the Viking enterprises. It is also true that landowning peasants already showed some tendency to decline to the position of tenants. Nevertheless, the yeomen still dominated the *ting*, as they had done in the Viking age, and in this more law-abiding period the decisions made there dominated the country. It was still the right of the individual to summon the *ting* for his own cause by sending arrows from farm to farm—like the use of the fiery cross in the Highland clans. But by the 11th century its purely local functions had come to matter less than what was done in bigger areas by the great *lagtings*, though even their jurisdiction did not cover the entire country.

They appointed the king. That is to say, when a king died, those of his descendants who claimed his royal estate sought approval from the *tings*—a circumstance which resulted in there often being joint-kings (as in the case of Magnus and Harald) and which gave great importance to one *ting*, usually the Öreting, which was likely to influence the decision of the others. As the repository of traditional law and ideas of justice, they provided the forum where all disputes were heard, even private lawsuits between joint-kings: this is the more remarkable as the king's thegns were expressly excluded from membership of the judicial committee which was set up within the *lagting* for each session. New law emanated from the *tings* or, as in the case of St. Olaf's church law, was adopted with such modifications as each might approve for its own district. Norwegian law therefore long continued to be local rather than common law in the English sense, based on the intercourse between neighbours instead of the dictates of a superior.

> If men go on a bear hunt and approach the den above the stockade and drive the bear out: then they are to pay the damage if the bear attacks people's cattle.
> If a man is injured by a dog or a horse, or gored by an ox, or bitten by any other farm animal . . . the owner shall bind it and hand it over to him that was bitten.
> If a man shoots at a whale and hits it, and drives the whale ashore: then he who shot owns one half and the owner of the land the other.
> If people row a fully-manned boat against a farmer and use force and break into his buildings and carry off the chattels: then they that do this are outlaws.[1]

Even the church law might be given a democratic twist by the *lagting* in the south-east, where German missionaries had been at work, who were less hierarchically-minded than the English: if the priest wished to absent himself from his parish, he is instructed to obtain leave from his parishioners on the preceding Sunday.

In the main, however, the growth and consequently the control of the Church comes from above. In Norway, as we have already noticed, the old gods died hard. Heathen gravemounds on old farms were sometimes the object of a traditional cult until almost within living memory, and the folklore of later generations teems with the adventures of heathen deities. The courage of the Christ who chose to ascend the cross made an immediate appeal to the hearts of the

[1] The Gulating Law, Sections 94, 147, 149, 142.

Vikings, and St Olaf's church law was able to demand one or two acts of mercy — for instance, that in future unwanted infants, unless seriously deformed, were no longer to be killed by exposure. But the Church of Norway grew up, less through spiritual causes than through an increasing realization that it was necessary to belong to Christendom in order to belong to civilization. St Olaf's successors on the throne put themselves at the head of this movement. Relations with the English clergy had already been made easier when Aelfgifu ruled on behalf of Canute, and the work of bishop Grimkell was taken up by at least two other members of the same, probably Northumbrian, family.

One of the ways in which Norway followed the English rather than the Continental practice was in the use made in church services of the vernacular. But Latin nevertheless provided the basis of any Catholic liturgy, and for the use of either language by the Church it was necessary to train a priesthood that could read and preferably also write. An English monk who visited the Norwegian court about the year 1070 was taken by the king as 'his master in learning psalmody', for which he had particular need as he was accustomed to assist the priest at the altar. Olaf the Peaceful, as this king was called, was the first of his line who could read and write, from which fact it is easy to infer the uphill struggle to train a native priesthood, which moreover could only be raised from among the peasants. For heathendom had had no priestly class in Norway, as each chieftain celebrated the rites on behalf of his own people. What heathendom had left behind, however, was an elaborate gradation of temples, serving respectively the large districts or *fylker* (such as the eight in Tröndelag), subdistricts, and the private properties of great men. To replace all these by churches was in the first instance impossible, even if there had been the priests available to serve them.

To begin with, therefore, the Church was essentially a missionary Church, with English, and to a smaller extent German, missionaries as its leaders, working under the direct patronage of kings like Harald Hardrada. When the German archbishop of Bremen, acting under the authority of both the Pope and the Holy Roman Emperor, tried to exercise his power over the Norwegian Church, Harald answered him, 'I know of no archbishop or ruler in Norway except myself alone'. The bishops were still at that time primarily court officials, whose missions the king directly controlled: no church building can be definitely traced which is earlier than 1050 and very few from any part of the 11th century. But the following century—the time when the great Cistercian abbeys flowered in England and elsewhere —saw the growth in Norway of parish churches, some of them squat stone buildings in which the English influence can be clearly discerned, others the wooden *stavkirker* with their dragonhead ornamentation, steep roofs, and short walls, so reminiscent of a Viking ship keel uppermost. These were, of course, manned by native clergy, though England's link with Norway continued to be traceable in connection with the foundation of dioceses and monasteries. The monastic orders did not become prominent until a rather later period, but by 1120 Cluniac monks had settled on a little island off Trondheim, and three Benedictine houses were also in existence, one of which, significantly dedicated to the English saint Alban, occupied a second island site north of the modern Bergen. This spot became associated with the legend of St Sunniva, an Irish king's daughter who fled overseas to escape the attentions of a heathen suitor and, together with some part of her retinue of 11,000 other virtuous virgins, disappeared into a cave there. The shrine of St Sunniva was second only to that of St Olaf in medieval Norwegian hagiology, and was transferred to Bergen when the growth of the town was seen to justify its selection for a bishop's see.

The location of the four first regular bishoprics at Trondheim, Bergen, Oslo, and Stavanger marks both the end of the pioneer stage of church history and the advance of another civilizing influence in Norway. Town life grew very slowly in a country which had never known the urbanizing influence of the Roman empire: in the time of St Olaf there was nothing which we should call a town, though Tönsberg may have inherited from the earlier and neighbouring harbour of Skiringsal a position as a market centre of more than local importance—it at any rate claims Harald Fairhair as its founder. A bishop's see attracted population, not merely for the building and service of the cathedral, but for the handicrafts and trade which might hope to flourish on the rents received from the surrounding countryside, rents chiefly paid to the bishop in kind. Stavanger, for example, as the nearest point to England, was a natural centre for the English trade. Its first bishop was an Englishman, a Benedictine monk from Winchester, who dedicated his cathedral to St Swithun. English materials and workmanship used in its building would be paid for by the export of produce from the episcopal estates. Oslo, like Trondheim, became something more than a local market when it could claim the shrine of a native saint. But St Hallvard — a rather shadowy figure, who lost his life quixotically defending his enemies from his friends — never had the same international vogue as St Olaf, and both the see and the town of Oslo remained of minor importance throughout this early period: as late as 1300 Oslo contained only about one-quarter of the number of churches to be seen in Trondheim or Bergen.

Bergen, however, began as a trading centre — we might almost say *the* trading centre. Since it was to have no serious rival before the 19th century its foundation, traditionally associated with the reign of Olaf the Peaceful, is the outstanding cultural event concurrent with the growth of the Church. The impetus came from without — in western Europe's demand for dried fish, stimulated by the fast-days of the Church and the need to find a cheap and virtually imperishable foodstuff for the growing town population. In return, they could offer textiles, metalware, and other products of their more experienced craftsmanship, together with some surplus of corn and salt and honey, of which the north stood always in need. Bergen, with its convenient harbour and easy approaches from north and south, quickly established itself as the place of exchange. Thither the fishermen sailed from the Lofoten islands and all the long stretch of the Nordland coast, the decks piled high with the tight-packed bundles of dried fish. There, merchants from a dozen lands, with the English to begin with perhaps in the lead, bought as cheaply and sold as dearly as the economic needs of the more primitive Norwegians permitted. And the men of Bergen, who acted as middlemen, learnt sometimes to outwit the foreigner and more frequently to depress the earnings of the native fishermen. The result was the growth of a city of European dimensions, bigger throughout the middle ages than any other in the north, and distinguished from nearly all its southern rivals by the fact that it remained a mere staple-port at the head of its fiord, cut off by a semicircle of steep mountains from intercourse with its immediate hinterland.

Relations with England were close but not necessarily harmonious. The English records show that there was considerable trade, not only with London (where Norwegians and Danes had special privileges of residence, denied to other foreign merchants) but along the east

D

coast as far as Northumbria. It is probable that the English corn was already being exchanged for Norwegian timber, though the Norway product which is most often named is the gerfalcon, much in demand for the royal mews. Commerce was, of course, facilitated by the ties of language and race. But Canute's empire left another heritage — a Norwegian claim to the throne of England. When Canute's only legitimate son, Harthacnut, was preparing the expedition from Denmark by which he gained the English crown, he made an agreement with Magnus I of Norway by which whoever of them survived the other should unite the three kingdoms. Harthacnut's unlamented death 'as he stood at his drink at Lambeth' in June 1042 therefore opened a period of high Norwegian ambition. Magnus made himself master of Denmark, and a Dano-Norwegian army under his command saved Jutland from a rising tide of Slav aggression by a famous victory at Lyrskog Heath over the heathen Wends. Magnus's claim to England had influential backing from Canute's widow, and what English opinion regarded as an overwhelmingly large fleet was being fitted out to cross the North Sea when the Norwegian king died suddenly in October 1047. His successor, Harald Hardrada, was at first preoccupied with an ultimately unsuccessful struggle to keep the throne of Denmark, but in 1058 a rebellion by the earl of Mercia gave him a chance to launch an expedition against the realm of Edward the Confessor. About this English chroniclers are strangely silent, but the Welsh and Irish write of the devastations achieved, and of a conquest which was only frustrated by the will of God. Eight years later came the final and more familiar trial of strength at Stamford Bridge, from which twenty-four ships carried away all that was left of a host which came in three hundred ships. But in assessing what the Norwegian threat to England had been, it is important to notice that five days earlier, at Fulford, the Norwegian force had routed the northern earls, won control of the northern capital, and secured a treaty with the citizens of York, pledging them to march south in support of a Norwegian conquest of all England.

After the gigantic frame of Harald had been laid to rest in his 'seven feet or more' of English earth,[1] Norway ceased to be a direct

---

[1] Snorre: *Heimskringla*, X, 91, is the source of the famous story that the English Harold before the battle would cede to his namesake no more than 'seven feet of ground or as much more as he is taller than other men'. The body was later reburied at Trondheim.

threat to England, except indeed as an ally of a potential Danish aggressor. But at the end of the century Harald's grandson, Magnus III, led more fortunate expeditions—and acquired his cognomen of Bareleg (the Kilted)—in the Orkneys, the Hebrides, the Isle of Man, and Ireland; he even landed and fought with success against two Norman earls on Anglesey. Dublin fell into his hands, and he may have entertained ideas of further conquests, but all that is certain is that Magnus met his death within a decade of his accession, during a more or less casual landing foray in Ulster. Suzerainty over Man and the Hebrides was reasserted for a time, and in particular their Church, though having earlier antecedents than the Church of Norway, came to form eventually one of the Norwegian dioceses. The Orkney earldom was on the whole more closely linked with the mother-country. The earls, who also claimed Caithness and Sutherland from the nascent kingdom of Scotland, were often anxious to secure the support of the Crown of Norway against the Scots. Here too the Church provided a strong connection. In the person of Magnus, an Orkney earl who was imprisoned and murdered by a rival in 1115, the Orkneys had their own saint. He was recognized as such in Norway, and the cathedral erected at Kirkwall in his honour, in a style copied from Durham, stands second only to Trondheim cathedral as a memorial of mediaeval Norwegian Christianity.

The banners of the Norsemen went farther even than the outermost islands. In 1107, when the kingdom had passed under the joint rule of the sons of Magnus III, Europe saw the novel sight of a Viking king, Sigurd I, faring forth as a crusader. The expedition, which started with sixty ships, probably from Bergen, was in no hurry to reach its destination. The first winter was passed in England at the court of Henry I, the second in Spain, the third in the Norman kingdom of Sicily. But there was fighting against the Moors on the way, and in 1110 the fleet duly contributed to the capture of Sidon. Royally received in Constantinople, the Norwegian king left ships and men there in the service of the Eastern Empire and himself returned to Norway overland. It is difficult to trace any direct results of Norway's participation in the greatest movement of the age, except indeed that the king fulfilled a vow taken in the Holy Land to introduce tithes. But the episode is a dramatic illustration of the fact that the kingdom of Norway stood now on a level with other champions of Christendom, as 'a people called the Norsemen, whom God had stirred up to journey from the western ocean to Jerusalem'.[1]

✳

Sigurd the Crusader followed his brothers to the grave in 1130. The sequel was a period of civil war, not altogether unlike the English 'nineteen long winters of Stephen' in general character and effect, but differing in the all-important circumstance that in Norway the period of upheaval, though not quite continuous, lasted almost six times as long. As in the case of Matilda and Stephen, there were rival claimants to the throne: but in Norway the number of possible claimants was multiplied by the fact that primogeniture gave little advantage and illegitimacy little disadvantage. Support of claimants provided a cloak for private ambitions of every kind, and respect for law and even the obligations of common humanity was lost in the confusion. But the reign of Stephen had as its one redeeming feature the glory of the new Cistercian foundations in the Church. Similarly, the Norwegian civil wars gain interest through the opening they gave for the assertion in the north of the spiritual claim to supremacy in temporal affairs, which pope Gregory VII had asserted against the emperor Henry IV in the wintry scene at Canossa.

Sigurd's son, Magnus IV, was ruthlessly robbed of the throne, blinded, castrated, and imprisoned by an adventurer from Ireland, Harald Gilchrist ('Christ's gillie'), who claimed to be an Irish-woman's son by Magnus III. He was soon killed, however, by his own alleged half-brother, who in turn was tortured to death after a battle in which the blinded Magnus was also involved and lost his life. These cruel deeds gave the throne to the sons of Harald Gille, the youngest of them a small child with a hunched back acquired when he was carried into battle, the trophy and victim of war. Of the four brothers only this one, Inge I, was legitimate: he was forced to share the royal dignity, but he found a natural ally in the Church. The position of the clergy had recently been strengthened by the arrival of the Cistercian Order from England: they came from Fountains Abbey to the neighbourhood of Bergen and from Lincoln to an island close by Oslo. The Norwegian monasteries, though small and few by the general standards of Christendom, were centres of piety and learning, made rich and powerful by the accumulation of landed estates—and they maintained close relations with their brethren

[1] Fulcher of Chartres: *Historia Hierosolymitana*, c. 36.

overseas. Gregory VII, as part of his far-sighted plans to render the papal and ecclesiastical power supreme, had urged the need to make up for the language-barrier against Rome's influence in Scandinavia by bringing Scandinavian candidates for the priesthood to be trained in the south. In the case of the higher clergy at least, this was beginning to be done, and in the great clergy schools of Paris—to a less extent also in England—they learnt to resemble the members of the monastic orders in their devotion to the papal claims. Inge was served by, and served, the Church: we can perhaps trace the growing influence of the churchmen at court in the circumstance that his reign seems to be the first in which royal decisions were recorded in writing.

Thus the greatest event of the reign of Inge and his brothers was the visit paid to Norway in 1152 by a cardinal legate, Nicholas Breakspear, the only Englishman to ascend the papal throne and the man who brought England's daughter church in the north into direct allegiance to that throne. The way had been prepared by Inge at a meeting of lay and ecclesiastical leaders from all the Norwegian lands, held in Bergen two years before, with a view to the establishment of a comprehensive archbishopric of Trondheim. Nicholas accordingly consecrated at Trondheim a metropolitan to take charge of eleven sees. Five of these (including a new inland bishopric at Hamar) were in Norway; the others stretched from far-off Garde in Greenland, through Iceland (two dioceses), the Faeroes, and Orkneys, to the eleventh see of Sodor (the southern islands or Hebrides) and Man, whose name survives in the English episcopate of today. The Norwegian ecclesiastical empire was a source of pride and might be made a source of power. But the main point of the action which the cardinal had been sent from Rome to take was, of course, to bring about a closer relationship between the whole of this remote area and the pope. Half a century before, responsibility for the Scandinavian Churches had been transferred from Bremen to an archbishopric of Lund, then in Denmark. The papacy was now setting up a separate metropolitan for Norway—as also for Sweden —who, like the English Primate of Canterbury, must receive the pallium from the pope, so that it would become easier to control appointments, enforce Church rules, and to influence men's thoughts towards the Gregorian ideals. Those ideals roused strongest opposition in the mainly German territories of the Holy Roman Emperors, which made it particularly attractive to outflank the German influence in the north.

Nicholas used the fact that he found three joint kings in Norway as a strong argument for making episcopal appointments the business of the cathedral chapters which he organized, but this was only slowly and partially conceded. He seems to have been more successful in claiming, like his contemporary archbishop Becket, that churchmen should be tried by church courts. Another change which required the approval of the *tings* was the concession of the right to free bequest of a tenth of inherited real estate and a quarter of other property. The Church, which taught people to will their land for the benefit of their souls, would be the chief gainer by the change, to which the Frostating agreed at once, but the fourth of the great *tings* only after an interval of more than two generations. The papal tax, which we call Peter's Pence, was also introduced at this time. But it is significant that no attempt was made to introduce the celibacy of the clergy, a measure by which Gregory and his successors set great store as the best means of setting aside from the secular world a disciplined and single-minded class of devotees of Church interests.

The opportunity for a further advance of Church power in Norway came very quickly. The slumbering quarrels of the kings revived. Inge killed both his surviving half-brothers, was himself in turn killed by the supporters of a nephew's claim, and, when this boy-king fell in battle at the age of 15, the nominal victor was a still younger child, Magnus V, claiming through his mother, the daughter of king Sigurd. The war had been won by his father Erling, a stern and ambitious nobleman and Crusader, with Danish support. He was fully aware that the claim to inherit from the female side was one which had not previously been accepted. Negotiations were therefore opened with the archbishop of Trondheim to strengthen the king's position by having him crowned as the Lord's anointed — a practice well established in other countries but without foundation in Norwegian custom. Archbishop Eystein (Augustine), who was sprung from one of the chieftain families of the Tröndelag, had newly returned with high ambitions from receiving the pallium at Rome. He had already doubled the income of his see by inducing the *ting* to agree that all payments due to him must be made, not in debased current coin, but in terms of pure silver. He had in view the completion of a great cathedral, which should fittingly express the wealth and power, the beauty and unearthly aspirations of his religion, high above all kings.

As Trondheim cathedral still existed chiefly in the mind of the archbishop, it was at Bergen that the seven-year-old Magnus was duly crowned in the summer of 1163. He was thus the first king to rule Norway 'by the grace of God', and the change involved other changes, both symbolic and practical. The king undertook to hold his kingdom in name as the property of St Olaf, in token of which the crown was to be placed at the end of each reign upon the high altar at Trondheim for each new king to receive it anew as from the saint. The 'realm of St Olaf' was a concept which clearly helped to ward off ideas of Danish suzerainty and to emphasize indivisibility; but at the time it also served the Church's purpose by suggesting that the king was a vassal of a saint, whose interest in the affairs of this world was represented above all by the Church. On the other hand, the realm was to pass in accordance with a definite law of succession. To ward off the evil, so often experienced, of the rule of joint kings, the priority was agreed of the eldest lawful son, unless debarred by incapacity of character or intellect. Failing such an heir, the choice from among other sons, other heirs, or—in the last resort —other candidates for the throne was to be made by the archbishop, bishops, and twelve leading men nominated by the bishops in each diocese. And, failing unanimity, the will of the majority was to prevail, but only if the majority included the bishops.

What did all this mean in the life of the ordinary man? There was perhaps a hope of an end to the dynastic quarrels when Magnus at the age of 21 successfully disposed of his rival—another nephew of Inge—in a battle near Tönsberg, so that 'it seemed to everyone that he surpassed all others, and that he would become a warrior as much greater than his father as he was younger'. But public opinion was probably more closely concerned with the effect on landed property. A marked feature of the age had been the increase in the proportion of peasants who were mere tenants. As population grew, farms became smaller or were located on inferior land, so that the payment of a fine or tithe or some other emergency meant recourse to borrowing from the wealthy, who from what we should call mortgagees quickly became full owners of the farm. Hence the growth of the class of large landowners who took part in, and often fomented, the dynastic struggles. Its lay members shared the interest of the Church in the conditions which gave rise to large estates; they were therefore disinclined to fight against the kind of ascendancy which archbishop Eystein had in mind. It looked as though the only struggle to be continued any longer would be one which was remote from questions of ecclesiastical power or other matter of principle, actuated merely by the discontent of landless peasants, and rapidly forgotten by history. But then came King Sverre.

This remarkable and enigmatic figure makes his first definite appearance in 1177, as a leader who rallies a band of refugees retreating from Tönsberg into Sweden, contemptuously nicknamed 'birchlegs' because poverty compelled these outlaws of the woods to improvise their own footgear. Their claimant to the throne having been killed in the battle, they accepted Sverre—who may have served some time already in their ranks—in his place. 'A little low man from an outlying island' is his own description of himself: for he was brought up in the Faeroes, where he was educated for the priesthood, moving thence at the age of 25, when (according to his own account) his mother had revealed that he was the bastard son of Inge's half-brother and fellow-king. The genuineness of the story of his royal birth, or even of his belief in it, is indeterminable: perhaps it represents a deduction by Sverre from his strong faith in 'kingship by divine dispensation'. Be that as it may, for a quarter of a century he exercised a more than royal influence on Norway's fortunes.

Sverre's campaigns do not greatly interest posterity, though they fascinated even English chroniclers at the time. One pointed out admiringly that he defeated fifteen kings in fifteen sea-fights; another, less enthusiastic, claimed that in a crisis he used witchcraft to engulf the vessels of his enemies in the Sognefiord. The reference is to the final battle at Fimreite (1184) against king Magnus, Erling having been overcome by stratagem at Trondheim five years before. Sverre was trapped in the fiord and heavily outnumbered, but it was Magnus who lost the day and his life. The details of the long and bitter struggle show the workings of an unusual mind—that of a Churchman turned strategist, with mobility, deception, propaganda, and economy of force as his chosen instruments. Even so, it is doubtful whether his Birchlegs, who seem to have enjoyed little popular support except in the Tröndelag, would have triumphed in the end, if Sverre's social programme had been anything more radical than

Spoils to the Victors. His offer to his men before a battle was: 'He who proves that he has cut down a lord, shall be a lord, and he who kills a royal retainer, a royal retainer shall he be; everyone shall be such a man as he contrives to make room for.'[1]

As Sverre was fighting to dispossess the king whom Eystein had crowned, his opposition was inevitable, and he was forced to spend three years in exile in England, watching the glories of Canterbury grow over the grave of Becket. He then made his peace with Sverre and devoted the remaining years, until his death in 1188, to the building of the gothic cathedral at Trondheim. His successor, however, renewed the most absolute claims of the Church in such matters as the appointment of bishops; refused to crown Sverre king; and rather than accept a verdict by the *ting*, which supported the king's demand for a reduction in the number of his armed retainers, sailed for Denmark, where he was received with open arms. The other bishops, though they consented to the coronation, eventually followed their leader into exile. As usual, there was no shortage of claimants to the throne—five are named in ten years—and the east of the country became practically a separate kingdom under the control of Nicholas, the highly-born and machiavellian bishop of Oslo, who even secured the support of the local proletariat, once the nucleus of the Birchleg party. Pope Innocent III placed Norway under an interdict, and the deposition of its excommunicate king was weekly proclaimed by his own archbishop from the safe refuge of the cathedral of Lund. In reply, Sverre's party issued his famous Speech against the Bishops, written by priests—it will be remembered that Sverre had been trained as a priest—yet making its appearance, not in the Latin of the clergy but in the vernacular of the common people. The arguments are many of them derived from the emperor Frederick Barbarossa's conflict with the papacy more than a generation before, but as a whole this remarkable document is ahead of all other contemporary contributions to the Imperial cause in the fullness of its claims for what came to be called the Divine Right of Kings.

> Kingship is created by God's command and not after the ordinance of man, and no man obtains kingship except by divine dispensation. A king would not be more powerful or mightier than others

[1] *The Saga of King Sverre*, Section 35.

if God had not set him higher than others in his service; for in his kingship he serves God, and not himself. Duty binds him to answer to God himself, and to render an account of his protection and care of Holy Church; and duty binds a minister of Holy Church to be obedient to the king, to afford him hearty worship and a guileless loyalty.[1]

Guileless loyalty was the last quality which could be attributed to bishop Nicholas of Oslo. His so-called Croziermen outlasted the great king, who died in March 1202 from an infection caught during his last campaign, when a brutal diversion from a force of skirmishers, lent by king John of England,[2] enabled him to lay successful siege to Tönsberg, in the heart of his enemy's territory. Nevertheless, Sverre left his mark in state as well as church. His wars had largely destroyed the old territorial aristocracy, which had provided the backing for rival kings, and the stone forts he made at Bergen and Trondheim helped to give the monarchy a secure base in the towns. As we have already noticed, he did not seriously disturb the class structure of society, which was then growing up in Norway: but he made the king's place in it much more influential than before. His new aristocracy was a court aristocracy, which lent iself to a more centralized form of government. Thus the office of Governor — a royal deputy sent from the court to rule a large district — came into common use, as for example in the Orkneys after a famous rebellion against Sverre by the 'men of the isles'. He also encouraged the introduction into the *tings* of Lawmen, royal officials to give legal advice, who developed into a separate court of first instance under royal rather than popular auspices. The king's army and fleet, too, had obviously become more efficient, since Sverre preferred to do his fighting with forces of retainers, on whose loyalty he could rely : he therefore often commuted the compulsory service of the *leidang* into a fine or tax. But it is impossible to say what features were wholly new in a reign which we see chiefly through the eyes of an Icelandic historian, who began his book in Norway 'when King Sverre sat over him and settled what he should write'.[3] What

---

[1] The complete text is in J. Sephton: *Saga of King Sverri*, Appendix II.

[2] Probably Welsh archers (G. M. Gathorne-Hardy: *Royal Impostor*, p. 258).

[3] *The Saga of King Sverre*, Prologue.

is certain is that Sverre prepared the way for the golden age of medieval Norway, which stretches from the reign of his grandson to those of his grandson's grandsons.

❦

The 13th century began inauspiciously. Sverre's death was followed within two years by that of his son, Haakon III, and of his only known grandson. The next heir, Inge II, claimed from the female side, a claim which had been disputed in an earlier case. This fact did nothing to weaken the Crozier kingdom in east Norway, which remained in existence (although the bishops had returned to their sees when Sverre was no longer there to defy the ban) up to 1217. In that year they gave their allegiance to Sverre's other grandson, the posthumously born child of Haakon III by a girl who lived in the Croziers' kingdom, smuggled to Trondheim as a baby in the depths of winter, brought up at Inge's court, and accepted as Inge's successor. Even then, with the Crozier party formally disbanded, three circumstances long delayed the consolidation of the royal power. One was the interest which the kings of Denmark had in anything which weakened Norwegian authority in the border region. Another was the disturbed social conditions in that part of the country, part cause and part effect of the religious partisanship which it had displayed. These caused it to become the scene of a series of further risings—of the landless against the landed, of the freeholders against the owners of greater wealth and power. The last rebel chieftain was hanged in 1228 after a number of campaigns led by Inge's half-brother, Skule, a kind of Warwick the Kingmaker, whom the young king, Haakon IV, had rewarded with the governorships of one-third of his kingdom and the novel title of duke. His ambition was the third and last cause of unrest: he induced the Öreting at Trondheim to accept him as king, and it was not until he had been hunted down and killed in May 1240 that internal peace was finally established.

The coronation of Haakon IV at Bergen in 1247 was performed by a cardinal legate sent by pope Innocent IV at his request. It was a splendid ceremony, designed to display a monarchy resting on as good foundations, both political and economic, as any in Europe. The cardinal's speech at the coronation banquet touched upon the latter point in terms which have had their echo in the speeches of facetious visitors ever since.

I was told that I would find few people here, and if I found any, they would resemble animals in their conduct more than human beings. Now I see a great assembly of the people of this country, and it appears to me that they show good manners. I see here so many men from foreign lands and such a multitude of ships that I have never seen a greater number in any harbour; and I believe that most of these ships have been laden with good things for this country. They scared me by saying that I would get little bread or other food, and what I would get would be of poor quality; but it seems to me that there is such an abundance of good things that both houses and ships are full.[1]

The activities which the cardinal noticed as he walked on the quays of Bergen were based mainly on the ever-growing trade in dried fish, which we have already mentioned, but they also owed something to the fact that this was the reign in which the realm of St Olaf expanded to its maximum. Sverre's reign had brought in Jemtland, the remoter hinterland of Trondheim, a no-man's-land which had been christianized from Sweden but had its main economic connection, the fur trade, with the west: this was all the more valuable as the older fur trade with Russia was dying out. In his suppression of rebels he had also been led to put the Shetlands directly under the Crown and to appoint Crown governors for the Orkneys; the Orkney earldom had since passed as a title into Scottish hands, the islands themselves remaining a Norwegian dependency. More important was the change in the status of Iceland. Like the island groups already mentioned and the Faeroes (a Norse colony about which medieval history records almost nothing) Iceland had always had close economic and cultural ties with Norway. Safety from foreign intervention had given the republic a long period of peaceful development, but in the end the great families failed to settle their mutual disputes or even to keep up the shipping needed to secure their supplies from abroad. Finally, in 1262 a considerable period of civil war ended in a voluntary submission to the Norwegian Crown, which guaranteed to keep up supplies in return for the right of taxation. In the preceding year a similar agreement had been made for Greenland, where the bishop of Garde's flock of perhaps 3,000 souls were able to maintain their precarious existence on

[1] Cardinal William of Sabina, in Sturla Tordsson: *The Saga of King Haakon.*

the edge of the polar wastes so long as timber and iron came with some regularity from abroad. Animal husbandry was practicable there, though walrus- and seal-hunting gave them their chief livelihood: but many of these most distant citizens of this far-flung Norwegian empire probably never knew the taste of bread, which they could neither grow nor afford to import.

In Norway itself trade flourished sufficiently for a few other towns to rise in the wake of Bergen, Trondheim, and Oslo—the three which had definitely attracted a non-agricultural population of traders, craftsmen, and officers and servants of the households of the great. The archbishop of Trondheim received the rents of something like a thousand farms, paid almost entirely in kind: he and his men almost inevitably came to conduct the biggest export and import business in the country. Just as the archbishops used some of their wealth to embellish their great cathedral, so the king displayed his in the building of a banqueting hall in Bergen, which still bears his name—a stone structure in the English style of the day, a fitting memorial of the reign in which the first trade treaty in Norwegian history was signed with our King Henry III. This was in pursuance of a 'policy of plenty': in other words, successive kings were eager to attract foreign goods to Norway, and it is likely that foreign merchants already dictated the terms of trade, which was conducted to a very considerable extent in foreign ships. An important matter was the supply of wheat for the growing population in the west coast fisheries, called into existence by the demand for the dried cod from Lofoten and elsewhere. This was met largely from English ports such as King's Lynn and Boston, to begin with; but there was increasingly keen competition from German traders in the Baltic, who may already have seen the possibilities of a monopoly. Meanwhile, the supply of foreign luxuries—a stimulus Norway had not experienced in any large measure since the days when the Vikings imported free of charge—enabled a European culture to flourish inside a limited upper class. And their rising standard of life was to some extent shared by a wider circle of the more substantial peasantry, witness the fact that the largest group of craftsmen were the shoemakers, whose shoes of properly tanned leather were beginning to replace the article produced at home from skins.

The national economy could now support a fully organized national government. A chancellor, with custody of the royal seal and a staff of priests as clerks, issued the king's orders and kept his records, much as in England. The body of the king's intimate advisers began to take shape as a privy council. For a few years it even looked as though a larger council including a representative element, like the meetings already authorized to settle a doubtful succession to the throne, would become a regular part of the constitution. Medieval Norway did not, however, develop a diet, much less a parliament; and the traditions on which she could base her modern public life were to that extent the poorer. But she inherits from this period another rich evidence of civilization, in the shape of a school of historical writing, closely connected with the court, which at its best had no parallel in medieval Europe. Reference has already been made to the *Saga of King Sverre*; the author of the masterpiece of the following generation, *Heimskringla*, was likewise an Icelander who visited Norway and found his subject in the romantic deeds of the Norwegian kings. Snorre Sturlason's hero was clearly St Olaf, but he told the whole story from Harald Fairhair to Sverre with a psychological insight, vividness of description, and sense for historical probability which restore for modern readers the drama and colour of the long-dead past. As Thomas Carlyle pointed out, *Heimskringla* is 'to be reckoned among the great history-books of the world'[1]; but it is more, for in many generations of Norwegian readers its idealized picture of the Norway that had been helped to kindle the hope of future greatness. Snorre was fortunate in having a source of unique quality in the work of the skalds, whose poetic technique he describes in detail in the *Prose Edda*. Snorre, who while in Norway had been in some degree a supporter of duke Skule, returned to Iceland against the royal orders and forfeited his life in consequence in 1241. But his study of the kings was continued by his nephew, who wrote the *Saga of King Haakon*, and an unknown author rounds off our picture of Norwegian society as Snorre knew it in the dialogue of *The King's Mirror*. This remarkable book was planned as a functional study of the four main classes of the king's subjects—merchants, the *hirdmenn* or retainers of the court, peasants, and clergy—and was most probably designed by a high Norwegian cleric for the education of Haakon's son, Magnus. Though only the occupations of the first two classes are actually examined, the effect is to bring into view the all-important social background of what Norwegians call

[1] *The Early Kings of Norway*, London, 1875, p. 2.

the Age of Greatness.

The reign of Haakon IV closed in disappointment. He met the Scottish challenge to his overlordship of Man and the Hebrides by organizing an expedition to the Scottish coast. It was the largest force that had ever been sent out from Norway, and recalled some of the glories of the Viking era, especially when a mission came from the almost forgotten Norse possessions in Ireland inviting Haakon to deliver their towns, now under English rule. But the conscript fleet was unwilling to serve, so that the campaign began late, and this exposed the ships to the autumn storms. The defeat at Largs on October 2, 1263, although it involved only a part of the Norwegian force, about 1,000 men, who had been put ashore beyond reach of help from the main fleet, led therefore to a discomfited withdrawal to the Orkneys. A good many ships deserted, and the king died there before the close of the year. His saga gives us a last glimpse:

> In his sickness he let Latin books be read to him at first. But then he thought it great trouble to think over what that (the Latin) meant. Then he let be read to him Norse books, night and day; first the sagas of the saints, and when they were read out he let be read to him the tale of the kings from Halfdan the black, and so on of all the kings of Norway, one after the other.[1]

The position which Haakon IV had attained at home and abroad was broadly speaking maintained during the reigns of his son and two grandsons. Magnus VI, known as the Law-mender, cut short the dispute with Scotland by selling Man and the Hebrides for a substantial sum down and a small annual payment, to keep up the idea of a tributary land. But the principal achievement of his reign was the working out of an agreed body of common law, based on the existing systems used by the *tings* and gradually accepted by each of them in replacement of local practices. The innovations went in the direction of the reception of Roman law, of which the principles were taught in every European university to which Norwegian clerics and others might go for training. They also went in the direction of an increased humanity, sometimes indeed farther than modern practice, as in the provision that no public prosecution shall occur 'when one that cannot obtain work for a livelihood, steals food and thereby saves his

[1] *The Saga of King Haakon*, Section 329 (Sir George Dasent's translation).

life from hunger'. But the biggest innovation of all lay probably in the fact that crime was to be treated no longer as a matter of private injury, the concern primarily of the injured person or of his family, but as wrong done to the state—and to the king in whom was embodied its outraged majesty. Special codes were enacted for the conduct of courtiers and the court, and for the towns, in which we can trace the beginnings of a town council. There was also a third code drawn up, for the Church: but from this a dispute arose, which reached its climax after Magnus's death in 1280, during the minority of his elder son, Eric 'the Priest-hater'.

Throughout the century the wealth of the Church was steadily on the increase. About 1,200 churches existed, served by at least 600 priests, in rural Norway—a larger provision of priests than is made nowadays for six times as many parishioners. The total of church rents, including monastic rents, can be calculated at the equivalent of 150,000 kilograms of butter or at least a million kilograms of meal. In some parts of the country, at any rate, one-third of the land was in ecclesiastical possession. Moreover, in Norway as in England, this was the period in which the friars were setting up their Houses in the towns, bringing with them new skill in medicine and in the art of preaching, so that theirs was a cure both of men's bodies and souls. In the circumstances it was almost inevitable that a new champion of ecclesiastical predominance arose in the person of archbishop Jon the Red—the complexion was that of his beard, not his policy—who induced the *ting* at Trondheim to support his claim that the king was debarred in principle from legislating for the Church. The result was a compromise, formulated in the friary at Tönsberg in 1277. The archbishop gave up the right to control the choice of king, so long as there was any lawful heir to the throne; and the idea that the realm of St Olaf was in some sense held from the Church, symbolized in the obligation to offer the Crown on the altar at Trondheim, was likewise abandoned. In return the Church courts got full powers over the clergy and, in matters of religion, over the laity as well, a source both of revenue and pride; and the king confirmed the right of the bishops to appoint the parish priests and of the episcopal chapters to choose the bishops.

Thus the death of Magnus found the Church at the height of its power. But the barons who acted as regents for his young son resented the further claims which appeared in the new form of the coronation oath, and within 18 months of the crowning Jon died in exile. A compromise was reached with his successor: for nearly two centuries the Concordat of Tönsberg remained a dead letter, but clerical ambitions could only be restrained by positive action. Eric's younger brother, Haakon V (1299—1319), shared his father's view of the high nature of the kingly office as a gift from God. He for the time being at least increased the royal power over the Church by building up the position of the fourteen royal chaplains, whose dean, besides serving the royal chapel in Bergen, supervised the others on the king's behalf with a status almost equal to that of bishop.

Haakon V was a builder of stone and brick fortresses, emblems of royal power—an ordinance of 1308 aimed at the entire abolition of the power of the nobles in state affairs—and bases of future policy. One was at Vardöhus beyond the North Cape, designed to assert Norwegian against Russian claims to the no-man's-land of the Arctic coast. The construction of Akershus, the little citadel overlooking the harbour of Oslo, marked a momentous change of capital from west to east. Together with the new forts at Tönsberg and Baahus (a strong position in the extreme south-east of the kingdom, near modern Gothenburg), it showed a new concentration of Norwegian interest in Continental affairs. Haakon's German queen, Euphemia, is famous for her introduction of romance and the literature of chivalry to the court. But there were other new trends of a more serious character, which had been developing since the days of his elder brother's reign.

Eric had married the daughter of Alexander III of Scotland, who had died at the birth of their only child, Margaret the 'maid of Norway'. At the age of 6 she was formally recognized as queen of Scotland; at 7 she was betrothed to Edward the first prince of Wales, and set out to claim her kingdom in the finest ship that Yarmouth could furnish. Towards the end of September (1290) she reached the Orkneys, storm-tossed and doubtless homesick, where she died in the bishop of Bergen's arms.[1] This was the signal for the fiercest of all Anglo-Scottish quarrels. But the plan to foster close relations between Norway and Scotland was continued by a second marriage, with Isabella the sister of Robert the Bruce, and in 1295 Norway figured for a short time as the ally of France for the contemplated deliverance of Scotland from the English yoke. The

---

[1] A. O. Anderson: *Early Sources*, II, 694-5.

E

anti-English policy was continued by Haakon V, who was indeed given some cause for it by an episode in which English fishermen killed a provincial governor and ten other Norwegian subjects. But the consequences were disastrous to Norwegian interests. Trade with England suffered serious interruptions, which meant on the one hand fewer voyages by Norwegian merchants with their own ships to King's Lynn (where they had numbered as many as thirty in a year), Hull, and other smaller ports, and on the other hand, fewer English voyages to Bergen, where they were the only serious rivals to the German Hanse.

Hanse privileges had begun in a very modest way under Haakon IV, but they had been extended under his two successors, so that German traders while in Norway enjoyed many of the advantages of a native citizen, while escaping taxes and other civic obligations. The struggle was continued in the reign of Haakon V, who tried to stop the foreigners from establishing themselves ashore except as tenants of Norwegians, and the internal trade of the country was successfully kept out of German hands. But the external trade even of his new capital at Oslo was made over to the men of Rostock. As for Bergen, German craftsmen had entered in the wake of the merchants, and a growing dependence upon the corn supplies which the Hanse brought from the Baltic already foreshadowed a situation in which under weaker kings the Germans would always have the last word in any controversy.

The way for weaker kings was, alas! being rapidly prepared. Haakon V fought a long war against Denmark, in which he was mainly successful. But he was tempted to marry his only child, a daughter, to duke Eric, a younger brother of the king of Sweden, who had an ambitious scheme for setting himself up in a central Scandinavian state composed of fiefs from all the three kingdoms. Duke Eric's career of intrigue was cut short when the king of Sweden captured him and another of his brothers by treachery; but thereupon the Swedish nobles rose against fratricide and in favour of Eric's son, the baby prince who was already heir to the throne of Norway. Thus the death of king Haakon, which soon followed, not only closed the direct line of descent from Harald Fairhair or Sverre, but opened the dangerous prospect of a union of thrones. A premonition of evil caused the dying king to swear the members of his council to admit no foreigner to civil office or the control of any fortress within the realm. But nearly five centuries were to elapse before this injunction was obeyed, and 586 long years before the realm of St Olaf could re-establish its wholly separate throne and line of kings.

CHAPTER IV

DECLINE AND FALL

WHEN Haakon V died in 1319, his power was at least comparable with that of his English contemporary Edward II (who had recently lost Scotland at Bannockburn) and his subjects could look back upon a long period during which their country had played an active, sometimes even a leading, part on the European scene. The leading English chronicler of the 13th century, Matthew Paris, after a prolonged visit to the Norwegian court, had seen nothing absurd in making the claim that Haakon IV had been offered command of the French crusader fleet by St Louis and that the pope would welcome his appointment to the office of Holy Roman Emperor. But the sequel was to be the decline and fall of the Norwegian kingdom—two centuries in which its position steadily deteriorates and then the nadir of its fortunes, reached in 1536, when its formal status became that of a mere province of Denmark. Norway seems to dwindle and vanish both from history and from the history books, for she remained as it were in the shadow of Denmark until the last stages of the Napoleonic wars. The story of the transition lacks the dignity as well as the oecumenical proportions which attract us in the decline and fall of Rome, but it raises on a very small scale some of the same puzzling questions about the underlying causes of such a change. The bare outline of the facts which follows represents a subject which has been worked over again and again by the historians of modern Norway, seeking to explain and condone the fortunes of their ancestors, but there seems to be no certainty—except that the realm of St Olaf fell on hard times and that European civilization throughout many generations was the poorer for it.

The three-year-old Magnus VII inherited the throne of Norway, but that of Sweden he received by election at the hands of the

Swedish nobility. The fact is doubly significant. Both the Swedish and the Danish monarchies were elective, so the possibilities of intrigue and conflict were enormous. Sweden, and still more Denmark, was a land of feudal lords—castles dominating wide estates, armoured knights on horseback the deciding factor in the battlefield and the unquestioned masters of a largely servile peasantry. The elective system stimulated royal ambitions towards Scandinavian unity, while the feudal nobility saw in the same movement the opposite possibility—that of a nominal Scandinavian unity giving them the best means of securing agglomerations of semi-independent fiefs. Whichever motive prevailed, Scandinavianism spelt disaster for Norway. She was outmatched by the other two countries in population, available natural resources, and the compactness of the settled area: any partnership would be dominated eventually by Swedish or Danish interests.

For thirteen years, however, Norway was ruled by a council of regency, composed of bishops and native nobility, which succeeded in checking the attempt of the new king's mother to continue duke Eric's scheme for a central state under her personal control. But Magnus on coming of age showed the same feudal rather than national attitude, when he assigned Tönsberg fortress as part of a big Norwegian fief created for the benefit of his queen, Blanche of Namur. A few years later his personal preference for Sweden found expression in a scheme by which he assigned Norway to his younger son, Haakon, but carved out from it for the duration of his own life the queen's and other southern fiefs, together with North Norway and the island colonies. Haakon VI took over the rule of a diminished but separate Norway at the age of 15 in 1355—in theory an independent monarchy again, in practice all too closely identified with Magnus's long-continued struggle to keep, and later to recover, the throne of Sweden. The Swedes eventually made good their claim to set up a new king, Albert of Mecklenburg, but part of west Sweden continued to side with Magnus and Haakon, so that the main unshot of the struggle from the Norwegian point of view was the frequent appearance of Swedish nobles at the Norwegian court, where they obtained high office and often intermarried with what there was of native nobility. Moreover, Magnus and Haakon had sought to strengthen their position during the struggle by gaining for the latter the hand of the king of Denmark's daughter and co-heiress, Margaret.

Magnus died in 1374, Waldemar of Denmark in 1375. Haakon, whose personal sympathies were Norwegian, was left with the Norwegian Crown, possessions in west Sweden, a claim on Denmark for his five-year-old son, Olaf, and a wife whose statecraft was to unite three kingdoms.

But before we trace the extraordinary achievements of queen Margaret we must notice the event during Haakon's childhood which had caused the three kingdoms to become pale shadows of themselves. In England the Black Death occasioned a temporary interruption in the glorious opening phase of the Hundred Years War and social upheavals which led up to the outbreak of the Peasants' Revolt in 1381. But none of the Scandinavian countries was as well organized as England to withstand such a shock. Denmark and Sweden, the prizes for which queen Margaret contended, became very much poorer than they had been before the cataclysmic year 1349, feudal armies were raised with great difficulty from partly uncultivated estates, and each fighting man was a loss to agriculture when the lack of so many hands had gradually to be made good. For Norway, however, the Black Death appears to have been more disastrous than for other countries, even her own neighbours: it is claimed that crippling effects can be traced all through the 15th century. Its ravages may therefore mean something more than an interruption — they may help to explain how Norway came to play such a purely subordinate part in a Scandinavian union, the prime mover in which began her career as a Norwegian queen consort.

The way in which the plague entered Norway is a reminder that, though the Germans by now had the lion's share in Norway's external trade, Bergen still had English connections. In August 1349, when England had been plague-stricken for a twelvemonth, a ship from there had begun to be unloaded in Bergen harbour when the disease disclosed itself among the crew. They all died on board, the bodies with the rest of the cargo being left to sink, no doubt as a precaution: but it was too late. The disease would spread fast in the crowded, insanitary alleys of the port — Icelandic annals, our main source for these events, say that eighty corpses were laid out in a single church there in one day — and from Bergen it ran in both directions along the coast and into inland valleys. By September it was in Trondheim, where the archbishop perished and every member of the Chapter except one. Oslo, which had the only surviving bishop, perhaps suffered least, but it was from east Norway that the disease next year continued its course into Sweden.

How large a part of the population perished we shall never know. Almost the only statistical evidence, for Norway as for England, is provided by episcopal or monastic records, which are very hard to interpret. The mortality among parish clergy would be very high, since they were bound by law, not to speak of duty, to carry the sacraments unflinchingly among the dying. The monks, too, were particularly vulnerable because they lived a community life. Nevertheless, such well-attested facts as that the Trondheim diocese had only forty clergy a quarter of a century after the plague, as compared with three hundred before it, are at least consistent with the Icelandic statement: 'The disease caused such mortality that not one-third of the people of the country remained alive.' The Icelanders themselves were the only west European community to escape scot-free for the time-being[1], because the plague cut off their communications with Bergen, but their version represents the sort of view which must have been current in Norway itself soon after the catastrophe. The only other evidence, if evidence it can be called, is the remarkable persistence in Norway right down to modern times of stories bearing upon the belief that whole areas were completely depopulated. The 'ptarmigan of the Jostedal', for instance, is the name given to a young girl who was found running wild when people came over the mountains the year after the plague into one of the innermost districts of the Sognefiord: she had survived the winter alone among unburied corpses. Another tale tells of a hunter in a much later generation, whose stray arrow strikes a bell in the depths of the forest, leading to the discovery of the church of a forgotten parish, with a bear hibernating in front of the high altar. Stories like these do not show that the loss of life in Norway was necessarily any greater than the proportion of about one-third which is commonly accepted for England or Sweden or Denmark; but they may at least cause us to suspect that the effects of the loss were greater.

In each of the countries which it visited, the Black Death weakened the administration and the legal and military systems, because skilled persons had suddenly to be replaced by unskilled; caused the Church to open its benefices to candidates below canonical age or disqualified by bastardy; and ruined towns (where the mor-

---

[1] The Black Death visited Iceland in 1402-4 (Gjerset: *Iceland*, p. 257).

tality would obviously be at the maximum) through the interruption of industry and commerce. But the biggest factor by far was the withdrawal of labour from the soil. Some land everywhere went temporarily out of cultivation: mankind had suffered a reverse in its endless struggle against the forces of nature, which include pestilence as well as fertility, and was obliged to beat a retreat. Farms were therefore to be had for the asking, which meant that tenants everywhere secured for themselves easier terms at the expense of the owners of land. The Crown, the Church, and the secular feudal lords were thus left poorer. So also was the class of yeoman farmers in so far as they had been accustomed to hire labour, either for a day-wage or (as in Norway) by subletting a small piece of the less fertile ground: who would choose to work for someone else when he could get good ground of his own? Of course there were statutes of labourers passed, with the object of keeping people in their old places, in Norway as well as in England—but in England the general effect was an increase of liberty, which no doubt helped towards a quick recovery of the economic strength that had been lost. The Canterbury Pilgrims, however, have no counterpart in late-medieval Norway.

In Norway the margin of cultivation receded, not for a decade or two but for two centuries. The higher parts of the valleys were left unoccupied, and a bird flying over the country, especially in the west and north, could have noticed the woodland and wild slowly reconquering what had once been won from them by the axe. It is estimated that one-quarter of all the farms were still disused in the first part of the 16th century, and that rents paid on the farms which then were in use averaged only a quarter of what was paid before the Black Death. Many experts believe that a worsening of the climate is partly responsible: there is some scientific evidence in favour of this view, and it might account for the contemporaneous disappearance of the Norwegian population of Greenland. But is it not sufficient to consider how precarious the livelihood of the farmer on the higher ground in Norway was in any case, by comparison with his counterpart in Sweden or Denmark (to say nothing of England), so that it did not need a worsening of the climate to tip the scale in his disfavour? The thinness of the soil, the scarcity of fodder for cattle, the short summer, the long distances—all made it a very slow task to restore the carefully balanced system of agriculture, which had made the poorer farms just worth cultivating before the plague. It may be significant that restoration, when it came, often took the shape of farming more cattle and less corn, leaving the bread supply of the people to be imported largely from more fertile lands—as it still is today. Returning to the middle of the 14th century, we may conclude that the immediate effect of the Black Death was to reduce the national capital of Norway by two-thirds—a meagre basis for the far-reaching enterprises of queen Margaret.

❀

Margaret, daughter of Waldemar IV of Denmark, was married according to the custom of the day at the age of ten, and was sent to be brought up in her husband's country, where she resided chiefly in Oslo, at the castle of Akershus. This Danish princess who was now the wife of Norway's king was given a Swedish governess—a significant touch—but even so she might in these early impressionable years have acquired something of a Norwegian outlook, had it not been for the grinding poverty of the country to which she had come. A letter survives, which she wrote to king Haakon in the autumn of 1370; she was then seventeen and awaiting the birth of her only child.

> I have to inform you, dear my lord, that I and my servants suffer dire need of food and drink, such that neither they nor I get the necessities. And I therefore beg you, dear my lord, to find some way of improving matters, so that my people may not leave me on account of hunger. And I beg you to write to Westfal that he may advance what I ask him for and require, and tell him that you will pay him well for what he advances to me. . . . And if you can come to an agreement with Hans, arrange it so that he can lend me money if any ship comes here.[1]

Westfal was a German trader in Oslo, Hans the master of the mint. Was it surprising that, as the queen grew older, her influence over her husband, her ambitions for her son, and finally the satisfaction for her personal craving for authority all led in the direction of a Scandinavian realm with Denmark as its basis, Sweden as its support, and the resources of Norway as a minor consideration, expendable in the interest of the other two?

The death of Waldemar in 1375 left the Danes with a choice be-

---

[1] *Norges historie*, III, Part 1, p. 144 (with facsimile).

tween his two grandsons, Margaret's son Olaf and Albert, nephew and namesake of the Swedish king. There was, however, a third party to be reckoned with. This was the rising power of the German Hanse towns, recently joined together in a formal league, which had defeated Waldemar and established complete control of the Danish trade and fisheries. Margaret hastened to Denmark and secured the election of Olaf to the throne: but the price paid, with the acquiescence of king Haakon, was the confirmation of the trade privileges for which the German towns had long been contending in Norway. The effect on Norwegian life, particularly, of course, in Bergen, was far-reaching. In the general politics of the North, however, the sequel was that, on Haakon's death in 1380, the boy-king Olaf added Norway to Denmark, with his mother controlling the foreign policy of both countries. She regained possession of outlying Danish territories, such as Schleswig; and when her son came of age in 1385 the position of the rival monarchy in Sweden, which had displaced king Magnus twenty years before, had become so insecure that Olaf assumed the title of 'rightful heir to Sweden'. But within two years this last scion of the old royal house of Norway, on whom so many hopes were pinned, died suddenly in Scania, part of the territory his mother had regained for the Danish Crown. The male line had failed, as we have seen, in 1319: it had taken only four more generations to extinguish the female line as well, so that Norway became completely a prey to foreign dynastic interests. Hopeful rumour even denied the fact of Olaf's death: 'The Danes said he was dead, but the Norwegians would not believe it'.

Norway's extremity was Margaret's opportunity. Though there were recent precedents in Naples, Hungary, and Poland, Norwegian opinion could not contemplate so drastic a breach of precedent as the election of a queen regnant to the vacant throne of Harald Fairhair. But this extraordinary woman, who consistently neglected the interests of Norway, nevertheless got its council to elect her their 'mighty lady and lawful master', to whom the members swore allegiance as permanent regent. Moreover, they accepted her choice of a male successor to the throne, from whom a new line of kings would stem, in the person of her three-year-old great-nephew, Eric of Pomerania. As her sister's grandson, the child had a claim to Denmark; he was also a nephew of the Swedish king, whose position Margaret had been undermining for many years. Seven years later he was elected in both countries, and the unification of the North was an accomplished fact. On June 17, 1397, Eric was solemnly crowned king of three realms at Kalmar; a joint seal was devised; and a committee set up to draft the terms of union. These never got beyond the drafting stage, perhaps because the Norwegians would not substitute an elective for their traditional hereditary monarchy. It may be significant that no Norwegian bishop except the bishop of the Orkneys was present at the crowning; certainly the fact that Norway had only four representatives on the drafting committee, to defend her interests against six Danes and seven Swedes, must have taught the lesson that, the closer the union, the more definite would be the subjection of Norway to her stronger neighbours.

As it was, Margaret up to her death in 1412 continued a centralizing policy. Denmark, with a greater population than Sweden and Norway combined and a position nearer to the main centres of European affairs, was the base; from there the great queen made her will effective through officials chosen from among her Danish subjects, often men of lower rank and even Germans by birth. After 1390 the Norwegian council, which represented the feudal nobility and bishops only, but in the sovereign's absence was the main institution of the state, had not a single full meeting. About ten years later, the seal was removed to Denmark, to the detriment of the powers of the Norwegian chancery. The noble families had been reduced in the course of a century from about three hundred to about sixty, chiefly of course by the Black Death; this had killed off some outright and ruined many more through the reduction of rent-rolls, so that they became submerged in the general mass of the peasantry. What was left was now denationalized by intermarriage with the wealthier families still to be found in Denmark and to some extent in Sweden, whose members might hold office in Norway; and in some cases the actual fiefs were granted by the Crown to Danes or Germans. On the whole, the Crown at this time took possession of less land in Norway than elsewhere; but a part of its profits went in any case to Denmark, to pay the cost of the queen's administration and Danish foreign policy.

One of the few redeeming features in the situation lay in the fact that Eric married outside the tangle of Scandinavian and German connections on which his patroness's policy turned. His wife, who was sent across the North Sea at 13, was Philippa, daughter of Henry

IV of England. She resided a good deal in Oslo, and was tireless in attempting to secure the redress of Norwegian grievances against what was becoming so largely a foreign administration. But the death of Margaret was followed by a further involvement in German quarrels on behalf of Danish interests, heavier exactions, and fresh efforts to bring Sweden and Norway fully under control. The result was rebellion, which began in Sweden and achieved lasting benefit for that country in the institution of the Riksdag or Diet, which helped to protect the interests of the four estates of the realm for the next four centuries. The Norwegian rising was the offshoot of the Swedish, and had similar national aims. But it left no permanent mark, though Danes and Swedes were sufficiently aware of Eric's shortcomings as ruler of Norway to round off a settlement of their own grievances with the following patronizing admonition:

> And then do not forget Norway, but send such officials and sheriffs as is proper, so that there may be a better government than we have heard that the country has now.[1]

However, none of his three countries could get Eric permanently to abandon the centralized system of government he had inherited from queen Margaret. Rather than compromise, he withdrew to the island of Gotland in the Baltic and turned pirate, leaving his subjects to find a more pliable monarch. The lords of Denmark and of Sweden elected his nephew; the Norwegian council, which did not regard their crown as elective, in the end reluctantly followed suit. Christopher of Bavaria was king of Norway for only six years (1442-8), his death being followed by a second interregnum in the three kingdoms, from which there finally emerged the Oldenburg dynasty, destined to govern the fortunes of Denmark and Norway for more than three-and-a-half centuries. Probably the most memorable thing about the short reign of Christopher is the way in which it focuses attention upon the activities of the Hanseatic league, which, after helping to secure his election, thwarted his attempts to reduce their powers in Bergen, exacted new privileges in Oslo and Tönsberg, and caused him finally to exclaim: 'The Hanse has more privileges and liberties in my countries than the king.'

This was, alas, no new phenomenon. In no respect did Norway suffer more acutely from the absence of a strong national monarchy

[1] *Norges historie*, III, Part 1, p. 302.

in the 14th and 15th centuries than in the opportunity it gave to the ambitions of the merchants of Lübeck and the other Hanse towns. The Germans of Lübeck were already an important factor in the commercial life of Bergen at the time of the cardinal legate's visit to crown Haakon IV in 1247, and their privileges always tended to grow. But it was not until the 1340's that the Bergen 'factory' became fully organized as a kind of state within the state[1] — a community of about 3,000 merchants, journeymen, and apprentices, living in their own closed-in quarter by the quayside, forbidden to intermarry with the local population, not amenable to the Norwegian courts of law, industriously amassing wealth from Norway's natural resources for their principals in far-off Lübeck. At about the same time the interests of Lübeck became allied with those of other German cities on the Baltic coast and elsewhere in a permanent political organization, the famous Hanseatic League. Having a particular interest in securing control of the rich herring fisheries of Scania, the League joined in the struggle for power in Scandinavia; exacted what terms they pleased from the Danes; and, as we have seen, took their privileges in Norway as their price for recognizing the claim of Margaret's son to the Danish throne. The only actual change made was that the privileges of any one city were extended to all other members of the League. But they were now more securely ensconced than ever before. How profitable the trade became in consequence is shown by some records of the principals in Lübeck: in the period 1378-85 the goods they sent to Bergen were valued at less than half as much as the goods received back in exchange.

The ruin of native enterprise in Bergen was completed, however, by the action of pirates, for which the Hanse was only very indirectly responsible. When queen Margaret was besieging Stockholm (where the last resistance was offered to her union of the three kingdoms), two Hanse cities encouraged some freebooters to run the blockade. Hence the name of 'victual brothers', which clung to their organization when it became a mere association of buccaneers, who among many other outrages perpetrated no less than three disastrous raids on Bergen. In 1427, the Hanseatic merchants sailed for home with all their movable wealth before the pirates arrived, and did not return for eight years. Meanwhile, the Norwegians made a desperate

[1] The Steelyard, its counterpart in the heart of the City of London, was established by 1320.

effort to quell the raiders by mustering a hundred vessels from the now obsolete *leidang* organization — but to no avail: the seven pirate ships captured the four Norwegian vessels which were of any size, whereupon the rest retreated as fast as their oars would carry them. After that the population of Bergen could only take refuge in the hills, leaving even the fortress (Bergenhus) to be burnt by the enemy.

The fact that Norwegian shipping was hopelessly out-of-date no doubt contributed also to the ascendancy of the Hanse merchants. Their 'coggs' were designed to stow the maximum of cargo and, as they were sailed only, never rowed, carried a very heavy load in relation to the size of the crew. The Norwegians had nothing bigger than the one-sailed fishermen's boats which brought the stacks of dried cod to Bergen. The Germans, it is true, supplied rather little corn in return for rather much fish, and in addition had a well thought out system of advance payments — supplies of food and clothing which the fishermen could not do without — to keep each fisherman in entire economic servitude to a particular merchant. Yet there is evidence also that Norwegians round Bergen preferred to buy from the German merchants' stores, and found a superior workmanship in the shoes and other articles produced by the numerous German artisans. Undoubtedly, the Germans made it their business to establish a complete monopoly of overseas commerce against foreign as well as Norwegian rivals. We read of their having murdered Englishmen in Bergen and smuggled the murderers away out of the reach of justice. They expressed grave displeasure when queen Margaret, a few years later, made a trade treaty with Richard II, with the result that some English ships continued to arrive at Bergen at least till the end of the 14th century. Even after the final return of the Hanse merchants in triumph from the temporary exile by which they avoided the attentions of the 'victual brothers' in 1427, the Norwegian Council tried to encourage the participation of the English and Dutch in Norway's trade. They were kept out, however, partly by the ill-will of the Hanse and partly by the fact, which is often forgotten, that only the Hanse was regularly in a position to meet Norway's increasing need of corn.

Bergen was the only big town in the country. To have a state within a state established there for many generations — three thousand often intemperate and occasionally murderously riotous Germans with privileges of complete extraterritoriality — was a political grievance that poisoned the life of the whole nation. But the economic grievance was of much smaller dimensions. The Germans brought in grain, flour, malt, beer, and some Rhenish wine; textiles, hemp, tar, salt, and household requisites; and a few luxuries from as far afield as Italy and the Levant. Norway at this time had no substantial middle class, no fully developed organizations for conducting trade abroad, no accumulations of capital resources: so she could not have imported on this scale on her own behalf. The Germans took out of the country hides and furs, some butter, and a little timber; walrus ivory and a quantity of herring; but the staple was always the wind-dried codfish of north Norway. German enterprise and existing trade connections found a vent for this last commodity all along the south shore of the Baltic and in the crowded cities of the Rhineland and southern Germany. This trade had been a very small affair in the centuries before they intervened; now it gave the means of livelihood, however exiguous, to a population which the bleak coast north of the Tröndelag could not otherwise have sustained at all.

By a strange chance the life of that distant region, whose wants the Germans supplied from their 'factory' at Bergen, is brought more vividly before us than any other aspect of 15th-century Norwegian society. The fact is the more surprising as north Norway was closed to foreigners by a ban on their trading north of Bergen, which the Hanse did not find it worth while seriously to infringe. On October 28, 1431, a noble Venetian merchant on a trading voyage from Crete to Flanders left the port of Muros in north Spain. He lost his rudder in a storm, became (like the apostle Paul in his voyage from the same island) the prey of the wind and the waves, and after nearly two months abandoned ship in midwinter, believing his position to be off the west coast of Ireland. One boat reached the shore of an uninhabited island, where a dozen survivors kept themselves alive in the snow, feeding on molluscs and the carcase of a whale, until they somehow attracted human attention — local tradition says, by smoke from a fire.

Their landfall had been made in the outer Lofotens, near the settlement of Röst, where the Italians spent the next three months among a population of 126 fisher-folk. 'We can in truth say that we were in the first circle of paradise,' declares one of the two accounts which these compatriots of Marco Polo wrote for posterity.[1] They were astonished to find religion and all the social virtues flourishing in these wild surroundings. A Dominican friar, who was able to establish communication with the strangers in Latin, proclaimed their needs from the pulpit, and they were allowed to share freely in everything the islanders possessed. Since this was the dark period of the Arctic winter, hospitality meant above all the sharing of the one-room round wooden houses, where the Italians could notice a high standard of chastity, honesty, and piety. They also noticed a Spartan practice of exposing infants at four days old by laying them under the opening in the roof, which served instead of a window, so that the snow might fall on them and harden them. This was matched among the adults by their habit of walking stripped through the cold to the bath-house: cleanliness in general was a notable trait, as it had been among the Vikings in Anglo-Saxon England.

'They neither possess nor use money.' Dried cod of their own catching provided the staple diet in winter, and the visitors found it palatable enough, after it had been pounded and mixed with butter and spices. Butter, milk, and some meat were produced by their own dairy-farming—a cow or two was kept, mainly indoors, by most families—and there would be plenty of fresh fish and birds' eggs in season. For everything else, however, the people of Röst, having neither grain of any kind nor even timber of their own, were dependent upon the voyage to Bergen. What became of the dried cod that they delivered there concerned them little—the Italians seem to have got the impression that its vent was chiefly within the Scandinavian countries—but by barter they obtained from the German merchants there the corn, woollen cloth (some of it English), and iron goods, without which they could not have lived in their island except as mere squatters. Wood they probably cut for themselves on the return trip: it was of course the outward voyage to Bergen which chiefly interested their foreign visitors, since it provided the occasion, in May, for their own departure on the long journey home.

They set out with their hosts on the slow passage through the Leads—'we rowed always', says the record—but were put ashore at Trondheim instead of Bergen, because king Eric's quarrel with the

[1] First printed in Venice, 1559. A full Norwegian version is to be found in *Norges land og folk*, Kristiania, 1908, Vol. XVIII, Part 2, pp. 869-908.

German states made it safer for them to travel overland. The arch-bishop was not in residence: they had already met him in the Leads, journeying northwards on an official visitation with a retinue of 200 men. But the governor entertained them in fine style with Latin conversation, numerous dishes, and clerical company, before send-ing them on their way to Sweden, furnished with horses, money, and a guide. The journey through the high mountain passes took them fifty-three days, and confirmed the impression they had already de-rived from their experiences in the far north, of a country very sparsely settled, handicapped by severe natural conditions—they learnt all about the making of bark-bread—yet in essentials civilized and astonishingly hospitable. When they reached their friends they calculated that their expenditure for twelve men and three horses had been no more than four florins. It would be interesting to know how this compared with their experience when, towards the end of the same year, the bulk of the party landed at King's Lynn and travel-led on via Cambridge to London, where Pietro Quirini, the Venetian nobleman, was welcomed by fellow-Italians as 'one returned from the dead', and it was observed with astonishment that his formerly precarious health had actually benefited by contact with the rigorous north.

On the death of king Christopher in 1448, the fate of the North passed into new hands. Denmark and Sweden elected different kings, both of whom claimed Norway, but Denmark's choice was even-tually accepted everywhere. In fact, his expulsion of ex-king Eric from Gotland, and the agreement—which later vexed all the European chanceries—whereby he became duke of Schleswig and count of Holstein on condition of their inseparability, made Christian, the first sovereign of the Oldenburg line, the ruler of the biggest northern realm since Canute's. Christian began the practice of granting to the Norwegians, as to his Danish and Swedish subjects, a charter guaranteeing their liberties; this was in return for their action in electing him to what was no longer regarded as a heredi-tary throne. But deeds speak louder than words. It was in this reign that the most famous of all Hanse outrages in Bergen occurred, when they stormed a monastery in which a Norwegian enemy had taken refuge, murdered the bishop and several priests before the altar, and killed altogether sixty persons in one day. The only

F

punishment inflicted was a charge for rebuilding the monastery! It was also in this reign that the Orkneys and Shetlands were made over successively to the king of Scotland, nominally as a pledge for the unpaid dowry of the Danish princess who became his wife.[1] There were other marks of Norwegian inferiority in the time of Christian I, such as his arrival in Trondheim with an escort of five Hanse ships for a coronation presided over by a German bishop. Norwegian fiefs were commonly granted to Danish nobles; the native nobility was diluted by marriages of heiresses to Danes; and people of lower rank succumbed to a natural temptation to abandon the pursuit of national interests and look after their own affairs.

When Christian was succeeded in 1483 by his son Hans, the power of the Hanse was better held in check; but, in spite of high-sounding promises made in his charter, Danish lords and their bailiffs (*fogder*, the Latin *advocati*) continued to oppress the peasantry. Hans sought to consolidate his realm as earnestly as his English contemporary, Henry VII, though he never managed to suppress the rebellious nobles of Sweden. The Swedish unrest spread readily to eastern Norway, where the king's son, duke Christian, put down a serious rising in 1502 at the age of 21, and on a later occasion arrested the bishop of Hamar, who had dared to sympathize with a peasant disturbance, and held him in prison without trial until his death. But the Norwegian peasants had no real leader, since the central figure in this period, a Swedish-Norwegian noble named Knut Alvsson, belongs rather to the type of 'over-mighty subject' than national hero. When he was governor of Akershus, his bailiffs were the most notorious of oppressors. When he was dismissed, he called indeed upon the people to throw out all foreign officials, but the patriotic programme was mixed up with a personal vendetta—and it was a personal enemy who ended his rebellious activities in 1502 by luring him with a safe conduct on to a ship in Oslo harbour, from which a dead body was soon flung overboard. Yet the lack of any better leadership for the national cause may be held to justify Ibsen's claim that the blow which stabbed Knut Alvsson was a blow at Norway's heart. For when the time came for the third

[1] The agreement stipulated for the retention of Norwegian law and institutions, which suggests that the pledge was originally meant to be redeemed. The Norse language lingered in parts until the 18th century; odal tenure still exists.

Oldenburg sovereign to be elected and to grant his charter, Norway had sunk so low that at the joint meeting of the Danish and Norwegian Councils half the representatives of Norway were Danes, and not even a pretence was any longer made of reserving Crown offices in Norway for Norwegians.

The new king, Christian II, had spent five years before his accession as viceroy of Norway. Besides his firm handling of rebellion, his rule had been marked by an attempt to organize an efficient centralized administration within his viceroyalty, and he had even forced the election of his learned and capable secretary, Eric Walkendorf, as archbishop of Trondheim. As king, however (1513-23), he revisited the country only on the occasion of his coronation, which was the last to be held in Norway for three centuries. But many Norwegians cherished his memory as that of a gallant and talented prince, who had actually lived in their midst and shown his goodwill towards the bourgeoisie of Oslo and other towns by supporting his father's policy against the privileges of the Hanse. It was in keeping with this that the passion of his life was for the daughter of a Dutchwoman who had a little baker's shop in Bergen. Both mother and daughter followed the new king to Copenhagen. where the 'little dove', as he called her, soon died, possibly from poison; but the mother's influence continued unimpaired. For those Norwegians who knew it may have been a consoling thought that both the king and the queen, who was a sister of the emperor Charles V, were largely governed by the political outlook of a Bergen tradeswoman at a time when Norway itself was passing into ever greater obscurity. So despotic was the authority of the Danish commandants of the three principal fortresses of Akershus, Bergenhus, and Baahus over their respective districts that we hear of a man being executed for attempting to convey a taxation appeal to the king at Copenhagen.

In external affairs, Norway had now ceased to be consulted even when her own interests were most obviously at stake. The trade with Iceland, for instance, had been legally reserved to 'the king's subjects', which meant in practice that it compensated Bergen to some extent for what was lost to the Hanse. But throughout the 15th century it had been tapped by interlopers from Bristol and elsewhere in England, and a treaty of 1490 gave the English liberty both to trade and to fish. The agreement was on a seven-year basis, and by

1510 the conduct of the Englishmen in Iceland had degenerated from high-handedness to open violence. But Christian II, after a vain attempt to browbeat Henry VIII, in 1515 renewed the treaty. A few years later, when he was busy hiring troops in Scotland and elsewhere in order to suppress the rebellious Swedes, he went further. In complete disregard of Norwegian rights, he tried to mortgage Iceland, first to the Dutch, and then to the English Crown.

Sweden, in significant contrast to Norway, had put up a stiff resistance to each of the Oldenburg kings in turn. With a view to its final subjection, Christian II perpetrated one of the most famous outrages of a bloodstained century. When the Swedish nobility were assembled in the capital for his coronation, a sudden *coup* placed those who had long opposed him in his hands, and eighty-two heads fell to the axe in a single day. But the 'bloodbath of Stockholm' of November 8, 1520, had the opposite effect from what was intended. In less than three years the Swedish peasants had fought a way to the throne for a native sovereign, the first of the Vasas, and threw off the Danish yoke for ever. Within the same short period the Danish nobles had also risen against a king whose numerous reforms did not in their eyes outweigh his tyranny. He quickly yielded and went into exile in the Netherlands, still accompanied by the old Dutchwoman, whose bourgeois influence at court was one of the main causes of his unpopularity. During these stirring events, only Norway had remained passive. Its Council did not meet during the reign. The only independent force in the country was the Danish archbishop of Trondheim, Walkendorf, who had quarrelled with the king and his Dutch *éminence grise* over abuses in the Church. He appealed to Rome, but died there, his case unheard, a few months before Christian's departure from Denmark.

The pope, we may suppose, had more urgent business on his hands, for by 1523 Luther's revolt against the papal authority, which he and the emperor had vainly attempted to extinguish at the Diet of Worms (1521), was spreading far and wide through Germany. Christian II had toyed with Lutheranism, when a papal legate offended him by selling indulgences under rebel auspices in his Swedish dominions. His uncle, Frederick duke of Holstein, whom the Danes now chose as his successor, soon became more definitely interested in the ideas of Luther — not least in the opportunity they offered for the transfer of wealth from Church to Crown, which was seized with equal eagerness and in the same troubled decade by his contemporary, king Henry VIII. But the Norwegian Council, though cowed by the Danes into electing Frederick, inserted a special clause into his charter requiring the suppression of Lutheranism.

The Catholic Church in Norway had been, as we have seen, to an unusual degree the creation of the state. Now that the state was no longer national, the Church was the one great national institution left in the realm of St Olaf. Because the country was poor, the Church was on the whole less corrupted than elsewhere by the abuses of wealth and power. Indeed, the power of the bishops was positively welcome to the people, in so far as they were the last element left to represent Norwegian against Danish interests. And because the country was remote, there was no infection of new doctrine preached by native zealots—no Norwegian Wyclif or Huss or Knox —to make the cause of the Reformation the cause of the scholar and the patriot. All this meant that when Frederick, in spite of his promise, began in 1529 to extend his support of Lutheran teaching from Denmark, where it was popular, to Norway, where it was not, the hour for a national movement of self-assertion seemed at last to have struck.

Norway had an obvious leader in the new archbishop of Trondheim, Olaf Engelbriktsson. He was a Norwegian by birth and had been educated at the university of Rostock, which in the 15th century largely replaced Paris and Oxford as a seminary for Norwegian clergy. He had learnt to safeguard Church interests as the friend and deputy of his predecessor, and was quickly accepted as the champion of all national interests on the Council, where he was president. But much of the power in the country rested with the holders of the great fiefs. Bergenhus, for instance, was granted for a time to Dr Vincens Lunge, sometime rector of the new Copenhagen university and a Reformation sympathizer; he married into one of the few surviving families of the Norwegian nobility, and was further enriched by the Crown with the plunder of Bergen's chief remaining monastery. Since the Hanse merchants there were the first to welcome Lutheran teachers to Norway, the west became a natural centre of opposition to the archbishop. Other fiefs also went to Danes, other monasteries were plundered. Lutheranism made its appearance in Stavanger as well, and was rumoured to be spreading as far afield as Finnmark. Engelbriktsson replied by organizing resistance in the Trondheim

area, where he had built himself a stone fortress on the fiord and accumulated soldiers and ships. He then negotiated secretly with the
king in exile, who was trying to convince his brother-in-law, the
emperor Charles V, that he was a good Catholic at heart, and so
secure Imperial help for a crusade to recover his lost kingdoms. In
October 1531, Christian set sail for Norway, with 25 ships and about
7,000 men.

Christian II, on his arrival in Oslo, was duly proclaimed king with
the support of the archbishop. But storms had depleted his forces,
which were unable to compel the surrender of Akershus by its
Danish commandant and failed in an attack directed against Bergen.
When the spring thawed the ice of the inner harbour, the Danes re-
lieved the siege of Akershus, and Christian rashly accepted the offer
of a safe conduct to treat with his uncle in Denmark; there he spent
the remaining 27 years of a long life, in castle dungeons. Vincens
Lunge was sent to deal with Christian's supporters in the northern
part of Norway, whereupon the archbishop paid a heavy fine and
was allowed to renew his allegiance to king Frederick. Engelbriktsson had failed to rally the Norwegian people in any effective resistance at the first opportunity: but a second quickly followed. The Reformation, which from 1527 onwards had gained the support of the
Vasa kings in Sweden, now seemed irresistible; but within twelve
months of the imprisonment of Christian II Frederick died, and the
fate of Denmark and Norway was again in the melting-pot.

Denmark for a time presented the strange spectacle of a three-
sided civil war. Frederick's elder son, duke Christian, was a more
active Lutheran than his father; and received help from the Vasas in
Sweden. The younger son, Hans, was put forward by the Catholic
clergy, who were hoping to avoid further deprivation and spoliation.
But the townspeople and the peasants, who hated the power of the
nobles more than that of the Church, pinned their hopes on a new
venture in the cause of the captive Christian II; he was also championed for its own ends by Hanseatic Lübeck. It was a situation by
which Norway might surely have profited. But at the time when
duke Christian was slowly fighting his way to recognition as king
Christian III, the archbishop left Vincens Lunge free to organize the
election of the duke by the Council in southern Norway, while he
contented himself with the control of Trondheim and the north. Not
until December 1535, by which time duke Christian was preparing

to starve his last Danish opponents, the burgesses of Copenhagen, into surrender, was Engelbriktsson at last ready with his own candidate—Frederick, count palatine, a good Catholic who had just married the daughter of the imprisoned Christian II and was promised the support of the Emperor. In the same month Vincens Lunge came north for a further meeting of the Council about the election of a king. He was murdered in an angry tumult, but that was the only effective action the Catholic party took.

The rest is anticlimax. Engelbriktsson called for a general rising, but none followed. He sent his own small forces to capture the main fortresses, but both Akershus and Bergenhus were too strongly defended. Frederick never put in an appearance, and no member of the Council dared to support what was now so obviously a forlorn hope. The forlorn hope did not even achieve the success of making martyrs. The archbishop himself vainly offered his submission to duke Christian, now that he was the victorious king Christian III, and when the royal forces approached Trondheim, he slipped away into exile by sea without a fight. The castle which he built but did not defend still looks out over the quiet waters of the fiord, a half-forgotten memorial of the unquiet past. Copenhagen surrendered to king Christian on July 28, 1536; the Catholic episcopate was at once abolished; and a new charter regulated the government of Denmark by king, council, and nobility. For Danes, the acceptance of Lutheranism, which was by far the most important event in this period, was a change in the national way of life confirmed by charter. For Norwegians, it was a change imposed from outside and tacitly accepted in consequence of an inferior status.

The new sovereign was never formally elected to the throne of Norway, and Norway received no charter from him. Instead, its position was defined by means of a promise addressed in his charter to 'the Danish kingdom, Council, and nobility':

Whereas the kingdom of Norway is now so far reduced in might and power, and the inhabitants are not able to support a king and lord thereof alone, and yet the selfsame kingdom is bound to abide with the Crown of Denmark for ever . . . it shall henceforth be and remain under the Crown of Denmark, the same as any of the other provinces, Jutland, Fünen, Zealand, or Scania, and it shall henceforth neither be nor be called a kingdom in itself, but an integral

part of the kingdom of Denmark, and subject to the Danish Crown
for ever.[1]

[1] Article 3 (*Det norske folks liv og historie gjennem tidene*, 10 vols., Oslo,
1930-35, Vol. 4, p. 112).

CHAPTER V

A NATION IN ECLIPSE

THE terms of the Danish charter of 1536 were not made public to the Norwegian people, and the stated intention to reduce their country to the rank of an ordinary province of Denmark was not fulfilled to the letter. The Danish kings for the next century and a quarter preferred to be regarded as kings of a second kingdom, especially as it was one in which their claim to the throne could be said to be hereditary, the Danish throne still being an elective dignity. Otherwise, the obliteration of the kingdom was now complete. The Norwegian Council passed out of existence, and for the first forty years there was not even a Danish viceroy to give the country a semblance of administrative unity — the main fiefs were ruled by Danish nobles in direct dependence upon the king in Copenhagen. The recent fruitless struggle had left the native nobility weaker and poorer than ever. The native middle class, which had long been ground under the Hanseatic heel, was not yet of any real importance. At least nine-tenths of the population were peasants, for whom the new situation meant chiefly an increased difficulty in asserting their rights against the bailiffs, themselves usually Danes of middle rank, representing the claims of a foreign king and foreign lords to taxes, fees, and services. Impoverished as they now were, and split into small groups as they had always been by the ubiquitous mountains, the descendants of the Vikings were not a militantly national class. The past lived on for them in historical legend and ballad, intermingled with a rich heritage of nature myths and fairy tales. The present was a struggle to win a livelihood from the soil and the sea; thought seldom ranged beyond the valley or at most the county; and government was something foreign and remote, to whose demands they submitted in peace and war, from custom or from fear rather than from any active loyalty or understanding of its aims.

The Norwegian peasantry in the main forgot the world, and were forgotten by it. In English history the case of Wales may be suggested as an interesting parallel. Of course, no such comparison is perfect. A Norwegian might object that they, unlike the Welsh, were by long tradition a nation of seafarers who could not be cut off from the world, even when the ships they served in were not their own. A Welshman, on the other hand, would point out that, when his Principality passed into eclipse, it was the Welsh House of Tudor which ruled in England and his people had representation in the English parliament. But Henry VIII's Act of Union belongs to the same year as Christian III's charter, described above; both countries waited until the 18th century for a great period of recovery; recovery, too, was closely associated with a nation-wide religious revival; and in modern Norway, hardly less than in Wales, language has been the banner of the nationalist cause. For the Norwegian today is wont to lay bitter stress upon the fact that Danish rule made Danish the language of goverment, learning, trade, and polite society, while the Old Norse of the Middle Ages was left to develop — as a spoken language only — into rural dialects, the use of which was the hallmark of the peasant. The preservation of Welsh as a cultural heritage by the Eisteddfodau and the chapels therefore has its counterpart in the revival of a non-Danish form of Norwegian, which, as we shall see, still plays an important part in Norwegian political life.

In 1536 the change of language was probably the aspect of the Lutheran Reformation to which the peasant was most sensitive. Predatory hands, such as those of Vincens Lunge, began to be laid on the monasteries at an earlier date; in any case, they never had the same place in the national life as in England. The appropriation of episcopal estates by the Crown meant only a change of master to the peasants who worked those estates. The fact that the new Lutheran bishops, for a time called superintendents, unlike the old were mere Crown officials, incapable of standing up for the people against the king, would not be realized immediately. The old priests were left in the parishes, so that it may be doubted whether the change in the doctrine of the mass and Luther's exposition of justification by faith were made very clear to the first generation of Lutherans in Norway. But the catechism, the service book, and the new hymns were all in Danish: so was the all-important Lutheran version of the

Bible—of which after twenty years there were less than 100 copies in the whole country. We read of parishes which asked if they need have a clergyman. Only slowly did the superintendents succeed in encouraging the development of the old cathedral schools as seminaries for a new Protestant clergy, whose livings were often handed down from generation to generation, so that the incumbents eventually constituted an important element in the growth of a new official class. But they preached in Danish; cultivated the glebe and lived as substantial proprietors; and lived always among, sometimes for, but never as, their peasant parishioners. On the one side, a grasping demand for tithe, of which before the Reformation one quarter had always gone to the poor; on the other, a clinging to old superstitions, a fear and love of magic, and moral standards often denounced from the pulpit without much visible effect on traditional local standards of behaviour.

Yet the picture is not wholly dark. If Norway experienced little or nothing of the intellectual ferment which characterized the age of the Reformation elsewhere, she at any rate derived more benefit than any other country from one of the practical inventions which also marked this as an age of change. The invention was the water-driven saw, introduced probably from Holland early in the century, now coming into general use. Norway had exported some timber in past centuries—rooms in Windsor castle were lined with Norway deals in the time of Edward III—but the quantity was severely limited by the manpower required to shape and cut with axe and handsaw. The new mills, smaller and easier to erect than the English cornmill, clustered at the mouths of rivers all along the south coast and to a less extent along the west coast as far as Tröndelag. The trees, in which the country was so immensely rich, were felled in the winter, when the snow made other outdoor work impossible but actually facilitated haulage to the rivers. In spring and summer the tall, straight trunks of the conifers floated easily downstream to be sawn and loaded for export.

In 1544 a trade treaty with the Empire, which then included the Netherlands, put the exportation mainly in the hands of the Dutch, where it stayed for about 150 years. The piles on which the great city of Amsterdam was constructed; the frames, and especially the masts, of their ships; the half-timbered fronts of Dutch houses; the supports for the famous dykes—all came from Norway. Not only so, but the Dutch re-exported to England, France, and the Mediterranean countries. Other countries fetched timber for their own use, particularly the Danes from the south and the Scots from the west of Norway; and the English interest in the trade grew, as Elizabeth I's war with Spain increased the pressure on the shipbuilders. But only to a small extent, and chiefly in trade with a poor country such as Scotland, did the Norwegians at this period succeed in organizing export in their own ships. Nevertheless, timber-felling put a little money into the pockets of the peasants, notably the one-third of them who were actual owners of the land they worked, and a good deal more into the chests of the middle class, which throve in the tiny new seaports frequented by the foreign buyers.

Bergen, having no wooded hinterland and no river, was not a natural centre for the timber trade, and in any case the Hanse obtained its own timber supply from the Baltic. But Bergen, too, underwent a change which favoured the growth of a native middle class. As late as 1523, when Vincens Lunge wanted help in securing Bergenhus fortress for king Frederick, the Hanse merchants had seized the opportunity for a large-scale riot, in which they destroyed the charters of the city and plundered their Norwegian, and especially some hated Scottish, competitors. But Lübeck, the Hanse state which had always hitherto predominated in Bergen, favoured the losing side in the Danish civil war of 1534-6; and when peace was made with the Empire in 1544, she no longer mattered as a political danger to Denmark. At the same time her economic importance was declining, as the Dutch began to take the lion's share of the Baltic trade, and Lübeck was unable to insist on her old rule that fish could only be taken from Bergen by those who brought the grain there. Lübeck and other Baltic Hanse cities continued to bring grain, but the Hanse cities of the German North Sea coast took most of the fish: there was at last a chance for the native merchant as middleman.

In 1559 there was a final trial of strength between Christian III's secretary, whom he had made governor of Bergen, and the German craftsmen, who had long flourished to the detriment of native rivals under the powerful protection of the Hanseatic factory. An order that the craftsmen should take up Norwegian citizenship was met by the threat of riot. But the guns of the fortress were then trained upon their shops: the craftsmen were forced to surrender, and left the city. After this the German factory ceased to be a state within the state; its members began to settle down and marry in Norway; and, while part of the harbour retained for centuries its close association with German trade affairs, conducted largely by Germans, elsewhere a second trading community began to grow up. This, too, had its nucleus of foreign merchants, chiefly Dutch, Danish, and Scottish, who came to Bergen to make their fortunes: but they identified themselves from the outset with Norwegian interests, and formed perhaps the most important single element in the growth of the Norwegian middle class. Out of a total of 232 ships which visited Bergen in 1597, no fewer than 181 still came from Hanse ports, but by then the once famous League had ceased to be a political power, not only in Bergen but in any part of northern Europe.

The politics of northern Europe, however, were now vexed by a new phenomenon — the rise of Sweden under her Vasa kings. Norway had no policy of her own: but whereas the struggle between Denmark and the League had concerned mainly the control of the Baltic and the Sound, Denmark and Sweden fought often for Norwegian provinces, and at times even the sovereignty over Norway was at stake between them. Beginning in 1563, the Swedo-Danish wars follow so closely on one another that the whole period up to 1720 might almost be called the Hundred-and-Fifty Years War. The earliest was among the most deadly, since both sides employed German mercenaries, who ravaged all three countries and at Hamar destroyed the largest mediaeval church in east Norway. Trondheim, a valuable prize and readily approached through the mountain passes from Sweden, was taken and retaken, but neither there nor in the struggle for the other border province of Baahuslen in the south-east did the peasants on either side show any patriotic enthusiasm. Peace was restored in 1570 without territorial changes. Perhaps the fairest comment on the Norwegian attitude on this and some other occasions was made by a humanist in Bergen, who wrote, 'It is not to be wondered at that the people are somewhat unwilling to defend their ruler when they never or very rarely see their king'. The king, for his part, thought of his Norwegian subjects, not as people needing or deserving the royal presence in their midst, but chiefly as a source of revenue, not to be taken from him by the Swedes. In September 1588, when wreckage from the very different Armada conflict was still being washed up on the coast of Norway, an Englishman made a manuscript note of the Norwegian position as follows:

As for the profit which the king hath from Norway, it consisteth most in such tolls as he hath out of havens, as Bergen and Warehouse, towards Russia, and in timber and stone, whereof is great abundance, for the making of masts and ships . . . great store of marble . . . divers skins, butter, and fish of sundry sorts as stockfishes and herrings.[1]

❊

Christian III, under whom Norway had been reduced to its purely subordinate status in the monarchy, was the first of ten kings—alternately Christians and Fredericks—who in general had so little to do with Norway that it would give a false impression to base a short narrative of Norwegian history upon the successive reigns. To this there is one great exception. Christian IV, who came to the throne as a child of 11 in 1588 and occupied it for sixty years, was not only the ablest of his line but the only one who ruled personally in his Norwegian kingdom. Most of the Oldenburg kings never saw their Norwegian subjects; a few made a single stately progress through the country from Oslo to Trondheim, returning down the west coast by sea; but Christian IV paid some thirty visits, and left his mark upon every aspect of the national life. It has even been said that Denmark, which he adorned with palaces and a numerous, mainly illegitimate family, 'was the land of his pleasures, Norway of his work'. And the work was that of a true Renaissance prince, inquisitive, enterprising, colourful, and gallant.

Christian came of age in 1596, but he went to Oslo for the first time as a boy of 14 to receive the homage of his subjects, ranged in four estates of nobility, clergy, burgesses, and peasants. These meetings of estates continued to be held for two generations, but acquired none of the functions of a parliament except the duty of furnishing the Crown with extra taxation. Nor did the recognition of an estate of peasants mean that they ceased to be exploited by the other estates. On the contrary, a letter from Christian's viceroy in Norway, written at this time, reveals one of the many ways in which they were placed at the mercy of lord and bailiff:

> If any poor man commits an offence so that he has to pay the bailiff or the lord for his neck, he is not executed for such a crime, but the lord or bailiff imposes so high a fine for the offence that he cannot pay it, and a poor fellow promises willingly, in order to

[1] *Den norske sjöfartshistorie*, 3 vols. (7 parts), Oslo, 1923-9, Vol. I, p. 352.

save his life, more than he or his family at any time can pay. Then he has to give the lord or bailiff a deed on his farm or possessions, as if the same had been bought.[1]

In later years the king, when he was in Norway, intervened in cases of similar injustices perpetrated by Danish lords in their capacity as governors of districts: but he did not change the system, by which grievances could only be redressed effectively by appeal to Copenhagen—hardly more accessible than the moon to a peasant in a remote Norwegian valley. But the administration of the law was to some extent improved by the issue in 1604 of a code, which consisted of a faulty translation into Danish of the laws of Magnus VI, together with the accumulated enactments of the intervening three and a quarter centuries. This was followed by a Church Law, the first since the Reformation, drawn up by the bishops in Norway, all of whom were Danes, and even so brought more closely into line with Danish Church law by the chancery in Copenhagen.

The Church Law included a requirement that every parish clergyman should have studied at Copenhagen or some other university, which helped both to danicize the lower clergy and to separate their interests more widely from those of the peasants. Norway, indeed, had no intellectual centre of its own at this time, very little contemporary literature of any importance, and—until the very end of Christian IV's reign—not even a printing press. The leading writer was Absalon Pedersson, the Bergen humanist referred to above; his work *On the Realm of Norway* shows a keen awareness of the contrast between the glorious past and the humiliating present of his country. Another *laudator temporis acti* published in 1606 a Latin verse chronicle of the kings of Norway, which was the first connected history to be available to the reading public outside Scandinavia; and in 1633 there appeared a translation of the royal sagas from Old Norse. But when the author of the latter produced a separate work on contemporary Norway, the Danish publisher struck out an allusion to 'a secret, inborn hatred for the Jutes'. Thus the Church Law corresponded to a restriction of the native culture —and made it harder for Norway to recover.

King Christian, however, concentrated his attention upon the practical uses of his Norwegian possessions. He was an enthusiastic

[1] Gjerset: *History of the Norwegian People*, II, 189.

sailor, who in 1599 took a squadron of warships round the North Cape to Vardöhus (*anglice* Warehouse), the fortress which none of his predecessors had visited. His object was partly to reassert Norwegian sovereignty over the Lapps of Finnmark and the Arctic coast beyond, and partly to exact toll from English and Dutch ships visiting these waters, for fishing or whaling or on the newly-opened English trade route to Russia via the White Sea. This last was a particularly sore point for a monarchy whose largest source of revenue was the Sound dues, paid by ships which brought Russian and other goods out via the Baltic. The sailor king also sought to vie with the Dutch and English in more distant waters. He sent three expeditions to renew contact with the Norwegian colony in Greenland, which had been lost for at least a century; no colonists were found, but a Greenland Company was formed, with a view also to whaling off Spitsbergen. In 1619 two ships set out from Bergen in search of the North-West Passage; three men came home again after a winter in Hudson's Bay.

The search for minerals was another feature of the age: Absalon Pedersson had based his hopes of a brighter future on the supposition that 'these hard mountains are full of good butter, silver, gold, and other precious things'. Christian, accordingly, established an iron-mining monopoly for Danish capitalists employing German technicians. These were not the first iron mines—English miners, for instance, had been at work round Oslo in 1558—but this large organization, the first purely capitalist undertaking in Norway, succeeded in developing a permanent, small-scale industry in many parts of the country. In 1624, following upon a chance discovery, he opened a silver mine at Kongsberg—the 'king's mountain', a town built for the miners—approached by the first carriage road ever to be laid out in Norway. The richness of the yield varied greatly, but at the height of its prosperity (about 1769) Kongsberg employed 4,000 miners and was the second largest city. A similar discovery, followed by extensive searches, resulted in the opening of several small and one big copper mines. The undertaking at Röros, began in 1644, is still active: for many generations its requirements in the way of limitless wood fuel and haulage were, for the peasants of a wide district, their principal source of ready money—and grievances.

The middle class, who were the prime beneficiaries by these enterprises, also profited on the whole from the great king's interest in the growth of town life. He strengthened the fortress of Akershus and extended it as a palace. Then, when Oslo was devastated by fire, he directed its rebuilding on a new site under the shadow of the fortress and gave it the new name of Christiania. Since 1925 the old name has been resumed, but from the market place of the modern capital the statue of Christian IV — the only Danish king of Norway to be so commemorated — still looks out upon the city of which he planned the nucleus. Kristiansand, the south coast port at the entrance to the Skagerrak, is purely his creation. A small fort had been built on an island near-by during the Swedish war; otherwise there was nothing until the king began to design the rectangular pattern of streets which still exists. Special privileges were assigned to its citizens, to the detriment of neighbouring towns, so as to populate what was planned as a centre of defence, government, and trade. Eight streets were intended to lie in succession behind the waterfront: but ten years after the first citizens moved into Kristiansand, only the first two streets had been fully built up with houses.

Christian IV left his mark on Norwegian military and naval organization. A small, separate army dates theoretically from 1628,[1] and by the end of the reign, at any rate, a force of about 6,000 peasant infantrymen and a few hundred cavalry was regularly in existence, on the basis that four full-sized farms provided one man and his equipment. To begin with, officers were often recruited from abroad: in the critical year 1644, for instance, two hundred and seventy-two Dutchmen held commissions in Norway. As regards the navy, Norway had for a century made a contribution in men and ships, but now began to have at least a squadron of her own; and a scheme was developed to provide defence-ships or merchant cruisers — specially built traders, which had certain privileges in peacetime and were at the disposal of the Crown in the event of war.

These events were of frequent recurrence. So far as Christian IV of Denmark and Norway is remembered at all outside his own dominions, it is for the part he played in the Thirty Years War. But even before this he had fought a war against Sweden in 1611-13, for which the Swedes recruited mercenaries in Holland and Scotland, whom it was proposed to march across Norway into Sweden for use on a front farther south. The smaller of two such parties, Scotsmen

[1] Three different dates are given in *Norway: Official Publication* (1900), pp. 135, 162, and 295.

G

under Ramsay and Sinclair, still lives on in Norwegian story, and legend because it was successfully ambushed and annihilated by the peasants in the Gudbrandsdal. The larger party, however, sailed up the fiord past Trondheim, landed in face of superior numbers, and crossed the frontier into Sweden unhindered—a sufficient comment on the indifference with which the peasant generally regarded any military operation not aimed at the occupation of Norwegian territory. Norway, accordingly, had little share in the disastrous campaign, in which Christian sought to champion the Protestant cause in Germany but was overwhelmed by Tilly at Lutter on August 27th, 1626—the event from which may be dated the decline of Danish power. The immediate sequel might, however, have affected Norway's fortunes vitally, for the Empire made an offer of partition to Gustavus Adolphus, Denmark to be allotted to the Empire and Norway to the king of Sweden.

Gustavus Adolphus, the Lion of the North, rejected the offer, preferring to bring to a glorious success the championship of Protestantism in which Christian had failed so dismally. Christian, having retired from the war, was roused to jealousy, and soon after the death of Gustavus in Germany in 1632 most unwisely provoked another conflict with Sweden. An old man now, he fought with great heroism: wounded so that he lost the sight of one eye, he still walked the deck of his flagship *The Trinity* in the thick of the fight. Norway, with its increasing economic resources, was better organized for war than before, thanks to her influential and ambitious viceroy, Hannibal Sehested, husband of one of the king's many daughters. But, though Norway was not seriously invaded, the Swedish army overran the whole of Jutland, and peace was bought in 1645 at the price of the two Norwegian border districts of Jemtland and Herjedal. Three years later the death of king Christian IV, worn out and disappointed, left Norway, which his rule had in many ways invigorated, attached to a Danish kingdom that had ceased to be the predominant power in the north.

Denmark, bearing Norway always with her, now passed rapidly from war for predominance to war for survival. An alliance was made with Holland, involving some passive support for the Dutch in their struggle with Cromwell, but no help was forthcoming when in 1657 the intended war of revenge was opened against the Swedes.

On the contrary, in nine months the Swedish army had landed in Zealand and threatened the Danish capital. Scania, the Danish province across the Sound, had now to be surrendered, along with the Norwegian district of Baahuslen, lying between the Danish province and the present-day Norwegian frontier near Halden. Farther north, the terms of peace were still more catastrophic. Not only must the Norwegians give back Jemtland and Herjedal, which they had re-occupied during the war, but Trondheim and Tröndelag passed into the hands of Sweden. The rest of northern Norway was also claimed by the Swedes, a claim which the possession of the port of Trond-heim would probably have enabled them to make good. In any case, the realm of St Olaf was now partitioned. When the Swedes after only a few months' respite renewed the war, and the Danish army was shut up in Copenhagen, it might well have seemed that the best Norway could hope for was to be transferred to Sweden entire — as conquered territory wrested from a permanently humbled Denmark.

But the Norwegians rose to the occasion. They recaptured Trond-heim from a weak and partly disaffected garrison of less than one thousand men. More important, the town of Halden, which at that time had little in the way of regular fortifications and, between September 1658 and February 1660, was attacked three times by experienced Swedish generals, withstood them all, and even served as a base for an advance into Baahuslen. The siege had just been raised for the third time when news was received of the death of the king of Sweden. In the preceding February the Copenhageners, reinforced by a Dutch supply fleet, had repulsed the attempt to take their city by storm. Other powers shared the anxiety of the Dutch lest the Swedes should become sole masters of the Baltic and its approaches, so the chance was seized to re-establish peace on the general basis of the *status quo*. But Norway, though Baahuslen was lost for ever, recovered Trondheim and the rest of the territory which had been torn from her west coast two years before. Thus the year 1660 marks the rescue of Norway, mainly by her own efforts, from the threat of partition, which the example of Poland suggests might well have proved a fatal blow; the establishment of her present-day frontiers; and an obvious recovery of self-respect from the nadir reached in the age of the Reformation. Moreover, the new frontier to the south-east interposed a stretch of Swedish territory, about five days' ride, between Norway and Denmark: distance lent disenchantment and would in the end make separation easier.

We must, therefore, beware of exaggeration and the temptation to anticipate the march of events. When the war resulted in a change of constitution in Denmark, quite as sweeping as the territorial changes, it was found sufficient to send the king's son, the future Christian V, to receive the formal consent of the estates of Norway to a revolution which had been completed in Denmark seven months before. Incensed by defeat and the sufferings of war, the third estate under Nansen, mayor of Copenhagen, joined with the clergy under the bishop of Zealand in attacking the privileges of the nobility, such as freedom from taxation and the all-important right of the Council to elect the king. Both demands were conceded; the existing charter of privileges, granted to the nobles by the king in return for his election, was withdrawn; and the king was invited by the estates to draw up a pragmatic sanction describing his position as hereditary monarch. This document declared that the royal powers, both in Denmark and in Norway (which had never willingly accepted the elective system of monarchy), were not merely hereditary but abso-lute—the two ideas being somehow conjoined, to the surprise of many members of the Danish estates, who nevertheless signed the document. This was in January 1661; the Norwegian consent, al-ready mentioned, followed in August; and four years later the all-powerful minister Griffenfeld set out the new system in detail in a Lex Regia, which it was not, however, found expedient to publish until 1709.

In theory, the Norwegians were now the legally defenceless sub-jects of an absolute despotism, the most autocratic monarchy in Europe, based on the ideas of Hobbes's *Leviathan*. Hobbes, however, was reasoning largely in terms of the English civil war when he declared that an absolute authority, whether exercised by a king or a parliament, was the best safeguard of men's lives and property: a Danish absolutism did not necessarily offer these advantages to Nor-way. In theory, therefore, the Norwegians were for the next century and a half delivered without possibility of redress into the hands of a foreigner, who could do anything he liked except alienate territory or abandon the Lutheran religion.

The king has the highest and most unlimited power, for he is the supreme head here on earth, elevated above all human laws, and he recognizes no other judge, either in secular or spiritual matters, than God Almighty. He can take no oath, nor make any declaration of any kind whatsoever, either orally or written, as he, being a free and unrestrained monarch, cannot be bound by his subjects through any oath or obligation.[1]

In practice, Norway gained more than she lost by the change. On the one hand, the autocratic rulers after 1660 sought to establish a unitary realm of Denmark-Norway, to which there was now no legal barrier whatever. On the other hand, the power of the old Danish nobility was broken; Danes and Norwegians were all equally subjects, set at the same great distance below the feet of Majesty; and though the civil service, which executed the orders of the autocrat, was still mainly Danish, he required some degree of efficiency in the management of what he regarded as the outlying portion of a great personal estate. The main spheres of administration were allocated among half a dozen 'colleges' or commissions, composed of high officials working in Copenhagen. Their orders, often extending to the regulation of the minutest details of private life, reached the public in both countries alike through a new and more bureaucratic type of county governor, the *amtmann;* this remained the title of the chief local official in Norway for two and a half centuries. Behind the officials of whatever rank stood the king, conducting his own policy, for better or worse.

A dramatic illustration of the weakness of personal rule was given in the very year of the Lex Regia, which was also the year of the outbreak of the second Anglo-Dutch war. Bergen harbour became the rendezvous for Dutch merchant ships, including ten East Indiamen, which were making the voyage home via Cape Wrath to escape capture by the English fleet. The cargo was valued at £6,000,000: admiral Lord Sandwich doubted whether such wealth had ever before been collected in one place. On the evening of August 1, 1665, he sent a squadron of ten men-of-war into the harbour; but they lost the advantage of surprise by stopping to negotiate for the forts to remain neutral, and when they attacked the Dutch at 6 a.m. next day the forts opened fire at a range of 150 yards. The English force withdrew after three hours with 118 dead. When all was over, it transpired that a messenger was on his way from Denmark, with final

[1] Second and seventeenth articles of the Lex Regia.

details of an agreement between the king and the English minister, by which the forts were to have stayed neutral and the king was to have had half the booty. The consequences were that the king acquired an additional reputation for bungling duplicity, and that he became involved in a short and indecisive, but not inexpensive, war with England.

Christian V, who succeeded to the throne in 1670, was the ally of the Dutch against France and Sweden in the war which ended at the Peace of Nymwegen (1678). Louis XIV was strong enough to forbid any territorial changes to the disadvantage of his Swedish allies: but the Norwegians could look back upon a grim struggle, in which they had re-entered lost possessions and contributed more than a proportionate share to some famous victories won by the Danish-Norwegian navy. The period is, however, chiefly memorable as showing autocratic kingship, not at its wisest but at its most active. Griffenfeld, the author of the Lex Regia, fell from power for opposing the war, was accused of treason, reprieved on the scaffold, and incarcerated for 18 years on a tiny island in the Trondheimsfiord. The king, who had visited and admired the court of Louis XIV, intended to be his own prime minister, though as regards Norway he generally allowed himself to be guided by his viceroy, Gyldenlöve, a half-German half-brother of the king. This remarkable man held his office for 35 years in all, but after the conclusion of the war, in which he had proved an enterprising commander, he remained in Copenhagen at the royal elbow, zealously watching the interests of the Norwegians, to whom he had become genuinely attached. Christian himself, however, had Norway much in mind: was it not the part of his patrimony of which his Swedish neighbour sought to deprive him? In 1685 he paid an eight-week visit to the country. Four thousand peasants were mobilized to row the royal party through the Leads from Trondheim to Bergen. He crossed the mountains, saw the towns, carefully inspected the fortresses, and was greeted everywhere, by a population which had never before set eyes on its king, with enthusiastic acclamation as the father of his people.

It was, indeed, in keeping with the spirit of the age that he treated his subjects almost literally as children. There was to be system in everything, from the insignia to be worn by licensed beggars to the hymns sung on Sunday, which were to be the same for every church in Denmark and Norway. Heaven, it seemed, had the same tastes as the king, for when it was decided to regulate private festivities according to the rank of the host—how many guests he might invite, what kind of clothes they might wear, and the number of dishes to be set before them—he prefaced his very detailed order with the reproachful observation:

> The extravagance of attire as well as food and drink at weddings, confinements, and parties is carried to such extremes that God thereby must be highly offended, and as one will not be inferior to the other in such matters, they waste their means until they are utterly ruined.[1]

It was, however, to this spirit of order that Norway was indebted for her legal code, published in 1688 and not yet completely superseded. Four Norwegians were originally entrusted with its compilation, but their draft was heavily altered by a Danish commission to bring it more into line with Danish jurisprudence. This meant that capital punishment replaced much of the old system of fines: but the most important feature was the retention of the old Norwegian land law, including odal right, and the judge was given a rather more independent position than in the Danish code of the same period. Another feature very different from the Danish practice was the inclusion, at Gyldenlöve's suggestion, of some safeguards for tenants against landowners.

But it would be wrong to infer that the peasants, the unobserved nine-tenths of the population, were a favoured class. On the contrary, the proportion of tenants to freeholders reached its maximum early in this reign, much land being bought and let out for profit by rich townspeople. In the absence of any important improvements in farming technique, the growth of population kept the rural standard of living very low: oats were still the main crop, and the average yield not more than threefold. Military expenditure and the upkeep of the court in far-off Copenhagen involved the levy of burdensome taxes. In addition, there were the various fees and dues and travel charges (including free use of the farmer's horses) exacted by the bailiff—usually a Dane and always the focus of ill-will, which sometimes rose to open mutiny; for what the Crown strove conscientiously to restrict, the man on the spot had both the will and the opportunity to expand. In 1662 the chartered towns, less than a

[1] Gjerset: *History*, II, 264.

dozen in all, had had their privileges extended, with a view to giving them control, not only of overseas trade, but of the internal commerce of their respective hinterlands. A further order of 1688, issued in pursuit of the same object of assigning appropriate functions to every class, established what were to be known for nearly two centuries as Quantum Saws. These were the 664 sawmills conducted by townspeople and authorized to saw a prescribed amount annually: except in the far north, or for local use elsewhere, all peasant-owned saw-mills were henceforth forbidden.

It was therefore in the towns that new growth began; and it is noteworthy that the thriving class of *entrepreneurs* was not recruited from the surrounding peasantry but from the foreigners, Danes, Germans, Dutch, and British, whom trade attracted from overseas. Timber was now the main staple, even more than fish, and about 1650 employed some 300 ships from Holland alone. The English Navigation Acts then intervened to give English shipping a larger share: [1] after the catastrophe of 1666, so much timber was fetched across the North Sea that the Norwegians were said to have 'warmed themselves well at the London fire'. Less successful was the attempt to replace foreign by native manufactures. Christian V, in imitation of Colbert, set up a new 'college' of officials to supply the necessary stimulus. He even employed an immigrant from Holstein to act as director of commerce for Norway, who planted a group of at least seven variegated factories on what might be called an industrial estate at Bergen. But they all collapsed, and a few years later manufacturing ventures in all parts of the country had subsided into one paper mill and one oil mill.

But Norway's future, and the future of her towns, lay with the sea. Seamen were so plentiful and ships so few that many Norwegians took service with the Dutch and, to a less extent, the English. Most of these emigrants disappear from sight among the miscellaneous maritime population of the Dutch harbour towns: but it was recorded with rueful pride that in the Anglo-Dutch naval wars Norwegians played a part on both sides, even among the captains. From 1672 onwards the government began to encourage the

---

[1] But, according to a tendentious broadsheet of 1668, *Inconveniencies to the English Nation which have ensued the Act of Navigation, in reference to the Growths of Norway*, Cromwell did not enforce the Act of 1651 strictly in relation to the Norwegian timber trade.

struggling native mercantile marine, especially the class known as defence ships, by a preferential tariff. This helped, and when the struggle between Louis XIV and William III began in earnest the distraction of mightier rivals enabled Norway to enjoy its first great shipping boom. In 1689 Bergen, still the seat of a Hanse 'factory', was visited by 350 ships—all but forty were Norwegian. An English pamphleteer of 1694 give a vivid picture of a growth which culminated in a fleet of 500 trading vessels, representing a 300 per cent increase in twenty years.

> In Norway little sea towns that formerly had either one, or two, or no ships at all, but sold their timber to the English and Dutch that came thither (the Dutch especially, being as it were their factors, carrying out their goods, and supplying them with all sorts of French and Spanish wares, which the inhabitants never fetched themselves). These very towns, which are not one or two, but most sea-towns in Norway, being in abundance all along the sea-coasts, now send yearly to England, France, and Holland ten, twenty, thirty, or forty large fly-boats, and ships of other building, as can be testified by the merchants who trade to those parts.[1]

When Christian V died in August 1699, the stage was already set for the outbreak of the Great Northern War. However, only the later phases of the long drawn out struggle, in which Russia seemingly for ever wrested from Sweden the hegemony of the Baltic shores, were of direct concern to Norway. For the first Danish attack on the dominions of Charles XII, only 20 years of age and hemmed in by enemies, was no sooner begun than ended. Fearing that France might reap the benefit of this distraction in the north, the English king William III sent an Anglo-Dutch fleet to the Sound. This enabled Charles XII to threaten Copenhagen, and Frederick IV therefore withdrew from the war exactly twelve months after his accession. The young king of Sweden continued with his at first overwhelmingly successful campaigns against Poland and Russia; but for many years Norway at least had a closer interest in the war which was simultaneously raging in western Europe. Denmark took no part

[1] [William King]: *Animadversions on a Pretended Account of Denmark*, London, 1694, p. 74.

in the War of the Spanish Succession (1701-13), but Frederick hired out a force of 20,000 mercenaries, including 6,000 Norwegians, who served under Marlborough on the Danube and in the Low Countries. More important, Norwegian shipping received a tremendous temporary stimulus by its neutral status in a world at war.

In 1709, however, the news of Charles XII's defeat by Peter the Great at Poltava far away in the Ukraine brought Frederick back into the fighting. So far as Norway was concerned, this meant chiefly a series of minor expeditions into Baahuslen, while the Swedes gradually lost ground to their enemies on the far side of the Baltic and their king lingered for years as an importunate exile in Turkey. But when he at last returned home (on Christmas Eve, 1715) to face a desperate position, the warrior king immediately resolved to rally the last energies of his subjects for a bold campaign against Norway. An outright conquest would provide a major compensation for his losses; a lesser success would still give him much-needed bargaining power at a general settlement.

Charles XII launched his attack against Oslo in early March. He was held up for a time by bitter weather, which enabled a strong garrison to be thrown into the fortress of Akershus, but he took the city itself without encountering resistance on the 21st. This gave him good quarters for his troops during an inclement season, but further advance was checked by the guerrilla activities of the peasants and a well-organized attack on his supply depot down the fiord at Moss. The king then abandoned his imperfect hold on the capital in order to secure Halden, the frontier town on the natural line of communication south into Sweden. The town itself fell, but when the Swedes went on to storm the castle, strongly built on a commanding height only half a century before, the people burnt their town, so that the enemy should have no place of shelter on which to base their operations. Norwegian towns, constructed largely of pitch-pine on cramped sites and exposed to Atlantic storms, were often burnt by accident; the deliberate destruction by their owners of some 330 houses was an act of self-sacrifice which made a great appeal to the popular imagination.

A second, more individual exploit followed a few days later, when Charles had adopted a second plan, involving a formal siege of the fortress. A Swedish squadron of forty ships, carrying his siege guns and supplies, lay in the Dynekilen, only twenty miles from Halden.

The entrance to the harbour was by a three-mile channel, 160-180 paces wide, with a battery of six 12-pound guns placed on an island commanding its mouth. A Norwegian captain, only 26 years of age, who had already been ennobled for his services by the name of Tordenskjold (lord thunder-shield), attacked with seven small vessels at daybreak. He had almost completed the passage of the entrance channel before his approach was signalled to the fleet, by which he was of course heavily outgunned even if there had been no battery to give support. Yet he somehow managed to close in upon the enemy, and after seven hours' hard pounding Tordenskjold was master of the harbour, from which he towed away nine warships and five transports — whatever else was left afloat was crippled. Two days later, the last Swedes had withdrawn from Norwegian soil.

This was intended only as a respite, while Charles collected fresh armies, twice the size of the Norwegian — a task which, in the condition to which Sweden had been reduced by nearly two decades of war, occupied him until the autumn of 1718. In September he sent one force to besiege Trondheim. In November he marched himself against Halden. The defences of the fortress had been improved, but the siege works duly advanced under the eye of the greatest military genius of the age, and the fate of Norway was still uncertain, when on the evening of December 11 a shot in the dark ended a career which had once involved the fortunes of half Europe. To the English poet the death of Charles at this juncture seemed an anticlimax:

> His fall was destined to a barren strand,
> A petty fortress, and a dubious hand.[1]

But for the Norwegians it spelt a great deliverance. Not only did the Swedes retire at once from south-east Norway, but the siege of Trondheim was abandoned in mid-winter and a large part of the retreating army was frozen to death in snowstorms as it recrossed the mountain passes to Sweden. The next year the Norwegians and Danes were on the offensive, and Tordenskjold scored his last triumph off the coast of Baahuslen. He died after a duel in November 1720, but by then his country had less need of him. Peace had been signed. Sweden, deprived of her Baltic provinces, was now so evenly matched with Denmark-Norway that neither side was tempted to any fresh trial of strength. A new era of almost uninterruptedly

[1] Samuel Johnson: *The Vanity of Human Wishes* (1749).

peaceful development, lasting eighty-seven years, was beginning. In it the Norwegian people gained much from the tradition of the spirit of unity and self-sacrifice which had been displayed against the invader, with Tordenskjold, the Nelson of Norway, as the greatest hero of them all.

CHAPTER VI

REVIVAL

THE end of the Great Northern War coincides almost exactly with the establishment on the other side of the North Sea of Walpole's famous peace ministry. But the years which brought such prosperity to Britain were for Norway a period of declining trade, in which recovery from war losses was slow and the life of the country felt the full effects of Danish commercial policy — a centralized economic system, firmly based on Copenhagen. As regards foreign policy, too, Norway played a less significant part than before. One of the terms of the peace provided for a commission, which in the course of the next thirty years completed the definition of the Norwegian-Swedish frontier in the desolate northern regions. So far, so good: but policy concerned itself instead with the Schleswig-Holstein frontier of Denmark, which meant a reduction in the importance of the navy, where Norwegians had distinguished themselves, and a drain on men and money for an army to serve purely Danish interests.

The most famous episode of the post-war period was among its many failures. In 1720 a company was organized in Bergen to revive the long lost connection with Greenland by means of a colonial settlement with missionary, trading, and whaling activities. The pioneer, Hans Egede, was a heroic clergyman from the Lofoten islands, who laboured on for fifteen years among the Eskimos and founded Godthaab: but before he returned (to become a bishop in Denmark) Bergen had already abandoned its interests to the Danes. There was also some Norwegian missionary activity among the long-neglected Lapps of Finnmark, but there the main concern was the economic needs of the growing Norwegian population of traders and fishermen, which Bergen and Trondheim were unable to supply, so this too became a Danish monopoly. Denmark had at the same time a monopoly of the importation of corn into southern Norway, which both kept the price high and diminished trade with England. To complete the mercantilist structure, in 1739 a Norwegian Company was started, which was to employ Danish capital for the exploitation of Norwegian natural resources: only when it had dwindled to a glassmaking concern without other interests did it became Norwegian in capital and management. It would be wrong to regard the Danish attitude as blindly selfish. Where Norway could supply the market, as in the case of iron, a monopoly was created for Norwegian benefit in Denmark. Again, the supposed need to regulate trade, which was held to justify Danish spheres of control in Norwegian economic life, also prompted an attempt to benefit Norwegian towns by a strong internal measure, assigning an appropriate rural district to each as its exclusive commercial hinterland. Above all, there was the fact that Norway still lacked the capital with which to develop her own resources apart from foreign intervention. For this the Danes were no doubt partly to blame; whatever its causes, the economic subordination of the Norwegian towns up to the middle of the century would make it premature to speak of any national renaissance.

The towns, however, contained only one-tenth of the Norwegian people. In country districts a slow process of change was already at work, which in the long run contributed an essential part to the national recovery. Population was now growing about twice as fast as it had done in the later 17th century, while the average standard of living was going up rather than down. Agricultural methods used by the Norwegian peasant had scarcely changed since the early Middle Ages, and he had no defence against inclement seasons —such as the period of increased cold which culminated in the 'black years' of 1738-42, when a third of the cattle were lost and many thousands of people perished of starvation or its equivalent in deficiency diseases. It is therefore evident that more land was being brought into cultivation by a laborious process of carting away stones, uprooting trees, and constructing buildings and means of access in newly won areas. History records little or nothing of this slow course of change—it was said to take a year to clear an acre— but without it Norway could not by the end of the century have achieved a population which was nearly equal to that of Denmark. Even this, however, was less important than the change in the social stratification of the land workers.

On the one hand, land clearance on property already attached to an existing farm, for which it served probably as rough grazing, gave rise to the growth of a new subordinate class of cottars. They were smallholders, but what was characteristic was not merely the tiny patch of ground, but the fact that their rent was paid to the farmer in work done by the smallholder, his family, and even his horse. Unlike other tenants, also, they had no legal security against dispossession. In 1750 this was remedied, indeed, for the cotter who had actually created the holding on which he lived, but otherwise his position remained as precarious as it was penurious—and by the end of the century this class, of which we hear almost nothing, is believed to have constituted about one-quarter of the rural population. Another quarter was made up of labourers without land, leaving one-half who were owners or tenants. Here, on the other hand, the trend was towards the increase of the more independent class— the yeomen freeholders who had for many centuries been on the decline. They had reached their nadir about the middle of the 17th century, at which period tenants are believed to have outnumbered them by about three to one. Since then the code of Christian V had intervened to protect tenants, so that to let out land became a less attractive proposition, as was shown when Crown land came into the market and—contrary to past practice—was left for owner-occupiers to buy. More important, there was a world-wide fall in agricultural prices, which made landlordism unattractive to those who sought a good return on their money, whereas to any peasant the purchase of his farm was the most natural use to make of his savings. By 1750 owners had become about twice as numerous as tenants, and were still increasing. Such men felt their rights of ownership in their own district most proudly and acutely, and were prone to regard the bailiff, the parson, and any other local representative of the Danish Crown as idlers or meddlers. Such men could be roused and organized to achieve independence beyond their district —for the nation at large.

All classes of the rural population were indirectly affected at this time by the religious movement of Pietism, which spread northwards from Germany and—chiefly after the great fire of Copenhagen in 1728—gave a more serious and puritan tone to the life of the Court and the clergy. Its direct influence on the masses was very slight, but among the middle class in the towns it inspired some saintly lives, a greatly increased attention to religious exercises, and an austerity of conduct which was sometimes tainted with hypocrisy. One consequence was the issue of a Conventicle Ordinance in 1741, which—like our own Clarendon Code in the days of Bunyan—enabled the local clergy to suppress any religious gathering which they regarded as fanatical or unorthodox. But the clergy themselves were deeply affected: hence, for instance, the mission to the Lapps and the support given to the Greenland mission. To put religious belief upon a sound and definite basis they therefore introduced (from Denmark) the rite of confirmation, which became established by law and custom as the means of entering into the privileges of adult life. No confirmation—no marriage, no rights of inheritance, and in principle no job. In order to be confirmed it was necessary to attend a course of instruction in Luther's catechism, organized by the priest, and to be tested orally by him in public. It was therefore necessary to learn at least temporarily how to read and a definite advantage to be able to write. Two further laws were made with a view to setting up schools and compelling attendance in every parish, but the peasants refused to pay the cost of the scheme and the country had therefore to make do with perambulatory teachers, often rejects from more profitable occupations, who travelled from farm to farm giving a few weeks' casual instruction in each locality. But confirmation, though it did not bring Pietism into the lives of the many, raised the standard of religious knowledge from practically nothing to one which affected the general level of ethics as well as churchmanship.

One of the by-products of Pietism at the Danish Court was a sudden interruption to the spontaneous flow of modern Norway's first literary genius. There had of course been earlier writers of talent, especially a half-Scots clergyman, Peter Dass, who ministered for a lifetime among the fishermen of the far north and recorded his experiences in verse-form in *Nordland's Trumpet*. He was a popular hero rather than a poet: on his death in 1707 his devoted parishioners sewed black patches on their sails, a custom which was not wholly discontinued for about 200 years. But with Ludvig Holberg of Bergen, Norway leaps to the front as producing a dramatist who was in quality most comparable to Molière but in impact far greater, for he transformed a nation's literature. Unfortunately and significantly, that nation was not the Norwegian: Holberg left Norway at the age of 22. His twenty-six most sparkling comedies graced the

Copenhagen stage in the years 1722-7, and in the more sober age which followed he turned historian — an art which he had first learnt to practise as a student in the Bodleian library at Oxford. His three-volume *History of the Kingdom of Denmark*,[1] realistic and would-be scientific in tone, was the first thing of its kind in northern Europe and necessarily shed much light upon the Norwegian people as well as the Danes. Apart from other major histories, Holberg wrote a largely historical *Account of Bergen* and a satire in Latin, on the lines of *Gulliver's Travels*, the hero of which sets out from Bergen for the centre of the earth. It is also claimed that many of the characters in the comedies are based on Norwegian rather than on Danish models. Yet Holberg lived to the age of 80, a Danish baron, a bachelor, and a man of wealth, without ever revisiting his native land. What is more, he applauded the results of the union of 1397.

> The Norwegians differ greatly from the Danes both in temperament and customs. But that difference does not prevent there being a complete union and agreement between the two nations, and ever since the famous union was made between Denmark and Norway they have been regarded as one people.[2]

Nevertheless, Holberg is a major figure in the renaissance which we are tracing. He belonged essentially to the cosmopolitan middle class of Norway's chief trading city: home background, even more than his admiration for England, gave him the feeling for reality and the humorous appreciation of character which pervade his work. What Norway gave him he repaid by helping his fellow-countrymen in later generations to understand themselves. Moreover, however busily they deplore his writing in Denmark for Danes, Holberg has always stood for them as evidence of their ability under the most unfavourable conditions to produce a figure of major importance in the history of the arts. In his lifetime the comedies were little known in Norway, which, even after the reopening of the Danish theatre in 1747, had no theatre of its own. But the Histories became fairly widely read by the middle class, and it was a Norwegian who translated the satire from the Latin. Thus the career of Holberg—

[1] A small part of this was translated into English by A. A. Feldborg. See G. L. Baden: *The History of Norway*, London, 1817.

[2] *Danmarks og Norges Beskrivelse*, Copenhagen, 1729, p. 25.

like the careers of Irish writers in England — showed how low the fortunes of his native land had sunk; but it also helped to inspire a change. His death in 1754 is separated by only six years from the foundation of Norway's first cultural academy, quickly followed by the opening of a long drawn out struggle for a university, so that her gifted sons might no longer be exiled to Copenhagen.

The last fifty years of the 18th century included at least twenty years of general war in Europe — war from which Norway again drew the profits of neutrality. War swelled the demand for timber, and enabled it to be sent abroad in Norwegian bottoms instead of its being fetched by the ships of the chief customers (England, France, Holland), who were not among the neutral powers. In addition to all this extra profit, there was a good chance for a neutral to break into the carrying trade, from which he was excluded in peacetime by the British Navigation Acts and their equivalent elsewhere. The wars of 1739-48 had already enabled Norwegian shipping to recover the ground lost earlier in their own struggle against Charles XII of Sweden, but it was the Seven Years War which provided the first big boom period and spread large profits among fish exporters, timber traders, and shipowners. The mercantile marine declined again after the restoration of peace in 1763, partly because a good many ships had been built in Norway with English capital which now took over their ownership. But the American declaration of independence on July 4, 1776, had for Norway an immediate economic, as well as a long-term political, importance, in that the general war which developed out of it produced a second shipping boom, which was not followed by a slump. In the last quarter of the century Norwegian tonnage increased by 250 per cent.

The economic life of the country profited simultaneously by the removal of trade restrictions. It became increasingly difficult for chartered towns to get the support of the government in their claim to restrict trade to their own narrow channels by suppressing a poorer or perhaps more enterprising type of merchant, who set up in an outlying suburb or in a town that had grown up without chartered privileges. In particular, the bitterly contested system, by which the peasants of a district had been required to trade only with one specified town, was by 1765 almost completely abandoned. Adam Smith's *Wealth of Nations* appeared in a Danish translation only three years after its first publication in 1776, and towards the end of the century his ideas became predominant. Thus in 1788 the Danish corn monopoly for southern Norway was finally abolished. Next year the Iceland and Finnmark trades were thrown open. Finally, in 1797 the tariff, which a generation before had been strictly mercantilist and teemed with prohibitions, became a tariff designed primarily to draw revenue—as close an approach to free trade as was achieved anywhere in modern Europe before the time of Huskisson.

Capital remained scarce, partly because Denmark, which had had a bank of issue since 1736, refused to extend to Norway a privilege which seemed likely to separate the economic interests of the two countries. Some Danish resources were invested in Norway, but as Norway was now developing the more rapidly of the two, the main effect was to extend commercial prosperity beyond the mercantile middle class of the towns to the two other groups which had capital available. On the one hand, there were the big freehold farmers, especially those with extensive property in woods—people who often converted their savings to silver plate for want of other opportunity. On the other hand, there was the official class. This now included a good many Germans as well as Danes, but families tended to become established in Norway, whence the younger generation returned to Copenhagen for the university studies which qualified them to occupy similar administrative posts, often in the same Norwegian district. Their capital came naturally to be employed in agriculture, industry, and commerce, which benefited at the same time from their superior education and wider knowledge. Agricultural improvements, in particular, began slowly to win their way through the example set by enlightened clergymen in the management of the glebe: the cant term 'potato parsons' speaks for itself.

In such circumstances the growth of national aspirations in a middle class conscious of its new wealth and importance was almost inevitable. But the beginnings were small. In 1760 the Trondheim Scientific Society was founded, on the model of an institution at Jena, with interests which ranged from the writing of Norway's history, so as to show its separateness from that of Denmark[1], to propaganda for the more scientific agriculture which might enrich its soil. For fifty years this remained the only centre of learning in

---

[1] For example, in 1763 the Society published parts of the Quirini narratives, translated unfortunately from a faulty version in German.

the country above the level of the old cathedral schools. In 1772, however, a Norwegian Society was started in Copenhagen. Its original object was mainly to protect Danish literature against German influences, but its members included at least one true poet, J. H. Wessel, as well as many bombastic versifiers, and it served for many years the purpose of keeping alive a rather uncritical enthusiasm for 'Norway Land of Heroes'. Since the members were mostly sons of officials in Norway, it helped to give a Norwegian outlook to a class which was in origin largely foreign and was engaged to serve a foreign government.

That service, however, was still being rendered unquestioningly to a bureaucratic system which had its centre in Copenhagen. This was shown in 1765, when the pressure of a poll tax caused a rising among the peasants in the coastal district adjoining Bergen, one of the poorest areas in the whole of the always impoverished, rock-bound west coast. Though the new tax was twice as heavy as all the existing direct taxes and the peasants, marching into Bergen, merely exacted a refund, without doing any serious harm to the terrified authorities, a force of 350 mercenaries was immediately shipped from Copenhagen, the money was re-exacted, and the ringleaders were sentenced to death (but not actually executed). It was only after an interval of seven years, during which there was passive resistance in many parts of the country, that the iniquitous tax was abandoned. In the meantime the strength of the system was shown still more strikingly, when it survived both revolution and counter-revolution in Copenhagen.

Of the three kings who ascended the Danish throne in the 18th century, Christian VI made some mark as a devout adherent of Pietism. His successor, Frederick V, who married a daughter of our king George II, imitated the morals of his father-in-law rather than his father, but he was quite insignificant as a ruler. There is perhaps something symbolic in the fact that, when he paid the last visit of any absolutist monarch to his Norwegian dominions, rain deterred him from penetrating beyond the vicinity of Oslo. With the reign of Christian VII, which stretched nominally from 1766 to 1808, the House of Oldenburg touched the lowest depths. A voluptuary at 17, he informed the court doctor that he would 'rage for two years', and degenerated rapidly into a helpless imbecile. He married, and mistreated, an English princess, Caroline Matilda, who was two years his junior. She precipitated a crisis which was in some sense inevitable by quickly falling in love with his German physician and subsequent master, Struensee. The power which he gained through conspiracy was overthrown by a counter-conspiracy after only sixteen months, whereupon Struensee was maimed and beheaded, and the unhappy queen, having been saved from a Danish prison by the determined intervention of her brother, George III, ended her brief days as a lonely exile in Hanover.

Yet 1771, when Struensee ruled supreme, was the year when the Enlightenment came to Denmark. This meant for Norway, too, a policy of reform, an opportunity of free discussion, and the rousing of hopes which were not destined to be satisfied until the dissolution of the union with Denmark in 1814. For Struensee believed in the ideas characteristic of enlightened despotism — humanitarianism, freedom of trade, religious toleration, liberty of opinion. It was the last which mattered most to Norway, where a torrent of publications exposed the selfishness of Danish policy in the past, and pleaded for the removal of the poll tax and the corn monopoly and the provision of a university, a bank, and a separate department of commerce. Of these five things only one, the freeing of the corn trade, had been achieved at the time of Struensee's fall — and that on a temporary basis. As the nature of the Norwegian demands suggests, it was chiefly the mercantile middle class which had been roused to agitate during that eventful year: uninstructed opinion seems to have been far more alive to the despotism of Struensee than to his enlightenment. Norwegians in Denmark had even demonstrated against him, and his overthrow by a clique of reactionaries was well received.

For the next twelve years reaction reigned in both countries, and even the movement towards freedom of trade was suspended. The removal of the poll tax, already noted, was the only concession to Norwegian wishes; a smuggling affray in Bergen in the same year as the Boston Tea Party (with which it has been misleadingly compared) the only serious protest against the system. Neither did Norway play any part in the *coup* which terminated the period of reaction in 1784, when the 16-year-old crown prince on his first attendance at the Council surprised the king into signing a new list of opposition ministers. The royal imbecile fled in panic from the room, but his signature was sacred. For Norway the return to enlightenment meant chiefly the progress of the free trade policy. For Denmark it meant also the final abolition of serfdom, brought about with other legal reforms by Colbjörnsen, scion of a leading family in Halden, whom Norwegians thought of with pride as bringing their traditions of personal liberty to the heavily oppressed Danish peasantry.

But Colbjörnsen was no Norwegian nationalist, and the programme of the Danish ministry in which he served was one of reform from above, imposing the imprint of enlightened institutions upon the obedient subjects of a closely united Dano-Norwegian kingdom. This appears clearly in the treatment accorded to a widespread movement of discontent among the peasants of south-east Norway, which came to a head in 1786-7. Its leader, Christian Lofthus, was a once well-to-do peasant who had lost money in shipping ventures at the end of the American War of Independence; but the public grievances which he voiced were genuine and their expression most moderate. The peasants thought of the increasingly wealthy middle class of the towns as leagued with the officials in order to exploit them: the king, on the other hand, was a father of his people, who had only to be brought to understand their grievances to ensure redress. Hence the organization of petitions, requesting such changes as the abolition of the Danish corn monopoly (reintroduced after the fall of Struensee); reduction of some of the thirty-six taxes payable by the peasant; stricter control over the fees and fines exacted by the bailiffs and other officials—a perennial grievance; and one striking novelty, 'that the king will give us as our superiors natives of Norway, who understand its needs'. But even the patriotic note was sounded without avail. The militia of the south-coast towns sided with the government against the peasants, whose mustering in support of Lofthus was illegal under a measure passed to suppress the disturbances of 1765. Though he had twice been received by the crown prince with respect as the people's representative, Lofthus was eventually hunted down like a dangerous criminal and chained to a block in the fortress of Akershus. Twelve years later sentence of life imprisonment was finally confirmed on a man who had been two years dead. The agitation also had long since passed into silence, leaving only scattered memories of the first great peasant leader who contributed, by example if not by achievement, to the renaissance of modern Norway.

✼

While Lofthus languished in his dark cell at Akershus, the fall of the Bastille proclaimed the opening of a new era of 'liberty, equality, and fraternity' in Europe. The direct effects in Norway were slight. The middle class in the towns discussed, indeed, the exciting developments overseas in their clubs and in the four small weekly papers, which existed almost entirely on local advertising. But this class generally combined a rather patronizing sympathy for the oppressed Frenchmen's struggle with the reflection that Norway already had all the freedom it needed. The philosophy of the revolution came more slowly into its own. In 1794 Colbjörnsen, for example, declared that the monarchy derived its powers from the people, but found in the existing autocratic form of government the expression of the 'general will'. By that time, however, the outbreak of the revolutionary wars had caused Norwegians to take sides in accordance with their commercial interests. Trondheim and Bergen had strong trade connections with France, which the British navy as far as possible interrupted: the tone of the press was correspondingly democratic and pro-French, especially in 1797, when British fortunes were at their lowest ebb.

> At last the Franks have mastered nearly all their enemies: only the new Carthage is left, and that is likely to experience the fate of Carthage of old. Our thoughts can hardly grasp the achievements of these republicans—although we see them—so colossal are they. We constantly ask each other what they worship that makes the Franks so brave, so unconquerable. The answer is: freedom.[1]

But all along the south coast and as far east as Oslo the timber trade and shipping enjoyed a golden age, which lasted—with one dramatic interruption—until the summer of 1807, and to which friendly relations with England were the indispensable key. The south and east now had the predominant influence in the country.

Since the age of Walpole, when Denmark-Norway was for a time a British ally, the good understanding between the kingdoms had only been interrupted twice. The ill-treatment of queen Caroline Matilda temporarily inflamed English opinion; and in 1780-82 Denmark-Norway joined with seven other powers to form the league in defence of their shipping rights, known as the Armed Neutrality of the

[1] Trondheim newspaper of December 15, 1797 (*Det norske folks liv og historie*, VII, 187).

North. But it is significant of the general trend of policy that the
Danish foreign minister, while openly supporting the league organized by Russia, had signed an abortive secret treaty with England, in
which the rights of neutrals were less forcibly asserted. Friendship
was also encouraged by cultural ties. Sons of well-to-do families received their business training in England, sometimes their schooling
as well. London had both a church and a club in which Norwegians
were the leading spirits. Chippendale furniture, Wedgwood china,
English oil-paintings, and the three-volume novels of the English
circulating library — all these in return found their way into Norwegian homes. Young's *Night Thoughts* and Thomson's *Seasons*
largely inspired the nature worship which found expression among
Norwegian poets in Copenhagen, to whom we have already referred.

This cultural influence was all the stronger because it was not
entirely a one-way traffic. In 1770 the translation into English of the
Swiss writer Mallet's *Northern Antiquities* began to arouse interest
in the heroic age of Scandinavian history, a study which was bound
to place Norway in the foreground. Before the end of the century the
future Mary Godwin in her *Letters* had inaugurated the long series
of semi-popular, half-accurate[1] expositions of the Norwegian way
of life as experienced by the foreigner in a quick tour, and the leading British economist of the day had visited the country in search of
confirmation of his classic theory. The study which Malthus made of
the 'checks to population' in Norway[2], while incidental to his main
argument, served to introduce a fairly wide public to some of the
distinctive features of Norwegian odal tenure and the status of the
husmann or cottar.

The main link, however, was neither diplomatic nor cultural, but
plainly commercial. Malthus in 1799 noted the evidence of prosperity as far north as the copper mines at Röros. It affected the big
farmers of the wooded eastern valleys, whose houses had become

[1] M. Wollstonecraft: *Letters Written during a Short Residence in Sweden,
Norway, and Denmark*, London, 1796, at first surprises the reader by its frequent mention of the expression of French republican sympathies in south-
eastern Norway. But the authoress, who largely sympathized with France
herself, provides the clue: 'I am persuaded that I have formed a very just
opinion of the character of the Norwegians, without being able to hold con-
verse with them.'

[2] Book II, Chapter I, in the 'new edition, very much enlarged' of T. R.
Malthus: *Essay on the Principle of Population*, London, 1803.

larger and lighter than of old, heated by highly decorative iron stoves and furnished with elaborately carved and painted cupboards and chests, bearing silent witness to new standards of comfort and artistry. But it is on the coast that we find a patrician class of industrialists, merchants, and shipbuilders—the occupations being very profitably intermingled—which seized with both hands the chances of wealth open to a seafaring neutral power. Best known among them, partly at least through the nostalgic memoirs he wrote in the 1840's, was an iron magnate, whose stoves found a sale all over Scandinavia. But it is significant that Jacob Aall had his interests near Arendal, which built more ships than any other port. The leading merchant family were the Ankers, who shipped timber from Oslo to London with such frequency that at least one of them satisfied a fastidious taste by having his laundry attended to on the other side of the North Sea. Another prominent figure in Oslo society was John Collett, English by origin as the name suggests, who ran a large model farm in what are now the suburbs, where he practised and popularized the improved English methods of agriculture. This was the class of people who warranted a poet's playful allusion to Norwegians who believed that human beings were born only in Norway or England.

For a time, everything turned to gold; even the activity of French and Dutch privateers off the southern coast meant profit, since their English prizes were brought into Norwegian harbours and sold cheap —nearly 100 ships, mostly very small, in three years. But the freedom of the seas, as this implies, was precarious at best, and in 1800, when Denmark-Norway rashly accepted Russia's invitation to form with her a new Armed Neutrality of the North, Britain in reprisal placed an immediate embargo on all the hundreds of their ships in British ports. There followed the defeat of the Dano-Norwegian navy by Parker and Nelson in the Copenhagen roadstead, by which they were forced to withdraw from the Armed Neutrality and accept English ideas of free goods and contraband. The golden years then reached their climax, particularly after the renewal of the struggle against Napoleon in 1803 had absorbed Britain's energies. Timber exports trebled in five years to a figure which was not reached again for more than a generation. The mercantile marine, swollen by this and the fish exports and the high freights to be earned in the foreign carrying trade, increased by about fifty per cent in six years. Moreover, this fleet was now larger than that of Denmark and Schleswig-Holstein combined.

The middle class had little fault to find with Danish policy in these years, except for its failure to maintain the value of the currency and the related and long-standing grievance of the refusal to allow Norway its own bank. Branches of a Danish credit institution had, indeed, been set up in 1797 at Oslo, Bergen, and Trondheim, but after a big financial crisis two years later they ceased to make any new loans. There was no strong separatist movement, and prosperity made the union more popular than before, especially perhaps with the less reflective elements among the people. But Norway's increased economic power, and the fact that her population was now only five per cent less than the Danish, made it easy to foresee a peaceful development towards greater equality within the union. What was not foreseen was the disaster of the naval war against Britain, which from 1807 onwards split the two kingdoms and in doing so gave Norwegian nationalism its greatest stimulus.

But before the English guns spoke for the second time in Copenhagen harbour, another movement, very different from the rise of a self-confident, luxury-loving middle class, had made its equally important contribution to the growth of nationality. The Norwegian peasantry, deaf to the call of the French Revolution, were roused by the call of religious revival to assert themselves — and men who began by taking responsibility for their own souls ended by taking responsibility for a nation. Hans Nielsen Hauge, like Lofthus, was the son of a peasant and a hero of the peasantry, who suffered the extremes of injustice on behalf of his class: but where Lofthus the politician failed, Hauge the lay preacher succeeded.

The parallel with John Wesley is a close one, and although the Haugeans owed nothing to Methodism, which entered Norway via America in the second half of the 19th century, there was even a common point of departure in the Pietist movement. This influenced Hauge's early home and, through the Moravians, had been a main factor in Wesley's conversion. Both men defied the conventional church teaching of their day, not by asserting any new dogma, but by their insistence upon the importance of a sense of personal salvation and the need to quicken and deepen the religious feelings by frequent devotional exercises and an all-pervading seriousness of life. They were both of them great preachers and travellers: in six years Hauge covered 10,000 miles in every part of Norway, visiting even the far north on foot. They had similar gifts of organization: in fact there is a very close parallel to the early Methodist societies in Hauge's scheme for establishing one of his 'friends' in every community, so as to provide hospitality, a meeting-place, and a means of following-up the work done by his travelling lay evangelists. And they suffered much the same kind of misrepresentation as wild fanatics, although they were both of them extremely practical men — one of Hauge's maxims was, 'Deny, but do not despise, the world' — and had if anything a rather exaggerated respect for civil authority. The Norwegian clergy denounced Hauge as a Jacobin just as readily and with just as little regard to truth as their English counterparts had shown when they called Wesley a Jacobite.

But there are also important differences to be noticed. Hauge had little formal education, though his most effective propaganda was his books. His influence, accordingly, was directed in favour of an improved standard of elementary instruction, so that his hearers might profit from their Bibles, hymn-books, and evangelical tracts. But Haugeanism for generations waged a bitter war, not only against the innocent traditional amusements of rural life, but to stop the advance of culture on a wide front. Economic life, on the other hand, gained directly by Hauge's missionary travels. He carefully observed the possibilities of each district he visited, planted out farming colonies on undeveloped land in the north, built up his own thriving business in Bergen as a wholesale merchant in corn and fish, and organized a paper mill and other industries for a kind of co-operative community planned and successfully managed by himself. His motives were not those of a self-seeker, but to rescue his followers from hostile surroundings which might weaken their faith, to enable them to develop their own latent abilities, and to break down class monopoly. His practical capacity was acknowledged even by his worst enemies, for when the hard times came they released him temporarily from prison to organize salt works as employment for the starving population.

Above all, the story of Hauge is a story of persecution. The experience which caused him to dedicate his life to the conversion of others came to him in April 1796 — a young man singing a German Pietist hymn while he followed the plough. His effective ministry lasted less than eight years, and was interrupted by frequent arrests on charges of vagabondism or breach of the Conventicle Ordinance. Finally, an official order was issued for him to be imprisoned without trial pending full inquiry. In October 1804, he was taken to Akershus in irons. The rigours of the first year of his incarceration ruined his health with scurvy, and temporarily broke his spirit, not so much because he was allowed no book or paper or visitor and was only three times in the fresh air, but through the realization that his persecutors were not merely the clergy and bailiffs but the king and government, whom he had always reverenced. The conditions were later relaxed and he was even let out on licence, as already related. But Hauge was not finally released until 1811, when it was thought that he would otherwise die, and the settlement of his case waited another three years, the sentence he had served in advance being rounded off eventually with a heavy fine. His brother bought him a farm, and he started another mill, the first in the modern industrial area of Oslo. By the time of his death in 1824 he had won the respect of the orthodox. But as late as 1812, a year of distress, we read of him ministering to the bodily and spiritual needs of the poor, while 'friends' kept watch against the approach of any well-dressed person — presumed to be inevitably an enemy.

The treatment accorded to Hauge is a vivid illustration of the gulf which still, in the opening years of the 19th century, separated the peasants from the official class. But the attempt to silence his 'friends' and to confiscate his writings, while it prevented the emergence of any separate Haugean Church, did not succeed in crushing Haugeanism as an increasingly aggressive force inside the existing Church organization. Hauge's 'friends' figured in the first Norwegian parliament, and the repeal of the Conventicle Ordinance (in 1842) was their tribute to his memory. In the course of time Haugeanism became the hard core of a fundamentalist opposition to the modernist clergy, and it still has its strongholds, particularly on the west coast. It has even been claimed that Norway was never thoroughly christianized before. Be that as it may, in the critical years from 1807 onwards it greatly affected Norway's secular development that the freeholding peasants, and even cottars, had been roused to a new sense of their own value and possessed the vestiges at least of a nation-wide organization.

❊

Meanwhile, the impact of the French Revolution personified in

Napoleon was reaching its maximum in Europe. The Danish crown prince watched his southern frontier from Kiel with mounting anxiety, as Austria and Prussia fell before the French armies and Russia was driven to make the famous compromise at Tilsit, by which the two emperors divided the European world between them. But it could only be the European world, since blue water marked the limits of their power. To which world did Denmark-Norway belong — the western continental mainland, dominated by Napoleon's marshals, or that of the islands and seaways, where the British Admiralty's word was law? The interests of Denmark pulled in one direction, those of Norway in the other; and the dilemma was inescapable. On August 2, 1807, before the agreements made at Tilsit were known in England, Napoleon wrote to his marshal Bernadotte: 'Denmark must declare war on England or else I declare war on Denmark. In the latter case your task will be to occupy the whole of the Danish mainland.' But Canning had already deduced what the next French move would be. He held all Danish and Norwegian shipping in British ports, while two expeditions steered into the Sound and Great Belt, ready to beleaguer Copenhagen and the whole island of Zealand from both sides, if the crown prince rejected the ultimatum dispatched to him at Kiel. This demanded the transfer of the Dano-Norwegian fleet to British service for the duration of the war, in return for a guarantee of 25 ships-of-the-line and an (inadequate) army of 40,000 men to defend his father's territories against Napoleon.

Frederick chose honour and an alliance with the then master of western Europe rather than a submission to naked threats, which would have benefited Norway at the cost of a French occupation of at least the major part of Denmark and all Schleswig-Holstein. The British landed on Zealand and by a three-day bombardment of Copenhagen forced the surrender of the fleet. The prince, who next year succeeded his insane father on the throne as Frederick VI, exercised a greater personal influence on government than his three predecessors — and used it all to maintain the alliance with Napoleon and the 'continental system' for the exclusion of British trade, through thick and thin, for the six long years that elapsed before Napoleon was driven back at last across the Rhine.

For Norway the first consequence was the severance of regular sea-route connections with the authorities in Copenhagen, in anticipation of which an interim commission of government was set up, together with a supreme law court to hear the criminal appeals which for so many centuries had been sent to the Danish capital. The commission, composed of leading officials, wrestled as best it could with three great problems. One was financial—to determine what measures were needed to avoid a complete breakdown of all economic activity. Merchant vessels and their cargoes had been seized without recompense in England; their crews were prisoners in the hulks at Chatham; and in any case the British naval blockade deprived Norway of any outlet for her timber and other products. A system of loans was organized under Danish sanction, but by January 1813, the paper currency had sunk to about one-fifteenth of its nominal value and, as a sequel to a kind of national bankruptcy, the Danes at last agreed to a separate bank for Norway. Work went on, but no amount of purely internal activity could enable Norway to feed itself. These were hunger years, when the use of Iceland moss was officially recommended to eke out the flour, and bark bread came back into extensive use. But the commission found an energetic agent in the youthful Count Wedel Jarlsberg, who bought up supplies in Jutland and brought them across to meet the first emergency. Lesser men then took up a perilous but essential trade, sailing in open boats across the Skagerrak by night and in all weathers at the constant risk of interception by British warships on patrol.

Defence was the third problem. Denmark-Norway had only one serviceable battleship left after the capitulation of Copenhagen, and this was lost in action off the Danish coast the following year. It was therefore impossible to take the offensive against the British blockade. But what could be done with brigs, small gunboats, and the support of shore defences was done enthusiastically. Privateers preyed heavily on British commerce, which had to be placed under convoy; the Norwegians kept their end up in a number of minor naval actions, fought in or near the Leads; and they repulsed landing parties, even as far north as Hammerfest. No new Tordenskjold appeared: but each small success had an enhanced value for the creation of a national tradition, because Norway under the commission was fighting its battles alone. It is fair to add that rather more might have been achieved, if Danish policy had not involved Norway at this juncture in a second war, against Sweden.

Sweden was now confronted by her traditional enemy, Russia, in alliance with France. In a previous conflict, just before the outbreak of the French Revolution, Denmark-Norway had given half-hearted support to the Russian arms, and the Swedes had retorted by an equally half-hearted attempt to organize an underground movement for seducing the Norwegians from their allegiance to the Danish Crown. But the storms of the revolutionary period and in particular the example of the partitions of Poland, over which Russia had presided, caused the growth of something like a Scandinavian spirit— a belief at any rate that it might pay the Scandinavian powers to stand together. However, when in accordance with the Tilsit agreements the Russian armies were on the march to seize Finland from the Swedes, and Bernadotte with his Frenchmen stood poised for the attack from Jutland across the water into Scania, the temptation to join in was too strong for Frederick. He declared war on Sweden; the British navy, as might have been anticipated, barred the way to Scania for French and Danes alike; and Norway was left to bear the brunt of the hostilities. Jacob Aall recalled the crisis long afterwards in his memoirs.

> It was regarded even by those citizens who were most devoted to the Danish government as a great mistake in Danish policy, and a presentiment was felt of the possible results which in the fullness of time revealed themselves. This war prepared the way for the separation of Denmark and Norway, and some Norwegians began, though vaguely, to think of the advisability of a union [with Sweden], the very possibility of which had hitherto wounded their innermost feelings.[1]

The actual fighting was on a very small scale. The Swedes invaded Norway at several points, but a national effort (which lived long in story) drove them out, a feat which was the less surprising as the main Swedish forces were heavily engaged in an unsuccessful struggle to retain Finland. The Norwegian troops showed little inclination to pursue across the frontier, in spite of Russian admonitions to do so. They had no interest in a Russian advance which must ultimately threaten their own safety; Wedel Jarlsberg, now a full member of the commission of government, drew his own conclusion from what had happened—that the interests of Norway could only be protected by a merging of the Danish and Swedish monarchies,

[1] Jacob Aall: *Erindringer*, 3 vols., Christiania, 1844-5, Vol. I, p. 336.

or by an outright transfer of allegiance to Sweden. For a moment the former alternative seemed possible. Disgust at the failure to save Finland brought about a revolution in Sweden, and if Frederick had been willing to accept the freer Swedish constitution, in which the power of the Estates had just been increased, he might have united the Crowns and changed the course of history. But he let the chance slip; a childless uncle of the deposed sovereign was elected king; and the problem became one of choosing his eventual heir. The choice fell on prince Christian of Augustenburg, head of the commission and commander-in-chief in Norway. Wedel Jarlsberg would have liked him to carry the Norwegian people with him to his new allegiance, but the new crown prince of Sweden was as high-principled as he was popular; in any case he lived only long enough to bring the war with Russia and Norway-Denmark safely to an end. Three months after his death, on August 21, 1810, the Estates of Sweden made their momentous choice of Marshal Bernadotte, whom the British fleet had so recently prevented from becoming their conqueror. The old king lived on until 1818, but Bernadotte began at once to direct the fortunes of his adopted fatherland—not towards friendship with France, as had been intended by the electors, but towards alliance with Russia in the war of 1812, and not towards the recovery of Finland, as they had also planned, but to the acquisition of Norway.

Meanwhile, the end of the war against Sweden had been followed for Norway by a period of respite, in which king Frederick tolerated the purchase of licences granted in London for trading with the enemy. In other words, Norwegian ships could buy immunity from the British blockade because they carried goods which Britain wanted, and in this way a precarious prosperity was re-established. Some money was thus made available for the promotion of three new national institutions, in which Wedel Jarlsberg was the moving spirit. The earliest of these was the Society for the Welfare of Norway, aiming at self-sufficiency in economic life and the general development of the country: it was partly modelled on the Prussian Tugendbund of 1808. The second was the long-desired university, for which the Society collected funds, and which, under charter from king Frederick, opened its doors on September 1, 1813, with a muster of five professors, one lecturer, and seventeen students. By then, however, the rigours of the blockade had been renewed, so that it was under the shadow of extreme poverty that an assembly of seventy-two leading citizens met in December, with powers also to set up the proposed independent bank, for which they could not find the means.

The renewal of the blockade resulted from the treaty of Stockholm of March 3, 1813, by which England promised support for the Swedish claim upon Norway. Russia had made a similar promise on the eve of the French invasion, and so far as the Allies were concerned, all that remained was to see that Sweden earned the gift of territory by loyal and effective support of the campaign against Napoleon. Frederick, who could have saved the situation by deserting Napoleon and competing against Bernadotte for the favour of the Allies, was at least no turncoat. He placed an army in support of the French in Jutland, and to keep Norway as far as possible within the control of his dynasty sent there as viceroy his cousin and heir presumptive, prince Christian Frederick. He landed from a fishing boat, disguised as a sailor, on May 21. He was only 27 years of age; a firm friend of the country he came to, and much under the influence of a Norwegian patriot, Carsten Anker. But he was a man of peace, not of war, and within eight months of his arrival he was confronted with the situation that the king, against his will, had ceded Norway to the king of Sweden.

After the decisive defeat of Napoleon at Leipzig in October, the Swedish forces together with some Russians advanced towards Jutland. When Bernadotte had defeated a small Danish corps in Holstein, the Council (which included the aged Colbjörnsen) advised the king against further resistance, although the main Danish army had not even been engaged. An Austrian intermediary tried to satisfy Bernadotte with a partition, by which Sweden would have received the Tröndelag, as in 1658. But the Russian Czar supported the full demands, and it is probably due to haste rather than design that the treaty of Kiel on January 14, 1814, signed away Norway only and not also the ancient possessions of the Norwegian Crown in Iceland, Greenland, and the Faeroes. The break-up of their empire in this way was later to be a source of additional bitterness; but this was of course a minor matter as compared with the claim to transfer the sovereignty over their native soil without pretence of consultation with the Norwegian people who lived on it. This it was which roused them to assert their independence in the face of Europe.

I

CHAPTER VII

A NEW NORWAY

IN Norwegian eyes the year 1814 possesses an almost mystical significance. A sense of national unity pervaded the people. A constitution, still the palladium of their liberties, was set up with astonishing rapidity. A king of independent Norway, owing his position to the will of the people, for a few brief weeks trod the stage. In the long run, indeed, Norway could not resist the wishes of the powers or even Bernadotte's army of veterans from the French war. But later generations forgot the two weeks' campaign against the invading Swedes in the 126 years of peace which followed. What they remembered, and treasured, was that their forefathers against all odds had banded together to defy the treaty of Kiel and the decisions of the great coalition, which in this same year sent Napoleon to Elba and carved up the territories of half Europe at the congress of Vienna. In the Norwegian view the union with the Swedish monarchy was a *pis aller*, but it was accepted on the basis of a free contract — Bernadotte's promise to maintain the Norwegian constitution unimpaired. The period which followed the crowded events of 1814 was full of disappointment and disunity, as we shall see. All the greater was the glamour surrounding the men of 1814 and the constitution which they left as the one effective rallying point for their successors.

The news of the treaty of Kiel, as it spread gradually through the country, roused a ferment of opinion. Danish policy, held responsible for the miseries inflicted by the war with England, now showed its selfish indifference to Norwegian interests still more clearly by offering Norway to an enemy without any serious show of fight. But to be joined with Sweden would be an unacceptable change, especially to the peasantry, who feared compulsory service under

Swedish noblemen in Swedish wars. Was complete independence a practicable third alternative? The ideas and ideals which had inspired the American and French revolutions were by this time widely known; and the official class, normally the most conservative, found itself cut adrift from the old centres of authority in Copenhagen and was anxious to secure a new basis for its traditional power. Moreover, in the person of prince Christian Frederick nationalist sympathizers of all kinds had a natural rallying-point. Time was short. He set off immediately for Trondheim, where he hoped to be acclaimed as king by divine right, on the ground that as heir to the Danish-Norwegian throne he could not be deprived of a part of his inheritance against his will. But doctrines of popular sovereignty were too strong for him. Towards the end of February he summoned a meeting of leading officials and businessmen to the home of his friend Carsten Anker, owner of an ironworks at Eidsvoll, and accepted the argument of one of Norway's first professors that as a result of the treaty of Kiel the Oldenburg dynasty had renounced its title to the Norwegian throne, which was now to be disposed of afresh by the Norwegian people. Christian Frederick, therefore, for the time being assumed only the office of regent. But this was enough to give an air of legality to what was in fact a revolution.

By an open letter, dated February 19, the regent called a meeting in every parish, at which his letter was to be read and two decisive steps taken. One was that the people should bind themselves by oath to 'defend the independence of Norway and offer life and blood for the beloved fatherland'. Having thus committed themselves to the defiance of the treaty of Kiel, each parish was to proceed to the election of two persons (of whom one must be a peasant) who would later participate in the choice of representatives for a national assembly, to be held at Eidsvoll on April 8. These eventual representatives would number three for each county (again one must be a peasant) plus representatives of the towns, allotted on a generous scale, and a small representation of the army and navy. It was an imposing appeal to the judgment of the people as sovereign, though we may notice that at least one-fifth of the entire population, including every one below the status of tenant farmer, was excluded from having any voice in the elections, just as automatically as women were excluded even in revolutionary France. Meanwhile the regent appointed a ministry, ranged his army on the frontier (where he had great difficulty in feeding it), sent an emissary to plead Norway's cause in London, and watched with growing anxiety the changing situation in Europe. On March 31 the Allied armies entered Paris, and the decision to restore the Bourbons soon deprived Christian Frederick of his forlorn hope that Bernadotte might be further distracted from his claims on Norway by hopes of gaining the crown of France. On May 1 Bernadotte left his native country for the last time, intent on gaining for his adopted country a due reward for his support of the victorious alliance. The Allies, apart from his friend Czar Alexander, grudged payment of that reward to a French revolutionary general who had changed sides. But the renewal of the British naval blockade and an order to the Danes to withhold all supplies of corn from Norway showed which way the wind was blowing.

It was, therefore, the great achievement of the Eidsvoll assembly — a medley of 47 officials, 37 peasants, 16 town representatives, and 12 from the Services — that it made a permanent constitution its business, rather than a foreign policy which could have achieved only temporary results. Apart from an unsuccessful attempt to stabilize the paper currency by a state guarantee, it concentrated its attention on laying down, first the general premises, and then the detailed contents (110 clauses)[1] for a single statute to replace the organs developed in one-and-a-half centuries under the Lex Regia of the Danish autocracy. Many precedents were borne in mind, from the American federal and state constitutions to the newest in Europe, which were those of Sweden (1809) and Spain (1812). A general impression of the British system of government, with which several leading members of the Assembly were practically acquainted through residence in England, also played a part. But in so far as there was any model, it was certainly the first French revolutionary constitution of 1791. The same principles of limited monarchy, separation of powers, and restricted franchise appear in both documents: but there the resemblance ends. For the native talent of the Norwegian people showed itself above all in the way in which the official class, many of whose representatives had made drafts from foreign sources, married abstract principle to the expression of law

[1] Since increased to 112. The English text, as published by the Norwegian government in 1814, is reproduced in T. Andenaes (editor): *The Constitution of Norway and Other Documents of National Importance*, Oslo, 1951.

in starkest detail. The latter had been characteristic, as we have seen, of the work of the *tings*; it now appeared in the clauses of the constitution, which succeeded in safeguarding in large measure the rights of men without any equivalent to the highflown Rights of Man, as enunciated for example in 1791.

Norway was declared to be a 'free, independent, and indivisible realm', governed by a limited form of monarchy. The executive and judiciary organs were to be wholly separate from the legislature, the former consisting of ministers nominated by the king and having no seat or voice in the deliberations of the legislature or Storting ('grand *ting*'). Each of the three main classes represented at Eidsvoll attempted to write into the constitution some safeguards for its own position. Thus the officials—who must in future be native-born or have resided for ten years within the kingdom—awarded themselves an extreme security of tenure. The peasants included the maintenance of the odal system among the provisions, and tried hard but unsuccessfully to abolish the immunity of the other classes from military service. The representatives of the towns were more successful in their fight, which was directed to the maintenance of their trade privileges, notably the exclusive right to own sawmills working for the export market. But in the long run what mattered was the nature of the legislature, which Norway was setting up at the very time when elsewhere in Europe such institutions were being fast disbanded as relics of the revolutionary era now ended. If the parliament was a workable device, minor imperfections could always be corrected later on.

The Storting was provided with the fundamental powers of passing all laws and levying all taxes. But in other respects its organization breathed the spirit of compromise. It was neither bi-cameral, as conservatives would have wished, nor uni-cameral, as the democratic French assemblies had been. Instead, it had a purely artificial division made after each election into two houses, the smaller division, one quarter of the whole, with the historic name of Lagting, being set to revise the bills proposed by the larger division or Odelsting. But in the event of disagreement the two houses were to sit together, and a two-thirds majority could then pass the bill through; finance matters were in any case to be dealt with jointly. There was another compromise over relations with the executive. Ministers were made liable to impeachment; but they were to be tried by members of the Lagting and Supreme Court together, with the latter casting one third of the votes.

There was compromise above all in the electoral system. It was to be representative without being democratic, for the vote was restricted to officials, townspeople who owned premises to the value of about £70, and farmers who owned their farms or held a lease for not less than 25 years. Election too was to be indirect, through representatives chosen by the primary electors, as under the French constitution of 1791 and, nominally, in the American presidential elections. A seemingly democratic provision awarded the peasants, who constituted four-fifths of the population, a minimum of two-thirds of the seats. That is to say, two-thirds of the members were to be elected by the peasant constituencies: but in the then state of popular enlightenment the officials calculated quite correctly that most peasants could be induced to choose officials from their area to represent them. The party system, which we think of as the lifeblood of a parliament, was likewise discouraged. Members were required to be residents of the area which they represented, and they came up to the capital for a single session at three-year intervals, though the king might summon a special Storting if he so desired. Consequently, in the early years at least, the members of each new Storting were largely new men, and those who were not had largely forgotten the events of the previous parliament after a gap of about two-and-a-half years since they last met.

The king was thought of as imposing his ministers upon the people, the people as imposing laws and financial measures upon the king. A direct echo of France in 1791 was the suspensory veto, which entitled the king to hold up a bill until it had been passed by three successive Stortings. This particular compromise, which had helped to bring Louis XVI to the scaffold, was fraught with difficulties for the sovereigns of Norway too, especially as the constitution nowhere stated whether the suspensive veto was also applicable to its own provisions. But the immediate issue was to match the constitution with a king and set it in motion. A pro-Swedish party, headed by Wedel Jarlsberg, had little following in the assembly at Eidsvoll. On the contrary, a clause, which helped to save Norway in 1940, entitled the king to govern from abroad: prince Christian Frederick could thus accept the crown of Norway without prejudice to his position as heir to that of Denmark. On May 17 the members of the national assembly subscribed their signatures to the constitution; on the same memorable day they elected prince Christian Frederick king of Norway.

❖

The independent monarchy, unlike the independent constitution, proved to be of short duration and small repute. Norwegian opinion at the time made a scapegoat of Christian Frederick, who was certainly no soldier and whom Wedel Jarlsberg, leader of the pro-Swedish party in the assembly, called the 'petticoat king'. Yet in later life, as Christian VIII of Denmark, he steered a kingdom through the difficult years preceding the 1848 revolutions with astuteness and a fair degree of success. As king of Norway in 1814, he could only have succeeded if the Allies had been willing to go back upon their pledges to Bernadotte, and if Bernadotte had then found his position too precarious to take what had been pledged to him by force of Swedish arms alone. These were big 'if's'. In point of fact, by the time he was proclaimed king the necessary support for Bernadotte was known to be forthcoming, and Colbjörnsen, who had been the young prince's mentor in past days, sent him a correct appreciation of Norway's plight and his own duty.

Now that the most powerful princes in Europe together make it a point of honour by their superior physical resources to compel fulfilment of the treaty for the withdrawal of Norway—you, my gracious lord, must also from your side weigh up Norway's strength in relation to that colossal power. That it is irresistible, especially when England gives way, is incontestable. . . . Try therefore to negotiate for this loyal people the best conditions that can now (perhaps never again) be secured as a federated state with Sweden. Then nobody will ever have benefited Norway so much as you.[1]

But the Norwegian people, sworn to resistance in February and in May enheartened by the achievement of a constitutional settlement by general consent, was in no mood to compromise its freedom, even if the implications of the European situation had been grasped—as they certainly were not. Their newly chosen king knew better, but he can hardly be blamed for preferring to enjoy his position for the time

[1] Letters of May 19th, 1814 (*Det norske folks liv og historie*, VII, 393).

being, while he waited optimistically for some change to occur that might yet enable him to retain it.

The prince's friend, Carsten Anker, had been sent to England in March to work up public opinion on behalf of an independent Norway.[1] There were debates in both houses of parliament. Mackintosh and Lambton, the future author of the Durham Report on Canada, pleaded for the Norwegian cause in the Commons; in the Lords, the Whig leader, Lord Grey, pressed the matter to a division, in which the Opposition mustered 34 votes against 115. The Opposition press likewise gave considerable space and support, and even the Tory *Quarterly Review* observed (in April), 'The tide of public opinion in this country certainly runs strongly against Bernadotte.' But liberal opinion was not at this juncture a serious threat to a foreign policy which Castlereagh was conducting with success, consistency, and a clear understanding of essential British interests. Bernadotte was neither liked nor trusted: but it was no part of British policy to break a treaty in order to vindicate an alleged claim to self-determination, particularly in a case where the claim was believed to be artificially stimulated from outside. For Christian Frederick's presence in Norway and the popular support which he was receiving there were regarded by the powers as the result of a trick, by which Denmark was trying to keep control of the country. Carsten Anker, and later emissaries from Christian Frederick, therefore achieved nothing directly. The naval blockade continued to exert its pressure; Allied commissioners were sent to Copenhagen; and the king of Denmark was required to issue orders to Christian Frederick as his representative in Norway for the immediate surrender of the country to the Swedes. On June 30 the commissioners went on to complete their business in Oslo.

But, as the Russian representative had already noticed, British interests were not identical with those of the other powers:

> No country, not even Denmark, has so many connections with Norway as England. Trade is the heart of Norway's life, and

---

[1] The Danish publicist, Andersen Feldborg, then resident in England, had been at work even earlier with his *Cursory Remarks on the Meditated Attack on Norway*, of which the preface is dated August 1, 1813. Twelve months later he returned to the attack in a second pamphlet, *An Appeal to the English Nation on Behalf of Norway*, dedicated to the ex-prime minister, Lord Grenville.

England is the heart of its trade. . . . It is the English they rely on, and there is a well-founded rumour going here that they want independence under English protectorate.[1]

While he and his colleagues were still collecting rumours in Copenhagen, Lord Liverpool had sent his private secretary, J. P. Morier, on a separate mission to Norway. Too late to address the Storting, as he had hoped, he made clear to Christian Frederick instead that the inescapable union with Sweden need not, in the British view, be a close one. Neither the aggrandizement of Sweden beyond the minimum contracted for, nor the abolition of a peacefully established parliament, nor the diminution of British influence in Norway—often emphasized during our emissary's journey from Kristiansand to Oslo—was a British interest. Accordingly, Christian Frederick was induced to accept British mediation and prepared to summon a special Storting, to which the need for his own abdication and the acceptance of Bernadotte's claims instead, and the prospect of an English guarantee for the retention of the constitution, could be duly explained.

Neither British mediation nor the joint mediation of the commissioners of the four powers could avert a recourse to arms by the Norwegians. Their patriotic enthusiasm and memories of their successful defence against the Swedes in 1808-9 made it impossible for Christian Frederick to make concessions, as he might have wished. His claims under the treaty of Kiel, the long delay in its fulfilment, and his own military reputation made it impossible for Bernadotte to waive concessions. War therefore began over the refusal to hand over the Norwegian fortresses of Kongsvinger, Halden and Fredrikstad. The fighting lasted eight days, during which the Norwegians were victorious on a small scale in the Kongsvinger area but were driven back elsewhere. Supplies were short, so the only chance left to Norway was to resort to a guerrilla campaign—a desperate measure which Christian Frederick, long resigned to the need to abdicate, was the last man to encourage. A short war was likewise long enough for Bernadotte: honour had been vindicated, and he was anxious to get a settlement before the meeting of the Allies at the congress of Vienna should invite a reconsideration of his case. On August 14 peace was re-established by the convention of Moss.

[1] General M. F. Orlov (*Det norske folks liv og historie*, VII, 396).

Swedish forces occupied a district stretching to the approaches of the capital—a sufficient guarantee that the special Storting would agree to place the Swedish king on the vacant throne; for Christian Frederick, now utterly discredited, was to return to Denmark at the first convenient moment. In return, Bernadotte accepted the Norwegian constitution, subject only to the changes required to implement the union of crowns. He was a generous man, when he got his own way: besides, had he not been a defender of that French constitution of 1791, which the Norwegian so closely and flatteringly resembled?

The membership of the special Storting, which met on October 7, reflected the national mood of disappointment. Only 19 out of the 79 representatives had been at Eidsvoll six months before; Wedel was the one survivor of the group which had then advocated the union with Sweden; and the rank and file of members were youngish men of the official class, who had apparently come together to carry through a disagreeable task. Fortunately, the small re-elected element included a Bergen official of Scots descent named Christie, who had served as secretary at Eidsvoll and seconded Carsten Anker's efforts in England. He was now elected president of the assembly, a post of leadership in which he showed such skill and sagacity that even a casual English source alludes to him years later as 'well-known for his sturdy and Hampden-like efforts for his country'.[1] There were two main problems. One was to convince members that the country lacked military and economic resources, even if it had the moral stamina, to continue the struggle for absolute independence. The vote for a union with Sweden was not passed until the last day before the armistice under the convention of Moss was due to expire: even then the members for Bergen felt themselves to be bound to vote against the inevitable, their fellow-townsmen having given them a mandate in all circumstances to oppose a union. The other problem was that of keeping to the absolute minimum the changes in the constitution required in order to implement the union. On the assumption that the king of two countries could only reside in one of them at a time, it was necessary to provide for a Statholder or, if he were heir to the throne, a Viceroy to act in Norway. More important, the ministry was to be divided, with three of its members residing in Stockholm to provide cabinet counsel for the

[1] F. G. Denovan, who figures in the Bodö Case (Gathorne-Hardy, p. 31).

king on behalf of the full body of Norwegian ministers in Oslo. But the Norwegians protected themselves against any intrusion of Swedes into civil service posts in Norway, and even braved Bernadotte's wrath by restricting to troops of the line and to defensive war the use which Napoleon's former marshal might make of Norwegian soldiery outside the borders of Norway.

November 4 was the date of a solemn election of the king of Sweden to the vacant throne. Norwegians could point with pride to the circumstances that since the formal abdication of Christian Frederick their own ministers had acted as an independent body of regents; to the fact that Bernadotte tactfully avoided any allusion to the rights which, in the eyes of the world if not of Norwegians, he might have acquired nearly a year before under the Dano-Swedish treaty of Kiel; and to the solemn oath by which crown prince Bernadotte and his young son Oscar bound themselves to observe the constitution. Next year the first regular Storting of the reign and the Swedish Riksdag ratified the agreement for the mutual relations of the two countries by means of identical legislation, the Act of Union, to which the Norwegians, wishing to make assurance doubly sure, attached the same special procedure for amendment as to the constitution itself.[1] Nevertheless, it was a union which could be differently interpreted and developed. Most Norwegians accepted it as a second best, but believed that by vigilance they could retain complete control over their internal affairs: external relations were little understood and the constitution left them in the hands of the king. Most Swedes accepted it as providing a new acquisition to the Crown in place of Finland — compensation for what they could no longer hope to recover from the Russians. Bernadotte, who was after all the chief author of the union, had a third point of view. He put first the increased security and additional force in international relations, which his dominions obtained by reaching to their natural frontier in the west. As long ago as 1806 he had told his Swedish prisoners, taken at the capture of Lübeck from the Prussians, that 'it was not in accordance with nature that Norway should belong to Denmark, but that she should be annexed to Sweden'. The 'annexation' had not taken quite the form he would have preferred: but time might work wonders for a ruler whose claim to reconcile and unify two peoples could be broadly based on impartiality — he never learnt

[1] A full translation is to be found in Norway — Official Publication (1900).

to speak any language except French—and a fatherly devotion to their welfare.

In 1815, however, and for many years to come, Norway's chief anxieties were not political but economic. The long period of trade depression, which England experienced after Waterloo, had its counterpart across the North Sea, to which English policy partly contributed. The ups-and-downs of the war years had left Norway with a merchant fleet of nearly 150,000 tons, but the strict enforcement of the Navigation Acts excluded it once more from the carrying trade. Not until 1825 did the first relief come, when Huskisson allowed Norwegian ships to carry Swedish timber from Baltic ports to England. Even then, it took a further decade to restore the position as it had been in 1815. The plight of the saw-mill industry all along the south coast was still worse. Britain gave an imperial preference to Canadian timber of about 65 shillings a ton, reduced after a few years to 45 shillings: even the lower figure still left a handsome margin of protection after the extra cost of transport across the Atlantic had been covered. Moreover, Norwegian timber merchants were put at a disadvantage in comparison with Baltic suppliers by the method of calculating the tariff on ready-sawn planks—a fixed charge for a fixed number, irrespective of size. This caused importers to favour the generally larger produce of the Baltic forests. Since Norway could not live without exporting timber, the result was, not a fall in quantities sold or the work done to produce those quantities, but a low level of prices, small profits, and starvation wages. Bankruptcies were the order of the day. The families which had made the union, with their patrician homes and English culture, disappeared from view. Old businesses were bought up cheap, partly with peasant savings, but mainly by immigrant capital from Jutland and Schleswig-Holstein, the owners of which centred their interests on Hamburg rather than London.

The financial chaos was extreme, and the institution of a Bank of Norway in 1816, with headquarters in Trondheim, did little or nothing to abate it. The unit of currency was still the traditional *daler* or dollar, which had become tremendously inflated by the reckless issue of paper money during the war. In 1816 the notes issued by the new Bank were given an official value of one-tenth of their nominal value in silver. But the Hamburg bank, which based its transactions on pure silver and had the dominant position in the trade of northern Europe, valued the notes, not at one-tenth but one-thirtieth. A silver tax was then tried — a proportion of every man's capital to be handed over in coin, brooches, spoons, or whatever he might have of silver in his possession. This inflicted much hardship, but the country was too poor — and in some parts too recalcitrant — to raise the full amount. The Bank of Norway therefore hesitated to make its notes redeemable in silver, as had been intended. A fluctuating paper currency continued to trouble the country until 1842, when — with the help of an improved output from its own silver mine at Kongsberg — the Norwegian state was at last able to guarantee its money. Such a guarantee had first been promised in the enthusiasm of the national assembly at Eidsvoll a generation before.

Town life at this time provided no basis for new adventures in politics. Bergen was still the one true urban centre in Norway, with its prosperity founded on pre-eminence in the northern fisheries, which its citizens defended tooth and nail. Newfoundland fish had to some extent ousted the Bergen staple from the European markets during the war, but Bergen's recovery was rapid. It is perhaps significant that Christie, who had played such a dominant role on the national stage in 1814-15, chose to spend the rest of his life in a government post in Bergen, its cultural leader and the founder of the Museum, which has since 1948 provided the nucleus for Norway's second university. Trondheim, as a foreign visitor noted with surprise, had no more than four buildings of stone; inter-urban rivalries, rather than any solid pre-eminence in trade, had brought the Bank there. The only fast-growing major town was Stavanger, where the profitableness of the herring fisheries now well established off the west coast doubled the number of inhabitants in a single generation. The towns of the south coast all languished under the regime of low prices for timber. Even Oslo, seat of government and — once in three years — of parliament, was 'a declining town', where an Englishman, as late as July 1826, was made uncomfortably aware of his country's responsibility for an empty harbour and deserted streets.[1] The three-day fair in February, when by immemorial custom the peasants came in with their sledges to buy and sell, was said to be the only time of the year when the capital woke to crowded life.

[1] Derwent Conway [H. D. Inglis]: *Narrative of a Journey through Norway, Sweden and Denmark*, Edinburgh, 1829.

The condition of rural society was no more encouraging. In 1818, when Bernadotte succeeded to the throne of the two kingdoms and came to Trondheim to be crowned, his presence in the country occasioned a rebellious demonstration of peasants: their object was a reduction of taxes, the means proposed—the abolition of the Storting and a return to paternal government by the Crown. If public opinion was like this in east Norway, for the demonstrators tried to converge on Oslo,what must be the feeling in the west, where conditions of life were always harder, and among the fishing population of the far north? There the houses were still windowless, in the remoter parts at least, as they had been in the middle ages. The stone hearth in the middle of the floor had usually, though not always, given place by now to an iron stove near the door; but the smoke from this still found its way out, eventually, through an opening in the roof of the single-storied dwelling. The cattle wintered in stalls built without light or standing-room, so as to give the maximum of warmth, from which they were lifted out as living skeletons when spring came; the accumulated muck was then shovelled out on to the fields. Methods of farming remained primitive in the extreme, both because of ignorance and through the fact that the strip system often made it necessary to work on a communal basis. But the same conservative instinct showed among the fishermen, who for centuries persisted in the use of line-fishing and sought legal and other means of protecting themselves against the more costly and enormously more efficient use of the net. Poverty breeds apathy, just as dirt breeds disease. Statistics, dating from the middle years of the century, give us a picture of the dirt expressed in terms of leprosy, which varied between one per hundred and one per thousand all along the west coast.

The situation of Norway at this time bore some resemblance to that of Ireland. The sudden, rapid growth of the Norwegian population, which averaged 13.4 per cent per decade during the first half century after the Napoleonic Wars, may be compared with an Irish increase of 14.2 per cent at its zenith in the 'thirties. In the absence of any large-scale industrial development, both countries experienced extreme pressure upon the soil as the available means of livelihood—in Ireland a multiplication of small tenancies, in Norway a doubling in the number of cottars and trebling of labourers. Some parts of Norway, too, resorted to the intensive cultivation of the potato which proved the bane of Ireland; and both countries adopted the happier expedient of sending their surplus population to share in the hazards and rewards of the opening-up of America. The first party of Norwegian emigrants, who sailed from Stavanger in 1825, was, indeed, actuated mainly by religious motives. Some prisoners in the hulks at Chatham during the war had been influenced by Quaker prison visitors[1]; were persecuted as nonconformists on their return to Norway; and organized an expedition to join their fellow Quakers in the New World. Their venture owed much, however, to a pioneer named Cleng Peerson, who ten years later sponsored a larger agricultural settlement at Fox River, Illinois. From that time the Middle West made a steady appeal to Norwegian farming families, especially perhaps the Haugeans dissatisfied with spiritual as well as material conditions in the home-country. Shipowners found their transportation a profitable business, because their vessels could at the same time bring Norwegian (and Swedish) iron on to the American market. Nevertheless, up to the American Civil War, emigration was limited by the need to find some initial capital, so that the very poor rarely succeeded in migrating farther than to the marginal lands of northern Norway.

Up to 1830 the official class had absolute control of the Storting, as it had planned. Some tentative steps were taken in the direction of freedom of trade. One measure, which left a serious mark on the national life, entitled every farmer to distil his own corn brandy: this became as cheap and noxious as gin had been in the London of Hogarth. Law revision began with the abolition of mutilation and corporal punishment, though the practice of employing heavily-ironed convicts on public works, such as the building of the royal palace in Oslo, was long continued. But the only drastic change was the abolition of titles of nobility. The Danish kings had replaced the great feudal families, virtually extinct in Norway, by a system of titles awarded for merit, such as those of Tordenskjold and Baron Holberg. But only three peerages and a handful of lesser distinctions of rank had been awarded in Norway. To demand their abolition was to some extent a logical result of the egalitarian principles em-

[1] *An Account of a Religious Society in Norway, called Saints*, London, 1814 [by Frederick Smith] shows that they were a group of Haugeans, eventually numbering 28, to whom a Quaker at Plymouth had supplied a Danish version of Barclay's *Apology*. On arrival at Chatham, they therefore asked the Quakers there for further help.

bodied in the new constitution. But chiefly the Storting sought to ensure that the king should not at some later date use titles to enhance royal influence in Norway. The royal veto was used to hold up the bill for six years; but it was forced through in 1821, to the king's great indignation. He replied by proposing the formal amendment of the constitution on a series of points, so as to secure (for instance) a right of absolute instead of suspensive veto on bills and a right to reintroduce nobility. The king's proposals were rejected unanimously and quietly buried: they are chiefly of interest as an anticipation of later and stormier conflicts between king and people and between their respective representatives, the ministry and the Storting. For the moment the predominant factor was suspicion of the king among the members of the official class, who still had their culture rooted in Denmark and their loyalty often directed to the memory of Christian Frederick. The ministry had little influence on the Storting, since the Statholder, a Swede, acted as its head.

Yet this was the heyday of Metternich and the European reaction, when disobedient subjects often received short shrift. Norway's foreign relations were therefore the most critical aspect of policy. Poverty and pride combined to cause the Storting to refuse payment of a due proportion of the national debt incurred during the period of union with Denmark. The obligation to pay rested on the terms of the treaty of Kiel, to which Norway was not a party. Moreover, by the same treaty a definite wrong had been done to Norway, in that her overseas possessions were kept by Denmark—a deprivation which further reduced Norway's capacity to pay. Let the Swedes themselves pay the debt, if they liked. Only after a sharp warning about the possible consequences of defiance had been received from the powers of Europe, assembled at Aix-la-Chapelle in 1818, did the Storting climb down to the extent of accepting mediation. The British minister in Stockholm then negotiated terms which were highly favourable for Norway; these were accepted after much murmuring in May 1821. But the king had already prepared a counter-action; it was too late for him completely to change course. On June 1 a circular note to the powers threatened a withdrawal of the constitution and a resumption of the rights which Bernadotte claimed as his under the treaty of Kiel. About a month later the arrival of Swedish troops and warships for joint manoeuvres with the Norwegian forces in the Oslo area caused many of his subjects to believe that the threat was to be carried out. But when the king himself came on the scene, instead of the expected *coup* he brought only his amendments to the constitution — and, as we have seen, he passively accepted their rejection. Bernadotte was after all a revolutionary king, who could never be quite sure of his standing with the autocratic sovereigns. They were busy that year restoring order in Naples and Piedmont: it is at least possible that the manoeuvres at Oslo were partly designed for their benefit — to suggest that intervention might pay in Italy, but not in Scandinavia.

The Norwegians themselves, however, now moved fast to the conclusion that foreign policy should not be left in the sole charge of the king, an arrangement which meant in practice a royal policy shaped and executed by the Swedish foreign minister and diplomatic staff. What Norwegians long regarded as a burning issue of injustice had already arisen at Bodö, though the facts did not come to light until 1827. Bodö was a new town, established in 1816 in the face of great opposition from Trondheim and especially Bergen, the citizens of which claimed an inalienable monopoly of the trade of north Norway. Besides its obvious relation to the Lofoten fisheries, Bodö offered great opportunities for the trade with Russians from the White Sea area. In addition, its weakness and remoteness made tariff and other laws harder to enforce. An English firm set up as smugglers in a big way of business; were eventually caught out; resorted to violence, which provoked counter-violence by the Norwegian authorities; and, at the point when most similar undertakings would have had to cut their losses and start afresh elsewhere, transferred their interests into the hands of a swindler of genius, who also had access to the foreign secretary, Lord Castlereagh. Castlereagh pressed the British minister in Stockholm to seek redress for what were made to appear as grave injustices committed by Norwegian officials. The minister received a favourable hearing, partly — it must be recognized — because the high-handed actions alleged against them were the sort of thing which Swedish diplomats expected of subordinate Norwegian officials in a far-away place like Bodö. But the king and his foreign minister also had very much in mind the circumstance that the person they were dealing with had just been appointed to mediate in the difficult business of the Danish-Norwegian debt.

The immediate upshot was that the English claimants secured the return of their goods, which may well have been lawfully im-

K

pounded, and monetary compensation in cash and privileges of free importation, to which they were certainly not entitled. From 1827 onwards the case provided angry Norwegians with their classic example of culpable disregard for their interests on the part of the Swedish foreign service. But the time was not yet ripe for a further development in Norway's position, where it was not clearly defined in the constitution. On the contrary, the 'twenties closed in a battle for a symbol. Which day was more deserving of public commemoration—May 17, for the Eidsvoll constitution; or November 4, for the acceptance of the union? Bernadotte not unnaturally preferred the latter, but in his goodhumoured way yielded to some extent to public opinion. However, on May 17, 1829, the students of Oslo university held an innocuous private celebration, which for want of better entertainment was treated by the public as a daring defiance of the Statholder. A crowd assembled to see the non-existent fun; failed to disperse when ordered by officious police to do so; and was dispersed without serious casualties by the cavalry. The over-zealous Statholder lost his appointment; the celebration of May 17 gained a place in easily kindled imaginations as having occasioned the 'battle of the market-place'. It was the day of small things.

In July 1830, the news of revolution in France gave a fresh impulse to political life even in far-off Norway. There had already been some economic revival, some stirrings of interest among the peasantry, some signs of the emergence of a new generation to take up what it came to regard as the unfinished work of the 'Eidsvoll men'. But it was the establishment of a constitutional monarchy in France which removed the fear of intervention by the despotic powers of eastern Europe. It also made it less likely that Bernadotte would in some mood of impatience try to shake off the role of constitutional monarch. A part which the Orleans family was willing to play in Paris was not one to be despised by a *parvenu*, even in Oslo. He continued to play it, and after another decade *The Times* declared: 'The secular hostility of the Swedish and Norwegian nations has given way to mutual confidence, cemented by kindred institutions and the enlightened government of the same sceptre'. In 1842 the British minister accredited to the court reported to the Foreign Office that Bernadotte was 'extremely popular in Norway'. When he died in 1844, the thoughts of Norwegians dwelt mainly upon the later part of his reign, in which the country had been steered into fresh paths of progress.

The exclusion of Norway from any voice in matters of foreign policy was mitigated by an agreement which guaranteed the summoning of a Norwegian minister to any meeting of (Swedish) ministers at which business affecting Norway was to be discussed. This was considerably less than Norway was entitled to under the letter of the constitution: but it was followed up by a rather more generous provision for consuls (not mentioned in the constitution) to be appointed at a joint session of ministers of both countries and to take an oath as Norwegian officials. Norway also secured, after a struggle in which the king impatiently dissolved the Storting, only to summon a special Storting the following month, a symbolic advance in the matter of her flag. Warships must continue to wear the flag of the union, but the mercantile marine in all waters might adopt a flag invented in 1821, styled a 'clean flag' by ultra-patriots because it incorporated no emblem of the union with Sweden. Another cause of friction was temporarily removed when the office of Statholder was given to a Norwegian, Wedel Jarlsberg, who thus presided over the ministry in Oslo until his death in 1840.

The triumph of free trade principles, expressed in the new tariff of 1842, and the adoption of a new code of criminal law are important measures conceived in the spirit of Bentham. But the most significant event, which had no real parallel in English life, was the emergence of the peasants as a force to be reckoned with in politics. Two-thirds of the seats in the Storting, it will be remembered, were seats placed at the disposal of peasant constituencies; in 1833 the peasants themselves began to occupy them. The actual majority which they obtained on that occasion was not repeated in succeeding elections, as officials and the urban middle class banded together to defend their interests. But the peasants had found a leader in Ole Gabriel Ueland, a self-made man from the hinterland of Stavanger, sharp-witted, narrow-minded, pertinacious, suspicious, and the sworn enemy of officialdom. He and his followers were zealous champions of the constitution, to which they owed their rights, but were not interested in any changes in it, even changes intended to assert Norwegian claims against the Swedes. Their great concern was economy in the administration: they came to the Storting to reduce expenditure, above all in terms of the numbers, salaries, pensions, and activities of officials. As a means to this end they demanded full powers of local self-government. As a result of exercising those powers, the peasants of the next generation came — long before the equivalent class in other non-industrial countries — to be the controlling factor in the life of the nation.

The local government law of 1837 fulfilled a requirement expressly stated in the constitution, to which indeed it is second only in importance. Local expenditure was henceforth to be controlled by the local tax-payer, the vote in local elections being given to the same groups as in the elections to the Storting. Each parish elected its council, but the main authority rested with the chairman and an executive committee composed of one-fourth of the total membership. The chairmen of councils in turn formed a county council, meeting annually under the presidency of the county governor, who also retained some rights of control over parish activities of any unusual kind. But the Council was entitled in principle to consider all matters of local concern. The same system was adapted to the towns, but as they still retained some vestiges of self-government the impact of the change was less there than in rural Norway, where men's minds could only hark back to the tradition of the medieval *tings*. Ueland himself had been a school teacher, but in the early days of the new system the peasants used it to restrict expenditure on schools. It is a measure of its value in broadening the peasant outlook that by 1860 they were supporting the introduction of compulsory elementary education — ten years ahead of England.

But Ueland was not a national leader: even the repeal of the Conventicle Ordinance in 1842 marked a class triumph over the government (which had used the royal veto to stop the measure twice) rather than a genuine assertion of the principles of human liberty. It was the great good fortune of the age that the leader whom the world of politics in the narrower sense had failed to produce stepped forth instead from the world of literature and youthful idealism. In the person of Henrik Wergeland Norway acclaimed its first genius since Holberg. But for history his importance lies less in what he wrote than in what he was. For in the short span of 37 years Wergeland contrived to embody in their most idealistic form the national aspirations which were latent in every class of society. He roused much controversy and made many enemies, but it is no exaggeration to say that for a century at least after his death in 1845 'his soul goes marching on'. It is a little bit as though Shelley had also been Cobbett.

Wergeland's father was a clergyman, a leading spirit in the promotion of the university and a prominent member of the assembly at Eidsvoll, where he later held the living. His earlier forebears, however, were peasants: in his temperament and its artistic expression the peasant character can be clearly traced. As a 21-year-old student he was present at the 'battle of the market place', and sent his coat to the military authorities with a note, explaining that it had been disgraced by a blow from the flat of a soldier's sabre. At 22 he published his most ambitious poem, *Creation, Man, and Messiah*, a chaotic welter of ideas sprawling over 720 pages but all tending, like its author's life, to the glorification of humanity. Shakespeare was his chief source of inspiration, England (and after 1830 France) revered by him as the great home of the freedom he incessantly preached. Two of the half-dozen lyrics, by which Wergeland's writing is best known in Norway today, handle English themes with sympathy and tenderness. Others of those that most fully express the poet in him were composed in the last 14 months of his life, when he lay on a sick-bed awaiting his end, his imagination unclouded by self-pity or by fear, reconciled to many enemies, a national figure one might almost say in spite of himself.

For one striking feature of Wergeland's career was its unorthodoxy. This clergyman's son, who proposed to follow his father's calling, was a great lover of wine, woman, and song: few theological students of any university have figured so frequently in the police court. The revolutionaries of all Europe, from Greece to Ireland, won his enthusiastic support; and he led an ultimately successful campaign for a constitutional amendment to admit Jews to Norwegian citizenship. He was also the central figure in a great and virulent literary controversy between his supporters and those of Welhaven, a rival poet and the exponent of a more polished style, a more Danish diction, and a ready acknowledgement of Norway's intellectual and aesthetic debt to the Danes. Yet Wergeland was not a nationalist pure and simple. Failing to earn preferment in the Church, he accepted a grant from Bernadotte's privy purse and then an appointment under the Crown as archivist, actions which many of his former friends denounced as the grossest tergiversation. To the poet the fact that he had often proclaimed his republican sym-

pathies in general seemed to interpose no barrier to his acceptance
of benefits from the generous Frenchman he had always admired.

In any case it might be pleaded that no one could hope to write as
voluminously as Wergeland without contradicting himself. His subjects included agricultural improvements for the peasants, and linguistic improvements for the intelligentsia; the temperance cause
and hygiene; the reform of prisons; and propaganda for any social
objective, from the provision of workers' housing to the discourage-
ment of emigration. He also edited an Opposition paper, and found
time to publish a major work on the Norwegian constitution. He was
not alone in the cultural field. Besides the poet Welhaven, whose
sense of form restricted his output but won him a chair of philosophy in the university, there was an important landscape painter,
J. C. Dahl, and Ole Bull the violinist, who made the name of Norway
known in musical circles all over the world. They too were national-
ly minded. Bull told the king of Denmark that it was the mountains
of his native land which had taught him his art. Dahl, though he
lived in Dresden, painted the Norwegian scene, founded the Norwegian national gallery, and also helped to found the society for the
preservation of antiquities, which dates from 1844. Nevertheless, it
was Wergeland who imprinted upon the Young Norway of his day
nationalist aspirations, transcending the rivalries of class and purely
selfish aims, to which later generations of Norwegians at their best
have been most true. His name is still the name above all others in
the celebrations of Norway's national holiday, as it was when
Björnson paid the tribute of a fellow-poet on May 17, 1864:

> If I should express a wish for Norway on this our freedom's birth-
> day, then I know of nothing finer than that all the dreams for its
> future, which took shape in the vast spirit of Wergeland, might
> also come to pass. For he willed a union of workman and king,
> law-breaker and law-maker, the wise man and the fool. And Nor-
> way's woods and mines and factories, her ploughlands, fisheries,
> and shipping—right down to the beasts and birds, he included
> them all.

CHAPTER VIII

SENTIMENT AND ACHIEVEMENT
(1844-64)

❋

THE death of Bernadotte in March 1844 marked the end of an era. As Charles XIV John he had been king for more than a quarter of a century, and before that his influence upon events in the north as crown prince, of Sweden from 1810 and of Norway from 1814, had been at least equally decisive. His son Oscar was a much less impressive figure—quiet and physically frail, but conscientious and mildly liberal in outlook. He was the author of a pamphlet on penal reform (translated into Norwegian by Wergeland), and on his accession showed an enlightened attitude towards his Norwegian subjects by small concessions about a separate man-of-war flag, a half-share for Norway in the union coat of arms, and putting its name before that of Sweden in Norwegian state papers. The changes gave satisfaction as earnest of a goodwill which the new king certainly cherished. But they are also a reminder of the fact that the sovereign could still initiate policy. His ministers in Norway worked under the presidency, not of a prime minister but of the Statholder—a Norwegian since the time of Wedel Jarlsberg, but a Norwegian who was the personal representative of the sovereign in Norway. It is to be remembered, too, that three Norwegian ministers were always in attendance on the king while he was in Stockholm, to conduct Norwegian business with him alone and joint affairs in session with him and the Swedish ministers.

The political programme of the next twenty years was not a parliamentary programme. So far as foreign affairs and relations with Sweden were concerned, it came mainly from the king. In purely domestic matters there was a compromise between the peasants forming the Opposition in the Storting, who could keep the Government chronically short of money, and the Government, which could use the suspensory veto vested in the Crown to hold up legislative changes of which it disapproved. All suggestions that ministers should be allowed to sit in the Storting were rejected by the peasant leader Ueland, because he thought that the ministers would then control the elected representatives of the people and not vice versa. That the system worked as well as it did may be attributed to the fact that the official class, now in its heyday, exercised a kind of national leadership. Officials and other middle-class men of similar education and outlook filled every ministerial post without exception: no peasant entered any government before 1884. In the Storting men of the same official stamp could often master the opposition through their superior knowledge of affairs; through the press and the pulpit they gave the tone to public life outside. Some idea of the strength of the 'unpopular front' may be gained from the matriculation figures for the university in its first decade, the students who would now be entering their forties — nearly two-thirds were sons of officials, at least 90 per cent came from middle-class families.

For the world at large, the most interesting feature of the age was the rise and fall of Scandinavian sentiment, which seemed at one time likely to reshape the north. Another predominant sentiment was a national romanticism which left deep marks, both in literature and in life. But the shaping of the nation was at least equally affected in the long run by an upsurge of prosperity and the reforms which accompanied it. Yet another contrast between sentiment and achievement is to be found in the sad, short history of the first Norwegian labour movement.

In the middle years of the 19th century Scandinavianism appealed to many people in each of the three Scandinavian countries as justified by past history and the current political situation. It lacked a firm basis of economic advantages for the member states, and — whether by chance or through its inherent defects — the movement never attracted the leadership of any first-rate statesman. It is easy to be wise after the event, and claim that the union of the north in 1397 by queen Margaret could never have been achieved again under modern conditions: but the unification of Italy and Germany provides some arguments in a contrary direction. Sweden and Norway were already united under one sovereign; in Denmark, when Christian VIII began his reign (1839-48), it was already clear that the dynasty terminated with his son, later king Frederick VII.

Language provided a bond which the world of learning at least could not ignore; and academic congresses prepared the way for a series of lighthearted rallies of students in the university cities of Scandinavia. In 1845 about 150 Norwegian students went to join a much larger number of Danes and Swedes in Copenhagen, where speeches were made and vows pledged for mutual support: as these were the young men of the class then ruling in each of the countries concerned, their governments had something on which to build, if they wished.

The year of revolutions, 1848, provided an opportunity to found Scandinavian unity, as German unity was to be founded, on comradeship in arms. The new king of Denmark defeated a rising among the German population of Schleswig-Holstein; but the Prussians came to the rescue of the rebels, beat his forces at the town of Schleswig, and threatened Jutland with invasion. He appealed for help to king Oscar, who promised men for the defence of Jutland, but not of the Duchies. Meanwhile, Czar Nicholas by a direct threat had induced the Prussians to withdraw from Jutland into Schleswig, and an armistice was signed. The Storting assented, indeed, to the use of Norwegian troops to defend Denmark, but with the significant proviso that there should not be 'any more permanent relationship with Denmark'. A Swedish-Norwegian army went down into Scania, but only Swedes crossed into Denmark, and the only soldiers who took any active part in the 1848 campaign were a little body of volunteers, 243 Swedes and 114 Norwegians. The armistice was prolonged through the winter, and king Oscar came to share the view of his Norwegian ministers that on strict grounds of nationality only the northern part of Schleswig ought to be claimed as Danish. He was therefore inclined to regard the Danes as the aggressors when a fresh outbreak in the Duchies next spring caused them to denounce the armistice. Neither king Oscar nor his subjects showed any great desire to fight in the new campaign; but after the Danes had again been beaten by the Prussians, he readily supplied a force of 3,000 Swedes and 1,000 Norwegians for a peaceful occupation of north Schleswig while the powers were settling the final terms of a Danish return to the ownership of the Duchies. Relations with the Prussians on the spot were as cordial as with the Danes. But a final settlement of the problem clearly awaited the death of Frederick VII, the king who had no heir; and it was a possible help that *The Times* (August

13, 1849) advocated Scandinavian union as the best solution.

Russia had done most to save Denmark in 1848; but it was not in Russia's interest that the country she had helped to save should ever form part of a united Scandinavia, which would be a serious menace on her northern flank. Conversely, the downfall of Russia and the aggrandizement of Sweden-Norway would bring union with the Danes much more within the bounds of probability. At the outbreak of the Crimean war in 1854 king Oscar coupled his declaration of neutrality with a refusal to oblige Russia by closing the Swedish ports in the Baltic to foreign warships. If the British and French had made that sea a main theatre of operations, he would probably have listened to the voice of the Swedish Junkers and tried to reconquer Finland. As it was, he hesitated, even when the British consul-general in Oslo produced elaborate evidence that the Czar had intended to engulf territory in Finnmark. But two important steps were eventually taken. In November 1855 after secret negotiations in Stockholm the king signed a treaty, for which the initiative lay with Palmerston, binding him to cede no territory in either of his kingdoms to the Russians, and giving him an Anglo-French guarantee in return.[1] From the Allied point of view, this constituted 'a timely threat against Russia'.[2] Sweden-Norway was not, indeed, brought into the war, which ended within a few months; but the guarantee, with its incalculable hypothetical effects on Russian policy, remained in force for a half a century. A more definite advantage was secured for Sweden at the peace conference, where king Oscar induced the Allies to remove a threat to Stockholm by requiring the Russians to demilitarize the Aaland islands, which had been one of the principal objectives of the Anglo-French Baltic squadron during the hostilities.

Thus the prime effect of the Crimean war upon Scandinavian politics was that it occasioned the abandonment of the pro-Russian policy of Bernadotte, who never forgot how Alexander I had championed his claim to Norway. It also had the effect of making opinion in Norway on the whole more interested in the idea of a united Scandinavia, as a defence for north Norway against encroachment by the Bear. In 1856 the crown prince was sent as viceroy to Oslo,

[1] The treaty was accepted by the three Norwegian ministers resident in Stockholm on October 30, 1855, three weeks before it was finally signed (*Det norske folks liv og historie*, IX, 208).

[2] *Cambridge History of British Foreign Policy*, Cambridge, 1923, Vol. II, p. 385.

where he at once set up a committee to consider steps by which the army could be increased in size, improved in quality, and above all brought under united control.

Two other events of the same summer seemed to bring the prospects of Scandinavian unity appreciably nearer. The largest of all the student meetings was held at Uppsala with the usual highflown speeches, but this time there was direct encouragement from both king Oscar and king Frederick. A few weeks later the northern capitals received a visitor, whose devotion to the cause rivalled that of the students, while his position as second in succession to the French imperial throne seemed to imply the support of Napoleon III, then for a brief space regarded as 'the master of Europe'. Prince Napoleon delivered himself to two leading propagandists, Swedish and Danish, in the following terms:

> It is a cause which must be carried further. We can never permit that a man who is under Russian influence ascends the throne of Denmark. Oscar has emancipated himself; he is our sincere ally, and he must go farther. The North must become one unit, one strong power, a counterweight both to Russia and to Germany. And this must happen soon.[1]

Accordingly, in March of the following year Oscar offered a military alliance to defend Denmark and Schleswig up to the line of the river Eider. But Frederick, badly advised by an anti-Scandinavian foreign minister, put off the day of agreement indefinitely by demanding the inclusion of Holstein, with its wholly German population, in the area to be protected.

Almost immediately afterwards, king Oscar fell fatally ill, and although he lingered until 1859 his son was recalled from Oslo to assume the regency. The change was an important one, for Charles XV's accession to power meant an attempted return to the ways of his Bernadotte grandfather. He would have liked to strengthen the authority of the Crown in both his kingdoms; took a special interest in the army; had visions of himself as the liberator, not merely of Finland but of Poland; and consequently pursued a Scandinavian policy with enthusiasm. An attractive, flamboyant figure, he won the devoted support of ministers in Norway as well as Sweden, though chiefly among the Swedish Junker class: but time revealed the

[1] Jorgenson: *Scandinavian Unionism*, p. 233.

fatal flaw—Charles was entirely lacking in strength of purpose. As regards Scandinavianism, he knew from his service as viceroy that the chief enemies of the idea were the Norwegian peasants: in his own contemptuous words, 'They desire to make of every province a little kingdom'.[1] But, in order to secure a favourable atmosphere for his military and other projects, the king agreed to mark the opening of his reign by a concession far larger than his father's.

Norwegian opinion had always resented the existence of the office of Statholder (or governor-general). It had never in later years been held by a Swede, but it was an institution to which Sweden had no counterpart and therefore emphasized the point that Norway was the less important of the two kingdoms, the one in which provision had to be made for the fact that the king was not normally present in person. For rather more than a decade the office had been left unfilled, but even so it had an adverse effect on the government of Norway: because the Statholder had originally presided over the meetings of the king's ministers in Oslo, there was no recognized post of prime minister. Hitherto the royal veto had been used to prevent a change. In December 1859, however, a bill was passed quickly and enthusiastically through the Storting, in the knowledge that the royal sanction had been promised in advance: an indiscreet newspaper editor named Björnson even published the promise. But the young king had reckoned without his Swedish subjects, whom the Norwegians had recently exasperated by rejecting proposals for a customs union and for making decisions by law courts binding in both countries, which had been found fully acceptable by the Swedish Estates. In other respects, too, the Storting had been tireless in its assertion of absolute equality within the union. The Swedes therefore seized the chance to declare that the post of Statholder was an integral part of the union, which could not be altered without their consent, and Charles's ministry in Stockholm threatened to resign if he kept his word to his other ministry in Oslo. Rather than face up to the threat he preferred to break his promise to Norway. This act of weakness did nothing to heal the breach between the kingdoms; it did everything to advertise the fact that Swedish interests mattered more than Norwegian to the house of Bernadotte. It also made Norway more wary in following the king in a fresh venture in the cause of a united Scandinavia.

[1] Jorgenson, p. 209.

In the summer of 1861 the new king visited his fellow sovereigns at the Tuileries and Osborne, but found them less forthcoming than Prince Napoleon as to his chance of supplanting in the Danish succession the candidate (Christian of Glücksburg) who had been conditionally nominated by the powers. The Danish king, however, had now come round to the view that Holstein would have to be surrendered to German rule, leaving Schleswig with Denmark to be defended as Scandinavian territory when the time came. On July 22, 1863, accordingly, Charles offered Frederick a military alliance: 20,000 Swedish and Norwegian troops would be used to repulse any German attack across the Eider into Schleswig. Success in such a war — and Charles thought only in terms of success — would give him as good a claim to unite the north under his sceptre as that which had just united Italy under Victor Emmanuel, with whom enthusiasts in Denmark were already comparing him. But it was not to be. When Frederick died in November, the position was that neither of Charles's ministries would agree to implement the alliance, pending assurance of support from France and Britain. Christian of Glücksburg duly came to the throne, and in January faced war with the German powers.

It seems likely that by this time Scandinavianism had rather lost its attraction for thinking people in Sweden but had made corresponding gains among Norwegians, inasmuch as Denmark in any union would naturally join Norway in resisting the claims of the predominant partner, namely Sweden. Be that as it may, Norway followed the lead of Sweden in a strictly commonsense policy, which refused any commitment to help the Danes against the invaders unless help was also forthcoming from one of the powers, so as to make the commitment worthwhile.[1] The Danes were thus left to be defeated by overwhelming forces, and had in the end to surrender Schleswig as well as Holstein. In Norway there were great meetings to express sympathy with the Danes, and some quieter but more effective references to the heavy commercial losses which would result from any participation in the war. The Danes had already been driven back as far as the Limfiord in North Jutland before the Storting had even formulated its opinion in favour of inaction. Scandi-

[1] The total war strength of the Norwegian army was calculated to be 55,666 men in 1866 (W. S. Cooke: *Armed Strength of Sweden and Norway*, London, 1875, p. 97).

navianism as a political programme was dead. King Charles XV had been obliged for a second time to eat his words, and nothing more was heard of a union of crowns in the north. That much more numerous body of opinion, which had praised vaguely understood Scandinavian ideals and looked forward to a vaguer form of union, had to face the fact that big words had been followed by little deeds. Three years later the mood of disillusionment found its outlet in a work of consummate genius, for *Peer Gynt* shows us the weakness and inconsequence of the Norwegian attitude to great events. At the close of the play, when that mysterious figure, the Button-moulder, threatens Peer that because of his uselessness he may be melted down 'at the next crossroads', a bitterly disappointed but not despairing Ibsen seems to be inviting his audience to wait and see whether his native land will yet match words with deeds.

❊

The poet was right in thinking that in this instance the Norwegian people had failed to turn sentiment into achievement. But in a world which was increasingly dominated by Bismarckian Germany strength was the first requisite for a nation; and the economic achievements of this same era, little regarded by Ibsen, were winning for Norway an independent position among the nations. In Schweigaard, who entered the Storting after a brilliant academic career in 1842, Norway possessed an economic reformer of the same type as his great English contemporary Peel, an ardent freetrader and a professed disciple of the Utilitarian philosophers. He never entered the government, since to do so it would be necessary to leave his lawmaking activities in the Storting. He was never a party leader, for the official class, which looked to him for guidance, regarded itself as standing above party and exercising a kind of paternal responsibility for the welfare of the people as a whole. But Schweigaard—the very opposite of the spirit caricatured in *Peer Gynt*—set his stamp upon the whole life of the age.

Commercial policy followed the lines of the English free trade movement, but at a distance. Thus it was as late as 1839 that the gilds lost their control of handicrafts in the Norwegian towns, and even after the actual tariff had been systematically reduced in 1842 most of the foreign trade of the country was restricted to the hands of townsmen. In the 'fifties the fall of the tariff on corn marked the fact that the peasants had become reconciled to free trade, which benefited their interests as producers of wood and fish for export, even though it also flooded the country with what they regarded as unnecessary luxuries. For the followers of Hauge often joined forces with the pure nationalists in a sentimental desire to avoid contamination with what was certainly alien and might be presumed to be also wicked. In the year following the German political triumph in the Duchies, Norway concluded important commercial and shipping treaties with France; and when the tariff next came up for revision in 1873, three years after the death of Schweigaard, the principle he had championed—duties restricted to the needs of revenue—was fully accepted. In twenty years imports had trebled, and Oslo, as the port through which they were mainly distributed, had shot ahead of Bergen to make for the first time a Norwegian town with large shops, hotels, and other facilities on a European level.

Expanding commerce demanded better internal communications. A newly established Ministry of the Interior had the ready support of the peasants in the Storting for a big programme of road building, to link the mountainous hinterland at as many convenient points as possible with the smooth passages through the fiords and leads. The new roads introduced the English macadamized surface; but the main feature was a systematic reduction of the maximum gradient from 1:5 to 1:20 by means of a spectacular zigzagging up the mountainside, which delighted tourists of the pre-motor age. The first railway was laid between Oslo and Eidsvoll in 1851-4, with Robert Stephenson as its engineer and mainly English capital. It followed the principal route of the overland winter haulage of timber by sledge to the Oslo sawmills, and was therefore sure of profitable freights: but in general, construction costs were far too heavy in relation to the anticipated traffic for Norway to be able to plunge like England into the planning and financing of a railway network. On the contrary, it took almost exactly a century before railways radiating from the capital gave direct communication with each of the three largest provincial cities, and the only rail route to Narvik is still that via Sweden. But the telegraph was a less difficult proposition from the technical aspect, and its value to a country of such vast distances and such a scattered population was enormous. Together with the introduction in 1854 of a cheap postal service, conducted chiefly by steamer along the fiords, the telegraph made nation-wide business activities possible. What business? Timber, cod, and herring were still the natural products on which the export trades mainly depended. But in the 'fifties there was something of a boom also in agriculture, associated with higher corn prices, greater variety of crops, and the increased efficiency brought about by the new agricultural schools. The Great Exhibition of 1851 also helped by introducing Norwegian visitors to the novelties of American farm machinery. The farms produced almost entirely for the home market, but the fact that their owners produced for a market at all and were no longer self-sufficing gave a big stimulus to all internal trade. Norwegians noted with pride that Oslo and Bergen, from the late 'forties onwards, had their own cotton factories, though they were dependent for their start on English technicians and for their day-to-day running on cheap delivery by sea of English coal. But their actual importance was very slight—insufficient even to start a protectionist agitation. The modernization of Norway at this era depended above all on the flood of foreign imports, among which English cottons were perhaps the most ubiquitous. The new business that brought them in was the ever-expanding Norwegian mercantile marine.

The ships which were Norway's pride owed little to government initiative; much to the keenness and ambition of thousands of men with little capital, whose united efforts built and sailed them; and most to favourable world conditions. Under the first head we may note the introduction of a compulsory mate's examination in 1840, and twenty years later a statute which standardized contracts and seamen's conditions of service. This was the work of Schweigaard, who brushed aside opposition based on the absence of any similar legislation in Britain by claiming that the Norwegian was unlike the Englishman in being accustomed to live under a system of written law. Under the second head, it is important to remember that the wooden sailing ship of those days could be built almost anywhere along the coast of Norway, by empirical methods, with mainly local material, and by local labour. One consequence was that the coastal population lived in an environment of ships and sails: its sons were already half-trained seamen before they made their first voyage at 13 or 14, and, as crews could be had for the asking, the Norwegian standard of wages, provisions, and quarters was correspondingly low. This helped to keep capital outlay to a minimum. Instead of the big shipowner of today, each ship had a multitude of small shareholders, often including persons who had contributed material or skilled labour to its construction. The skipper's share was usually one of the more substantial: in any case, he was employed, not merely to navigate his vessel from port to port, but to find the most profitable freights and, if necessary, to buy and sell cargoes all over the world.

The trade was of course partly founded on the rising exports and imports of Norway itself and of Sweden, which as early as 1827 had given Norwegian shipping the same rights as ships owned by Swedes: Swedish iron was commonly known in America as 'Norway iron', and from the 'forties onwards a lot of money was made on freightage of Swedish timber as well as Norwegian. Nevertheless, the cardinal event in the entire history of the Norwegian mercantile marine is undoubtedly the repeal of the British Navigation Acts in 1849. This threw open the trade of the whole British Empire to free competition for freights; was quickly imitated by other countries, such as Holland; and inaugurated a long period in which flag discrimination was out of fashion. The first Norwegian ship was unloading Canadian timber in the London docks within a week of the repeal, and builders, who had been content for generations to design 'tubs' for a type of cargo which was virtually unsinkable, began to vie with the English and American shipyards in the production of fast, slimly-built clippers for the China tea-run and other highly profitable trades. An additional impetus, temporary but highly valuable to a country which often lacked the capital for making the most of its chances, came from the Crimean War. Supplies for the Allied campaign in the Black Sea; blockade-running to Archangel for the Russians; neutral trades in which the war-making powers had for the time being lost interest—all these combined to make a golden age for Norway. It was followed by a brief collapse of trade in 1857, a by-product of the slump which marked that year in England, but the growth in shipping was virtually uninterrupted for about two decades.

The results can be measured in different ways. Most of the Norwegian ships of this era, whether home-built or bought cheap in foreign ports, were slow carriers for bulk commodities. Accordingly, their function in the economic life of the world was to convey firstly timber and then corn, from which they graduated as it were to the carriage of coal and iron goods such as rails. In other words, they served the growth of population and the development of the industrial revolution. They did not do it for nothing, of course. Statistics

L

from the later 'sixties reveal an average net profit, after fair allowance for depreciation, of 16 per cent: spread over the many small shareholders, this meant an immediate rise in the standard of life all along the seaboard. Results can also be measured in terms of tonnage. Between 1850 and 1868 it was trebled, by 1880 quintupled. Since the total in 1850 was already approaching 300,000 tons, this would represent a very important economic structure for any country. But in the last analysis the biggest fact about the mercantile marine was its ability to overhaul the shipping of other and much larger states. Up to 1850 it had been growing, for two decades at least, at the same rate as total world tonnage: in the next generation, it grew twice as fast. In 1850 it was the sixth largest in the world; by 1880 it had passed, not only France, but the Dutch and German mercantile marines which had once excluded Norwegian vessels from carrying their own exports, let alone the trade of the outside world. The Swedish flag covered a navy of only half the size of the Norwegian, a fact which tended to inflame the thought of ardent nationalists. As one of them wrote exultantly,

> Our glory and our might
> Are borne on sail-wings white.[1]

The poet Björnson, like his equally nationally-minded predecessor, Henrik Wergeland, would have been quick to point out that the glory and might of a nation consists of something more than the achievement of empire, even a peaceful economic empire of the waves. It is a remarkable fact that in Norway, as soon as the direst pressure of national poverty began to be relaxed, pioneering work of a broadly humanitarian character began gradually to establish her claim to be regarded as a civilizing influence in the world, not to be assessed in terms of her political insignificance. Mention has already been made of the interest taken in penal reform. This led to the building of a model prison in Oslo which would have delighted the mind of Bentham; the discontinuance of the old slave-gangs; and, as early as the 1870's, the complete disuse of capital punishment. A closely related movement was that which fought the intemperance resulting from the practice of distilling corn brandy at trifling cost on every farm. In 1845 Schweigaard in the face of strong

[1] B. Björnson: *Norsk Sjömandssang*, 1868.

peasant opposition got household distilling abolished, and a scheme of local option was introduced into rural areas, with the result that consumption was cut by half in twenty years. Up to 1914 at least, Norway appeared to visitors a more sober country than Britain. Even more striking is the fact that Norway in 1848 abandoned the then virtually universal practice of regarding the insane as persons requiring no other treatment than to be deprived of their liberty. The pioneer—the son of an Irish refugee from the '98 rebellion—was drowned a few years later while emigrating to America: but he had already prevailed upon the Storting to build the first modern asylum, which is still in use.

Education and popular enlightenment were other spheres in which Norway made noteworthy progress. Compulsory schooling from 7 until the 'age of confirmation' was established in all towns by 1848, that is to say, twenty-two years in advance of England. In 1860 the principle was extended to all country districts, and it was made obligatory to build a school wherever there were thirty children able to attend, with the result that teachers gradually took over the leadership of rural communities from the clergy. The content of the elementary school curriculum, which specifically included history, geography, and nature study, was rather broader than in England; and in the secondary schools the first definite break-away from the once universal classical course came as early as 1852. But we must beware of exaggeration. Enlightenment is partly a matter of accessibility. Norway contained vast regions in which thirty children could never be mustered in one place, and there the peripatetic schoolmaster made what impression he could as he travelled from farm to farm. On the west coast in particular, there were very many homes, too, where the influence of the schools was artificially limited by Haugean influences, which were said to eschew all reading matter other than the Bible and the constitution. Indeed, the painstaking investigation of rural conditions which Norway's first social economist, Eilert Sundt, conducted in the 'fifties and 'sixties showed up so many dark and primitive survivals that he was roundly denounced by a type of patriot which preferred an unrealistic picture of the noble peasant.

Sundt, however, was one of two remarkable social pioneers whom Norway threw up in the same seminal year, 1848. He made his name by an investigation into the racial and other characteristics of the gipsies, which stopped the Storting from imposing a penalty on nomadism. Thereafter he became a sort of one-man royal commission, enquiring into problems of population, poverty, labour, and social environment. He exposed bad living conditions in towns, especially unorganized ramshackle suburbs. But his main achievement was to publish a series of objective accounts, of peasant life in its different aspects, minutely and sympathetically observed while the old ways still maintained their hold on the remoter valleys, to which a modern economy had not penetrated. Few countries possess a comparable source for their social history. For contemporaries also Sundt did a great work of enlightenment, revealing to other classes the rich cultural contribution of the peasantry, for instance in the building arts, and at the same time revealing to the peasants the things which disfigured their way of life. He sponsored the propaganda in favour of English ideas of hygiene and cleanliness, which slowly banished the mediaeval dirt and infestation then found in most rural Norwegian houses. In the towns, too, Sundt influenced opinion through educational and insurance societies for working men: but here he built on foundations already laid.

The career of Marcus Thrane began with the French revolution of February 1848; it came to a disastrous end in the summer of 1851, by which date reaction was everywhere in the ascendant; and even then he was less than 43 years of age. Much was packed into a little space. In his early childhood his father had been found guilty of misappropriating the funds of the Bank of Norway, of which he was a director and chief cashier. Marcus therefore was by birth a member of Norway's governing class, but had personal experience of the poverty he sought to remedy. On a visit to France in 1838 he spent two months in prison as 'having no visible means of support', an experience which no doubt intensified his obvious interest in the ideas of Louis Blanc and the *droit au travail*. From Paris he made a brief stay in London, the London of the Chartist manifesto; returned home to lead a struggling existence as a private-school master; and in May 1848 first attracted attention by some newspaper articles, advocating self-determination as the best solution for the vexed problem of Schleswig-Holstein. This led to his appointment as editor of a local newspaper in the town of Drammen, near enough for his voice to be heard also in the capital. He was dismissed at the end of the year, but in the meantime he had made the grievances of the poor known as they had never been known in Norway before. In his own words, he 'felt a personal responsibility for improving matters'—an attitude more closely akin to that of the contemporary Christian Socialists in England, whose enthusiasm for the co-operative movement was shared by Thrane, than to the Marxian teaching, with which he seems to have been wholly unacquainted. From editorship he turned to organization. His first workmen's associations were founded in Drammen and Oslo, after which a special paper was started and Thrane began also to make propaganda tours about the country. The growth was phenomenal. After eighteen months there were 273 associations, with 20,854 members; and though we have no precise figures for the remaining year of their existence, there is no doubt that membership continued to increase.

At first sight the movement might be dismissed as a mere echo of Chartism. Manhood suffrage was the first and foremost demand, and the means of agitation employed included a petition (to the Crown) and a delegate meeting in Oslo which coincided with the meeting of the Storting. But this was a social movement also, making more definite claims than the English Chartists for such measures as the shortening of hours of labour, abolition of remaining trade monopolies, and provision of smallholdings through government action so as to reduce the competition for employment.[1] It is sometimes claimed that Thrane built up a socialist party at a time when it had already been crushed in France and had not yet arisen in Germany. The term socialist is perhaps too strong: but the astonishing thing, which certainly was achieved, was the formation of a class party. Industrial workers in Norway were few, but their interests were successfully welded together with those of two larger groups—the cottars employed by the rich peasants of the eastern districts and the impoverished small farmers of the west coast. In fact, some amelioration of the hard conditions, under which cottars paid rent in the form of work on the rich man's land, was the only legislative result of the movement. The government, the officials and the representatives of the richer peasants in the Storting, and even the judges conspired to crush a class party of the poor. Local disturbances provided a pretext. Thrane, who was no longer the actual head of the organiza-

---

[1] Their paper also gave enthusiastic support to an abortive scheme, financed by the violinist Ole Bull, for establishing 'New Norway'—a 250,000-acre settlement for Norwegians in Pennsylvania.

tion, spent three years in prison awaiting trial, and then served a four-year sentence. There were 133 convictions in all, and the movement lay in ruins. When Marcus Thrane was released in 1858, he was a forgotten man, whose once enormous following had been cowed into submission or — the more fortunate among them — caught up in a new wave of prosperity. As late as 1883, Thrane's return from America on a short visit created little stir in Norway: but the influence of his example upon the imaginations of a later generation of pioneers, who built up one of the strongest Labour parties in Europe, must be left among the imponderables of history.

❋

In the eyes of contemporaries among the educated class, the suppression of Thrane and his followers was a necessary piece of social discipline. Indeed, to them the gulf between the have-nots and the haves seemed altogether less important to society than the gulf between themselves, what were called 'the people of condition', and the primitive peasantry, both poor and not so poor. To bridge this gulf was the great task of national leadership, since without it there could be no complete Norwegian nation; and the cultural leaders seemed to many to be doing a greater work than any political or social reformers, because they were making the nation one.

For the English public folk-songs, folk-dances, and even folk-museums are minority interests: but on the continent an almost mystical significance has been atttached to the evidences of a past way of living, in which the spirit of the folk-group is believed to be handed down from generation to generation. In Germany the brothers Grimm had pointed out the special value of a rich heritage of folk-tales. For Norwegians, whose literature since the close of the saga age had been so sparse, the publication of their folk-tales was like the winning of a major victory. Asbjörnsen and Moe came respectively from tradesman and farmer stock, met first at school, and were inspired by reading Grimm to begin collecting the stories preserved by oral tradition in the neighbourhood of Moe's home. Initial success led the two friends on to comb a large part of the country for the best material; more than ten years' work was crowned by the appearance in 1851 of a definitive edition of *Norwegian Folk Tales*, with a scholarly introduction by Moe, who later became a bishop. To Asbjörnsen the stories had become a life interest, and he produced a separate collection of nature legends, in which he skilfully interwove the accounts of supernatural beings with a description of the people telling the tales and of the places where they arose. The two authors had enriched the world by their disclosure of a hidden vein of fantasy among the Norwegian mountains, beautiful, thought-provoking, and strangely original. German experts vied with their fellow-Scandinavians in acclaiming the stories as masterpieces of folk-literature; an English selection, translated by Sir George Dasent, was published in Edinburgh in 1859—the first Norwegian writing to interest a large public in this country; and the best of them took rank as children's classics everywhere.[1]

But for the Norwegians themselves they were something more than a national treasure and a source of pride in a national achievement. The language in which the tales were couched had been carefully chosen, so as to give the maximum of rustic idiom and local dialect which was consistent with their being fully intelligible and enjoyable for a town audience. Its enormous success with all types of readers had a general effect on vocabulary, the preference being for words of native origin as opposed to the traditional Danish—a form of 'patriotism' already preached by Wergeland. The tales themselves by their quaint and half-mysterious content gave the peasant a new place in the mind of the 'people of condition'—an imaginative, poetic figure, attuned to nature and steeped in the thoughts of his country's past. Even when the Storting met and reminded them of the existence of a peasant Opposition, economical, narrow-minded, and often cantankerous, the upper class now regarded the gulf between them as inevitable rather than desirable.

Other means of bridging the gulf were sought in the collection of folk-ballads, in which Norway proved to be disappointingly poor, and of the folk-tunes, which were later to inspire the genius of Edvard Grieg. But it is more to our purpose to observe how the work on cultural traditions was related to the study of history in the narrower sense. Norway's classic historian, P. A. Munch, promoted the efforts of Asbjörnsen and Moe and himself thought originally of writing history in the style of Scott's *Tales of a Grandfather*. His talent, however, lay not in popularization but in original studies of a teutonic thoroughness and magnitude, which brought back the great-

[1] A single story, 'The Master Thief', had appeared in *Blackwood's Magazine* as early as November 1851. A second, enlarged edition of the book was called for within three months, and a selection for children was made in 1862.

ness of mediaeval Norway for the admiration and emulation of the moderns. His vast *History of the Norwegian People*, which takes six massive volumes to carry the story down to the 14th century, is not easily—or often—read:[1] but it altered the whole climate of opinion about the significance of the middle ages for Norway. For example, at the time when Munch began to write it was seriously proposed to pull down what remained of Trondheim cathedral, Norway's chief heritage of gothic art and the focal point of her mediaeval history. Instead, it became one of Munch's innumerable by-employments to prepare the text of an appeal, which was published in 1859 in English and Norwegian, with drawings by a German architect. Today the enormous work of restoration continues as a national obligation, unchallenged.

Munch was not always right. From his predecessor in the university chair of history he took over a theory—which neither of them acknowledged to have been formulated much earlier—to the effect that the true Scandinavian stock entered its homelands north-about. The route of a race movement which took place many centuries before the Christian era might seem to us both indeterminable and insignificant. But to the Norwegian it would be a national triumph to be able to show that their country had been peopled in this way. For the 'Nordics' who came in round the north of the gulf of Bothnia could be pictured as a 'pure' race, spreading southwards through an empty land, the Norway which they made their home, until finally they spilt over into south Sweden and Denmark, where they became mixed with other racial elements. The theory was discredited, even in the course of Munch's lifetime, but it served his purpose in bolstering up a genuine claim, then often denied, that Norway had its own important and identifiable share in mediaeval Scandinavian civilization.

He was an indefatigable worker, with the memory of a Macaulay and an intense devotion to a national mission which it would be hardly possible for any English historian to feel. He died at the age of only 53, pen in hand, from the effects of a stroke sustained while he searched for Norwegian material in the Vatican archives; it was felt to be a national disaster. But by 1863 his main objects had been attained. The world of learning recognized the existence of a Nor-

[1] Only a sample is available in an English version—P. A. Munch: *The Norwegian Invasion of Scotland in 1263*, Glasgow, 1862.

wegian Historical School. A vast amount of archival material had
been transcribed and appraised from Danish and many other sources:
one of Munch's most sensational finds was that of the earliest manuscript, *Historia Norvegiae*, in Edinburgh. Above all, he had fought a
completely successful battle with Danish scholars to establish the
truth that the great mediaeval literature of the north, which culminated in the Icelandic sagas, was written by men of Norwegian
blood in an identifiably Norwegian language (Old Norse). Munch was
by no means an enemy of Scandinavianism, but Norway must first
lay claim to whatever was truly Norwegian and then develop the
interest in the larger whole.

> It is a distinguishing characteristic of our time that every people
> seeks not only to protect its nationality, as it exists at the moment,
> but also tries in a manner to strengthen and rejuvenate it by going
> back into the nation's inner self in order to eliminate from it the
> heterogeneous, unnational elements and, partly from folk-life,
> partly from history and legend, to bring forth and preserve what
> may be termed the common element, that which is peculiar to the
> national character, and on this common basis to plan the future
> development.[1]

Munch's programme appealed to two writers, who possessed all
the literary graces which he lacked. In the 1850's Ibsen and Björnson
were young exponents of the national idea in the world of the
theatre, where they had a double objective — to banish a Danish style
of acting and speaking and to introduce a Norwegian subject-matter
to the stage. Ole Bull the violinist used some of the money he earned
in America to establish the first 'Norwegian theatre' in his native
Bergen, for which Ibsen was employed to write the plays. After
five years he returned to direct a similar 'Norwegian theatre' in
Oslo, and his place in Bergen was taken by Björnson. But it was
Björnson whose agitation against the Danish actors had made the
new theatre in the capital a practical possibility — and when both
these new ventures went bankrupt, it was Björnson who became
manager of the Oslo theatre which dominated theatrical life for the
next generation. Meanwhile, the Danish accent had completely disappeared, and the national sentiment among theatregoers had been
notably fortified by a succession of mediaeval historical plays from

[1] Speech of January 13, 1847 (Jorgenson: *Scandinavian Unionism*, p. 141).

both authors, on subjects sometimes directly suggested by the work of P. A. Munch. Posterity finds most depth in Ibsen's *Pretenders*, which examines the characters of king Haakon IV and Skule. But for contemporaries Björnson was already an acknowledged national leader in this and other branches of literature when, in 1864, Ibsen departed for Italy, a poor and bitterly disappointed man. The fact that the public did not accept his work no doubt enhanced his indignation at its failure to accept the Scandinavian challenge of the same year, which Ibsen attributed to a frivolous irresponsibility in the Norwegian character.

His indignation, as we have seen, inspired *Peer Gynt*. Björnson was also disappointed by Norway's failure to support the Danes in their hour of need: Scandinavian sentiment had figured prominently in the original version of the national anthem, which he composed in 1859. But his optimistic nature quickly regained its poise and accepted the inevitable with a good grace. The vogue of the historical drama was now on the wane, but Björnson, who was a most prolific writer, while immensely active in the theatre and political journalism, had found time to establish a separate reputation in a different genre. His stories of peasant life breathe too much of a romantic spirit of sunny optimism to suit modern taste. But at their first appearance in 1857-61 they marked, not only the rise of the Norwegian novel, but the completion of the work inaugurated by Asbjörnsen and Moe in making a wide public sympathetic with the life of the peasant. It was Björnson's ambition to stand forth as representing the aspirations of a united nation. His personality was to influence the political thought of the next generation in Norway as much as Ibsen influenced the ethical thinking of a much wider public. But in the 'sixties the rift in cultural unity was already in one respect widening beyond control.

While others were busy interpreting the peasant to the world, two peasants had stepped forward to do their own interpreting. If the Norwegian of the 19th century was in any real sense the heir to the glories of mediaeval Norway, then a vital link lay in the heritage of Old Norse, as Munch had demonstrated. Moreover, the true path from the past to the present was that which most completely circumvented the alien influences bequeathed by the tyrant Danes. These two propositions combined to give enormous significance in Norwegian eyes to the work of a self-educated peasant philologist, Ivar

Aasen. He travelled through the western districts, collecting and analysing the local dialects, which had survived for four or five centuries as the language spoken on the farms, while Danish (pronounced in a distinctively Norwegian way) was the language superimposed by authority from the bench, the pulpit, and the press. The towns used only this modified Danish, which with the growth of popular education and easier communications might quickly have become universal: an English parallel on a small scale would be the replacement of local accents in our own day by the English of the B.B.C. But Aasen's grammar and dictionary of the synthesis of dialects, which he called the 'country language' *(landsmaal)*, gained point by their resemblance to Old Norse. Munch, in fact, would have liked the nation deliberately to have reverted to a language made out of Old Norse, in the same way and for much the same reasons as modern Greek has tried to go back to the language of Homer. What was of more practical importance, the publication of Aasen's books in 1848-50 coincided with the establishment of the peasant Opposition. What better way of asserting their dignity and basic value to society than to make the official and the townsman in general, who prated so much about national values, accept as a national language uncouth expressions they had always despised?

Aasen himself was the most modest of men, and the movement he had started grew very slowly at first. A likely compromise was provided by a school of thought, which Björnson for a time supported, having as its object the introduction by degrees of all kinds of words from the tongues of the people to enrich the language of literature. But in 1858 the peasant-poet A. O. Vinje began to publish his own paper, *The Dalesman*, in a language still more heavily impregnated by class, since he brought in the vulgarisms of the urban poor. It was a little as though Carlyle had written with a combination of scotticisms and cockney: but before he died in 1870 Vinje had produced in the new medium both poetry and descriptive prose of undeniable beauty. In particular, he wrote rapturously of the high mountains, to which he was one of the earliest regular visitors, and where he hoped his spirit might abide for ever, 'looking out over Norway'. Ibsen for his part ridiculed this alleged 'primeval right of screech',[1] and continued to write in almost pure Danish, while most other authors of note Norwegianized their language gradually at

[1] *Peer Gynt*, Act IV, the scene in the lunatic asylum at Cairo.

their own discretion. The upshot was that the users of *landsmaal* remained a minority with a minority literature; but they had started a controversy which tended to open a fissure in society and which still colours Norwegian politics in the middle of the 20th century.[1]

---

[1] A passage from a *landsmaal* author rendered into an equivalent style of English is to be found in *Across the North Sea*, pp. 127-9. A short general history of the problem is given by Professor A. Sommerfelt: *The Written and Spoken Word in Norway*, Oxford, 1942.

CHAPTER IX

THE DEMOCRATIC PROGRAMME
(1864-89)

THE German defeat of Denmark in 1864 marks the close of an era in which the policies of the Scandinavian countries had some bearing on the general course of international affairs. In the next quarter of a century the main interest lies in internal development. The bitterly disappointed Danes modified the liberal constitution which had been conceded under the influence of the revolutions of 1848 and was now discredited by their failure. The Swedish people in 1866 replaced the ancient estates by a parliament of two houses, but the authority of the nobles and other big landowners in the First Chamber of the Riksdag remained predominant. Norway, however, offers the spectacle of vigorous domestic controversy, culminating in 1884 in a liberal amendment to the constitution of 1814, which had the effect of putting the country once more in the van of political progress. The controversy produced Norway's first political parties and its only first-class party political leader, Johan Sverdrup, whose fall from power in 1889 left Norwegian Liberalism in the doldrums — not unlike the fate of the English Liberal party after the retirement of Gladstone. Meanwhile, the rise of Norwegian literature to world fame, the spread of the Norwegian people into the American midwest and other areas of development overseas, the shipping, and the vogue of Norway as a tourist land were among the factors which drew the attention of at least a few outside observers to its rising democracy.

Although Bismarck and Moltke had put an end to any prospect of a union of three Scandinavian powers, the German leaders at least interposed no barrier to the second 'Scandinavian' alternative, namely a closer union between Sweden and Norway. On the contrary, the fact that the house of Bernadotte was quick to cultivate the friendship of the new German emperor threw German influence on to its side. But there was a more important reason for supposing that the *impasse* which had been reached in the matter of the Statholdership need not be regarded as final. One consequence had been the placing at the head of the ministry in Oslo in 1861 of the highly successful Minister of the Interior, Frederik Stang. He remained at the head for nineteen years—always a conscientious administrator and never a party leader, but fully aware that the ascendancy of the upper class, which he represented, needed now to be bolstered up by the use of the powers of the Crown and the closest possible association with the far stronger upper-class ascendancy in Sweden. He therefore accepted the persistent Swedish demand for a joint committee to revise the terms of the union. Ueland was induced to serve on it; the report was unanimous; and its reception by the press so good that Stang felt strong enough to dismiss the nationalist poet Vinje from a minor post for daring to oppose. Whereas the report of a similar committee in the 'forties, set out in 150 sections, was never even printed by either of the governments which had ordered it, this time the report had been agreed by both. Many of the proposals amounted, indeed, to little more than a formal recognition of existing inequalities, such as the fact that the foreign minister of Sweden acted on behalf of both countries and that the king's court was established in the Swedish and not, except for brief intervals, in the Norwegian capital. But to recognize them would have been to recognize once and for all that Norway's position was that of a junior partner in the union. The idea of a united parliament had been rejected by the Norwegian members of the committee, but it recommended that a union cabinet should be set up and given a wide competence. These proposals were being launched in 1867, the very year of the inauguration both of the *Ausgleich*, which held Austria-Hungary together for more than half a century, and of the North German Confederation, which grew into the German Empire. It is impossible to say whether they could have given the united kingdoms of Sweden and Norway the means of satisfactory organic growth; but if they had grown together until 1914 (as did the other two composite states named above), they might well have remained united to this day. What is quite clear is that the defeat in the Storting by 92 votes to 17 marked the rise of a new generation of nationalist-minded youth in Norway, and their organization in party-form by Johan Sverdrup.

But before we turn to consider the career of the 'little general', as he was dubbed at about this time, it will be convenient to note that the Statholder question was at last laid to rest. Charles XV died young in 1872, and was succeeded by his brother, Oscar II. The new king was an impressive figure, with the temperament of an actor and some of an actor's shortcomings: but he had been cast for the role of 'the Norwegian prince' and chose as the motto for his reign 'the welfare of the brother peoples'. Accordingly, he made the abolition of the disputed post serve as an accession gift to his Norwegian subjects. The effect of the gesture was spoilt by its ambiguous form, since the Swedish government insisted on stating its right to object to the change, as on the previous occasion, though this time they agreed to waive the exercise of their alleged right. The details of such a dispute make tedious reading, and are likely to convey the impression that the Norwegians were not merely legalistic but petty-minded. The instinct, however, was a sure one, which taught the nationalists, throughout the period of their union with a neighbour state possessing greater wealth, population, and prestige than their own, to cling to every formal evidence of equality. Otherwise, there would be a tendency to drift into the closer relationship with the stronger state which, for better or worse, the nationalists sought to avoid. At all events, the change went through, and Stang in 1873 became the first holder of an office equivalent to that of prime minister in our own constitutional terminology. He was now 'minister of state for Norway', whereas previously the top-ranking member of the Norwegian ministry had been the senior of its three representatives in the Swedish capital, the 'minister of state in Stockholm'. The old arrangement had implied that the centre of authority was to be found where the king was, the new that—in theory as well as in practice—it lay in Oslo. If ministers did not depend on the king, who did they depend on? Sverdrup had his answer ready: the Storting.

Sverdrup's father had been estate manager for Count Wedel Jarlsberg, and later set up the first agricultural school in Norway. His mother was partly French, and there was a maiden aunt who brought the child up to be a lifelong admirer of the French Revolution. He was a solicitor by profession and dabbled in local government, thus acquiring an early familiarity with the growing petty bourgeoisie of clerks, small businessmen, subordinate officials, and ill-paid teachers. In 1851 his election to the Storting was one of the few direct results of Thrane's activities: but it took Sverdrup nearly twenty years to establish a reform party there—Thrane had directed his appeal chiefly to the unenfranchised masses. As an illustration of Sverdrup's difficulties we may cite his campaign in favour of a jury system. This was a natural extension of the principle of self-government established in 1814, and would have the effect of relaxing the grip which the officials had on every side of legal administration. But after nine years' work he had his plan rejected by the Storting of 1864, because the peasants at a moment of agricultural depression took fright at its supposed expensiveness. Two-thirds of the members were returned by peasant constituencies, which were not interested in reforms but were intensely interested in keeping to a minimum the sums extracted from their own pockets by the tax-collector. Moreover, they were accustomed by long experience to think of all public expenditure as tending to enrich the official class. For Sverdrup to acquire influence was made all the harder because just at this time a new peasant leader, who replaced Ueland, began to organize his electoral supporters through local branches of 'Friends of the Peasant' and the publication of a weekly paper—the first Opposition organ to achieve a steady circulation and influence in Norway. Jaabaek was a professed admirer of the English, who wrote in the first number of his paper: 'England—that is a name which rings through the world as no word has ever done before'.[1] He shared Gladstone's enthusiasm for peace and retrenchment, but Sverdrup had to educate him as to the meaning of the third liberal tenet, reform.

In January 1859 Sverdrup formed an enduring alliance, in which Jaabaek pledged his support for Sverdrup's far-reaching reform programme and received in return support for one reform which his peasant constituents had really at heart—abolition of the ancient servitude, whereby farmers must provide free post-horses for officials on their journeys about the country. On larger issues he became content to follow Sverdrup's lead, although the latter had behind him only the discontented element in the towns, the intelligentsia, and the youth movement. It was a great feat of leadership to combine a peasant majority with so different a minority. Something must be credited to the fact that Jaabaek was astonishingly free from personal ambition, which Sverdrup was not. But Sverdrup

[1] *Folketidende*, Mandal, July 1865.

was not merely an ambitious intriguer, as pictured by his opponents. He was an orator of rare distinction, who combined a Gallic charm with an impressive ability to reduce each problem that arose to first principles, so that in the French manner he seemed always to be advocating a strictly logical course of action. He was also a political expert working among amateurs—getting up his subjects with enormous care, always well informed as to the best practice in other self-governing countries, and having that sixth sense which enables the born politician to know which problems are ripe for solution.

The firstfruits of the alliance were the enactment of the first major change in the constitution of 1814, by which the meetings of the Storting were made annual instead of triennial. The proposal came from the ministry, which hoped for a quicker transaction of business as the main result; but as a constitutional amendment it required a two-thirds majority in the Storting. Many peasants were disposed to think of an annual session both as an irksome burden in itself and as likely to bring them too much under ministerial influence. But Sverdrup carried the day, and the consequences were those he had expected—more effective parliamentary control of the Budget, more political interest in the constituencies, and a better chance of organizing his political party. For another ten years, however, there was only one party—the Left or Liberal party, engaged in a bitter struggle for power against the ministry, which claimed to stand above party, to occupy a central position, and to be concerned only to preserve its existing constitutional authority. But in 1880 the larger landowners began to realize that the Stang ministry was fighting to preserve the power of the official class against its threatened seizure by a party of peasants and other enemies of 'people of condition'. They therefore began to organize a counter-agitation with public meetings, at which they expressed devotion to the prerogatives of the Crown and the union with Sweden as bulwarks of the old class system. It is, however, a measure of the primitive character of Norwegian political life that not until 1885, when this great fight was over, did the Liberal and Conservative parties develop permanent, nation-wide organizations of their respective supporters.

The chosen battleground was a proposal to amend the constitution by seating the ministers in the Storting, an idea which the peasants had previously rejected, in the expectation that any such change would enhance the control of the ministers over the members

M

and not vice versa. But Sverdrup put it before them as a natural sequel to the introduction of annual sessions, and argued that ministers who excelled in the bureaucratic art of fencing with memoranda would prove more amenable when their statements had to face the test of public debate. Whether he already realized that the result of the amendment would be to make the ministers directly subject to the control of a parliamentary majority is uncertain; but it seems reasonable to suppose that so farsighted a leader anticipated that in one way or another there would be a decisive change in the balance of power, if he won. It was a big 'if', even after the rejection of the new proposals for the Union (already described) had shown how big a majority Sverdrup could muster where it was a matter of negativing a government-sponsored proposal in the Storting. He now held the office of president there, a position which conferred some of the prestige and control over business associated with the Speakership at Westminster but did not demand any abandonment of the role of party leader.

But a positive constitutional amendment, solidly opposed by the government, was a much harder thing to carry through. It required a two-thirds majority: this was secured in 1872. In order to surmount the suspensive veto vested in the Crown, the bill had to be passed twice more, after successive elections: by 1880, this too had been done — and the majority had risen to 93:20. But the government then interposed the claim that, as the constitution was silent about the applicability of the suspensive veto to amendments of its own provisions, there was a presumption that in such cases the veto was absolute. This view is said to have been propounded by king Oscar himself, who had recently been incensed against the leaders of the Liberals by the renewal of the old agitation about the national flag, a matter in which he had been personally connected with the concession made by his father in 1844. Sverdrup replied by passing a resolution on June 9, 1880 — a memorable day for Norway — which attempted to assert the supreme authority of the Storting over the ministry by demanding that they should now promulgate the amendment as law. Stang, who was an old man, resigned, leaving the problem to a personally unimpressive but highly bureaucratic successor named Selmer. He secured a unanimous opinion from the law faculty of the university that the veto was absolute, Sverdrup a less formal support from the activities of volunteer rifle clubs, intended to prevent a royal *coup*.

The final stage in the long drawn out struggle is perhaps the least edifying. Sverdrup resolved to end the deadlock by an impeachment, a process which had been employed in other political cases but which was clearly designed in the constitution to protect the state against crime rather than against mere errors of opinion. At the next election a majority was obtained from a nation at fever heat, big enough to keep control of the Odelsting while completely packing the Lagting, the members of which plus the nine judges of the supreme court formed the special court for the trial of an impeachment. The result was therefore a foregone conclusion. Selmer and his colleagues were found guilty and sentenced to fines and loss of office, in spite of the fact that the professional judges were unanimous in favour of their acquittal. Selmer tried to persuade the king to disregard the decision of the court; and the king himself tried to impose a less drastic solution by substituting a new ministry of the same political complexion as the old. But within four months king Oscar was forced to accept the logic of a situation in which the will of the Storting majority could be resisted only by a hazardous resort to force. As an English Liberal paper, which watched developments with interest, had already pointed out:

> It is surely too late in the day for any constitutional king to think of forcing an absolute veto, which is now really the point of contention, upon his people at the point of the bayonet, and if the Norwegians do not belie their tradition, there seems but little chance of success for the king, if he were to attempt to thwart the national will by force of arms.[1]

On July 2, 1884, Sverdrup and other Liberal leaders took their seats in the Storting as the king's ministers, and responsible government in the English sense[2] became established in Norway. It remained the

[1] *Pall Mall Gazette*, October 10, 1883. On October 4 an article on the Norwegian constitution by H. L. Braekstad had appeared in the Conservative *Standard*.

[2] But in Norway the constitutionality of legislation which has been duly passed by king and Storting may fall to be determined by the Supreme Court. Mr C. J. Paal Berg, for many years Chief Justice of Norway, writes in G. B. Lampe (editor): *Norway*, Oslo, 1946, that this became the established practice in the 1890's. But Professor Frede Castberg (*The Norwegian Way of Life*, London, 1954, p. 58) observes: 'It is very rare for the Supreme Court to set aside a law on the ground that it is unconstitutional.'

practice for ministers to be chosen in many cases from outside the Storting, which they then attended by virtue of their appointment to office; but a new provision was at once introduced, giving ex-ministers the privilege of standing for election in any constituency without regard to the usual residential qualification.

The political triumph of Johan Sverdrup would have been impossible if he had not been backed by an ardent body of supporters, who watched every phase of the constitutional struggle with absorbed interest. They for their part could not have given so much attention and emotion to the political developments of the day, if the efforts of a less nationally-minded generation had not laid economic foundations which were still tolerably satisfactory. Thus the completion of the telegraph network and the extension of the coastal steamer services right up to the Russian frontier, both in 1870, made Norway more of an economic unit than ever before; and in the previous year the laying of a direct cable to Peterhead had transformed business communications with Britain and America.[1] Trade interests often cut across the rising national antagonisms, as when an agreement of 1874 removed the customs barrier for most goods passing between Norway and Sweden overland and for many exchanged by sea. At about the same time a Scandinavian monetary system was instituted, each of the three countries adopting a new unit, the Crown, which was to be freely convertible into gold. The era of world free trade, which had already done so much for Norway, was then reaching its climax, with record prices for timber, and in a four-year period (1869-73) Norway was able to double its consumption of sugar and coffee, silks and wines, and even of pianos. In the harder times which followed, Norwegian staples still had some advantages in the world markets. The woodworking industries, for instance, received a fillip through the growing demand for their new products, pulp and cellulose. The introduction of canning brought fresh prosperity to the fishing port of Stavanger, and the use of the harpoon gun (a Norwegian invention of 1868) stimulated whaling, which was still conducted mainly in Arctic waters.

The mercantile marine of course suffered severely during the world depression of the 'eighties, and in many respects was worse off than its competitors. The use of iron and steel instead of wood

[1] T. Rafto: *Telegrafverkets Historie 1855-1955*, Bergen, 1955, pp. 79-82.

for building even sailing-ships made it less easy to build at home; to change over quickly from sail to steam would require a capital expenditure beyond Norwegian means; and to run steamers successfully needed a type of operator, with up-to-the-minute knowledge of changing world markets, which the scale of Norwegian business hitherto had been too small to develop. So, by 1890 Norway had fallen back from third place to fifth in tonnage owned, and of that tonnage about three-quarters consisted of sailing-ships, considered obsolescent elsewhere. Only Bergen had as yet begun to develop the modern type of shipowner and had mainly a steamer fleet; even there the steamers were for the most part such as had been discarded by the big shipping companies of other countries in favour of newer designs which were more economical in use. In 1876 Plimsoll visited Norway, and a Plimsoll line was eventually introduced; but the use of old ships bought cheap abroad, especially of course the unwanted sailing-ships, caused a sinister rise in the number of shipwrecks. Nevertheless, the fleet remained a big factor in the transportation of the world's needs in the way of bulk commodities from overseas — wood, corn, coal, rice, jute, salt, petroleum — and was well established also in one or two of the semi-luxury trades, such as the carriage of fruit. Over the period 1873-1895, shipping profits covered nine-tenths of the deficit caused by excess of imports over exports. Norway was only the fifth power at sea, but the smallness of her population meant that the earnings of the ships nevertheless exerted a large influence on the national standard of life.

Agriculture was only gradually losing its pre-eminence as the source from which the Norwegian people through all ages and in every change of political circumstance had derived its main sustenance and whatever comforts it might aspire to. A minimal importation of foreign corn had been necessary, indeed, from the earliest historic times in certain areas: but the typical Norwegian was an almost self-sufficient agriculturist. In the period 1800-75, however, the total population doubled, and although the towns came to absorb twice as large a proportion of the people as before, this left 82 per cent residing in rural areas. When due allowance is made for fishermen and woodsmen — many of whom were part-time farmers as well — it is still evident that pressure on agricultural land was enormous. Holdings were subdivided to an uneconomic extent; marginal land was cultivated with an excessive expenditure of labour; and the condition of the cottars, in spite of Thrane and a new law, remained miserable because there was more demand for land than for services. Thanks to the agricultural schools, an improved technique was increasing the yield of the soil, acre for acre: but even so, most farmers found it very hard to win from it a return which met their cash needs. For self-sufficiency was going out of fashion; it was becoming socially desirable to buy clothes and furniture, for instance, instead of making do with the home-produced article which had satisfied earlier generations. From the 'seventies onwards the world price of corn was falling; the purchasing power of the Norwegian farmer was automatically reduced; and in the absence of industrial growth on the English scale, there was no solution to the economic problem — inside Norway.

But fortunately it did not require to be solved inside Norway. Lands across the sea eased the burden in the 19th century, as they had done a thousand years before. Emigration to the United States had afforded some relief, as we have seen, since the days of Cleng Peerson and Ole Bull. But after the end of the American Civil War a much bigger movement set in, when the Homestead Act with its offer of free land for every settler was being discussed by peasant firesides as the most glamorous of folk tales come true. English shipping firms and American immigration agents vied in providing facilities, and every spring boat-trains from Hull and Newcastle to Liverpool were full of Norwegians being shepherded on the first stage of the great adventure of the young.[1] Jaabaek's paper, which ran from 1865 to 1879, was packed with information from and about America. The movement reached its zenith in 1882, when the total of emigrants was 29,000, and there were four years in that decade when the net population remaining in Norway was actually on the decline. In the course of the half-century before the first world war interrupted the movement, 676,741 Norwegians made the voyage across the Atlantic and went for the most part to the four mid-western states where their descendants still flourish and abound. Hard times in the 'nineties drove some of them over the border into Canada, and after 1900 up to ten per cent of immigrants made their way direct to the Canadian wheat-growing provinces or to the fisheries of British

[1] When Mrs C. S. Sidgwick wrote *The Story of Norway* for English children in 1885, she ended with a description of an emigrant family setting out to cross the Atlantic, 'as brave as Vikings, and much more lucky than lemmings'.

Columbia. But it was in Wisconsin, Minnesota, and the Dakota Territory (where Rölvaag placed his *Giants in the Earth*) that Norwegian pioneers left their chief mark in the making of the New World — through forgotten lives in lonely shacks and unremitting labours on the endless prairies.

But what did the making of America contribute to the remaking of Norway? The first economic effect was to relax tension. The ill-used class of cottars, which had once consisted of a quarter of the population, sank by the end of the migration period to an insignificant three per cent. Some of the very poorest independent holdings in the west, which had never yielded a proper living, were left as they stood and have not attracted new occupants. But in the long run scarcity of labour encouraged the use of better implements and technique on the farms, while the same phenomenon in industry helped the growth of trade unions. The authorities, who had begun investigating the causes of emigration as early as 1845, viewed the draining away of the nation's manpower with increasing alarm; eventually (in 1909) a special organization was started to provide new soil for those who were willing to accept independence at home instead. It is to be observed, however, that economically Norway benefited very considerably by the capital which the emigrants from the earliest years sent home in remittances to relations, estimated at £2,000,000 in 1912. There was also a not unimportant influence exerted by those who went to America and came back with experience and often with savings — an average of about 400 persons a year and, in one emigration-prone south coast district, a total of three per cent of population. But the social influences, which cannot be measured so easily, may well have been more important. Norwegian Lutheran Churches were rapidly set up by the emigrants, but they could not fail to notice and describe the absence of a state church in America and the variety of its Protestant faiths. Methodism was brought to Norway from this source, and the Haugean tradition was greatly strengthened. If we could examine the hundreds of thousands of letters, often accompanied by the price of a ticket, in which emigrants described their new surroundings for those at home, we should almost certainly find a type of freedom extolled which bore (for people of that persuasion) a most enheartening resemblance to the programme of the Liberals in Norway. In 1880 Björnson visited the Norwegian settlements in America, collected some contributions for a financial testimonial to Sverdrup, and in a characteristically flamboyant utterance suggested when writing home that would-be emigrants retained an obligation to the Liberal cause. His support for emigration is in any case an important factor in its growth, for he fired the imagination of youth.

> One thought follows me here far away, where I have constantly (along with so many emigrants) to think about our attitude to our duty to the fatherland. . . . The fatherland cannot require us to cripple our abilities. If it lacks the conditions for their development, then one must go where the conditions are to be found. But —and of this I feel certain—if the fatherland is threatened by a great danger like war, if it passes through a crisis which is decisive for its future, then every one who can serve it must be in the fight. I must set that up as an unconditional obligation.[1]

In all Norwegian eyes, it adds lustre to the history of this period of political strife that great writers played a part in it. The greatest of them all, indeed, stood half aloof, for Ibsen lived abroad until the 'nineties. At the time it seemed very important that, on his visit home in 1874, he let himself be hailed as the associate of the official, conservative-minded class, whereas on the morrow of Sverdrup's victory over the ministers Ibsen expressed a general sympathy with the Liberals—this in spite of the fact that he had satirized both Sverdrup and Björnson in his early comedy, *The League of Youth*. But the truth is that what interested Ibsen was the warfare of the soul, not of the platform—the development of human character, never the social setting for its own sake. *A Doll's House*, which became widely known abroad within three years of its first appearance in 1879, has no rival in its importance for the emancipation of Western woman. For the author, however, what mattered was the character of Nora, one of the roles that every great actress aspired to play, not the effect on the fortunes of the feminist agitation in Norway.

This had begun as early as 1855 with a realist novel by Wergeland's sister, Camilla Collett, examining the lack of worthwhile opportunities for action in the lives of *The Governor's Daughters*. The

---

[1] *Dagbladet*, Oslo, July 19, 1881 (I. Semmingsen: *Veien mot Vest*, Vol. II, Oslo, 1950, is the source used for the quotation and all emigration statistics).

university and the professions were opened to Norwegian women without restriction in the early 'eighties and equal franchise rights were granted before the outbreak of the first world war: willy-nilly, Ibsen had helped to place Norway in the van of progress. It would also be possible to illustrate from several of the plays his encouragement of free discussion of ethical problems and the shortcomings of a conventional religion. The result was to intensify the bitterness of a peculiarly Norwegian conflict. On the one hand, the clergy were attacked as civil servants who in the name of religion conducted a systematic propaganda from the pulpit on behalf of political conservatism and the old order of society. On the other hand, they were denounced for a fundamentalist and puritan attitude in questions of belief, which in England at least found expression among the nonconformists rather than inside the Establishment. In Norway the sects had never been important: the followers of Hauge stayed in the Church, and their sons and grandsons in many cases became peasant-clergy. As the theological training in the university was given by men who bitterly opposed all Broad Church tendencies, the intelligentsia quarrelled even with those of the clergy who on social grounds might have been their staunchest allies against the old order.

Ibsen to some extent ventilated these grievances, while the whole of his work may be said to have preached the value of free development of the personality as the only supreme good. The individualism and self-reliance in thought as well as action which are characteristic of modern Norway obviously owe much to him. But his art matters far more than any supposed message for the Norwegians of his day. By producing the greatest dramatic genius of modern times Norway not only showed her ability to excel in the only way which is open to a small people, namely in the achievements of individuals; she also gave the play-going public of Europe and America a new awareness of the country's existence. Ibsen in the 1880's was becoming a household name in Britain;[1] no contemporary composer was more popular than Grieg; and summer by summer the steamer was bringing a greater number of tourists, drawn mainly from the more

---

[1] Gosse wrote his article 'discovering' Ibsen in the *Spectator* of March 16, 1872; Archer's translations began to appear in the 'eighties; and, as a sequel to the performance of *A Doll's House* in London in 1889, twenty-three translations and editions of the plays were published in the next eight years.

influential classes of society. Twenty years before, to travel in Norway had still been something of an adventure. Now, there were thousands who could supplement the impression derived from Ibsen's plays with some recollections of a different Norwegian type — the hardy peasant, encountered by fiord or fell, poor, picturesque, and unforgettable. He is sometimes denounced as grasping: but very few of the critics were in a position to realize that the money earned with boat or carriole in the summer weeks was perhaps the determining factor against emigration and the essential basis of the 'independent attitude' which was so often remarked.

Nevertheless, the vogue for Ibsen was not accompanied by any comparable interest, so far as Britain was concerned, in the other great literary figure of the age. Björnson had a big reputation in Germany, for he was often an ardent exponent of pan-Germanism; in France, where he was thought of as a revolutionary republican; and among many oppressed peoples, notably the Slovaks, for whom he stood as a champion of political liberty. He was also an important figure in the international peace movement. His best writing, which does not in any case lend itself to translation, is to be found among the short lyrics, the stories of peasant life, and the historical dramas, which have already been mentioned. His disappointment at the desertion of Denmark in 1864 led to a period of comparative silence, from which he emerged with a 'new course' for his country's foreign policy, namely to foster good relations with their racial kinsmen, the Germans of the mighty new empire which had swallowed Schleswig. This at least was consistent with his later advocacy of pacifism. More important was the conversion of this son of the manse to a freethinking position, which incensed many people who had formerly admired him as a patriotic writer and lent additional interest to his later plays and novels. These dealt with the problems of his own age directly, and have not survived it: but they confirmed Björnson in the position to which he aspired, that of a national conscience personified.

From 1869 onwards Björnson was the sworn champion of Sverdrup's line of policy, but it is characteristic of his desire to be regarded as a national and not a party voice that at general elections he always refused to vote. What in fact he did was to cause the intelligentsia, the peasantry, and the young people of all classes to identify whatever form of liberalism he chose to preach with a clear course of patriotic duty. Björnson looked and dressed like a sage; he had a magnificent voice; and though he was always idealizing and moralizing, his poetic fancy lent charm to his most casual utterances. Those utterances were indeed innumerable. His books were many, yet for years Björnson also found time to edit a popular paper and he wrote letters to the press of almost every country in Europe. He was an adept at occasional verse on public themes—rather in the style of Tennyson's poet laureateship work—but probably made the greatest impact of all through his speeches. Their sentiments would have sounded highflown to an English ear, the delivery rhetorical and unrestrained: but for his own people he embodied all they most admired in the character of the skald who accompanied the Vikings into battle, assisted their deeds, and sang their praises. May 17, the national festival in honour of the constitution, was in a special sense his day. He invented (in 1870) the processions of flag-bearing children which are still its most picturesque feature; for more than a generation his speeches imprinted its significance upon the mind of the whole nation.

Björnson's views lacked logical consistency: as a schoolboy he had always failed in mathematics. Christianity, the language question, republicanism, and—as we shall shortly see—the character of Johan Sverdrup are only four of the important subjects on which he gave a lead in two different directions. When he bought a farm in the Gudbrandsdal and went to live among the peasants about whom he had written so enthusiastically for years, the first result was a temporary wavering in his enthusiasm: if he roused them to political life, might they not after all prove to be a reactionary force? His farm was close to a folk high school, a form of adult education newly introduced from Denmark: there, too, Björnson met with disappointment, for the religious outlook was Haugean rather than liberal. But he was always an optimist, always an idealist, always receptive of something new, making an endless appeal to the twin forces of nationalism and youth. 'In Norway the Norwegian people shall be master, they and no other, now and for evermore.' That was the message with which he roused the slow-moving mind of the masses in the 'seventies and 'eighties. But the man was more than the message: it is hard to understand modern Norway unless one takes into account that Björnson—the artist in politics, the idealist plunging lightheartedly into public affairs—still has only one rival in the national affections, namely Nansen. When Björnson received the Nobel prize for literature in 1903, he made a significant reference to another great writer.

> Victor Hugo is the man for me. Inside his sparkling imagination it is the feeling of the richness of life which colours everything. Many people talk about his faults—all right. But for me every one of these faults is blown away by the tremendous breath of life which was in him.

The breath of life was precisely what he himself represented in the slow-moving society of his native land.

The first of Nansen's great exploits—his crossing of the Greenland icecap on skis in 1888—lies so near the end of this period that we may for the time being ignore the influence which was to rival Björnson's. The university already had its distinguished figures in the field of scientific research—among them a clergyman who helped to lay the foundations of the study of marine biology, and a brilliant Bergen doctor, who in 1873 isolated the bacillus of leprosy. There were at that date more than 2,000 lepers on the west coast of Norway; by 1910 the total had been reduced to 300, and the disease, a sordid relic of the Middle Ages, is now virtually extinct. A slow improvement in public hygiene was a result of educational progress which in the long run had incalculable importance for the life of the nation: but in the age of Sverdrup it was the build-up of public opinion which mattered most. The only influence comparable to that which Björnson exercised over the less sophisticated elements in the nation was that which a historian exercised among the intelligentsia. J. E. Sars was the son of the marine biologist mentioned above, and his work owes much to the scientist's desire for system as well as to Guizot and Buckle, the historians of civilization. He studied intensively as a young man in the Danish archives, and was able to show that the period of Danish rule in Norway had been fruitful in economic progress. This might seem to us a sufficiently innocuous conclusion: but the Norwegian nationalist had been plagued by what Wergeland called 'the false solder', that is, a vista of meaningless centuries joining up the 'true' Norway of the Middle Ages with the 'true' Norway of the 19th century. Now he was allowed to see the whole of his country's history as a continuous process of development, a viewpoint which took away most of the bitterness and sense of inferiority resulting from the memory of the Danish yoke. In 1873 Sars published the first volume of his closely-reasoned *Survey of the History of the Norwegian People*[1]. Next year he was appointed Professor Extraordinary on the motion of Johan Sverdrup. Thenceforth he was able to influence the bulk of the young men passing through the university, at their most impressionable age, towards a liberalism which saw in democracy and independence of Sweden, not merely the goal of legitimate Liberal ambitions, but the end of a course of national evolution.

❋

History, however, is often made or marred by the characters of a few individuals whom merit and luck have combined to bring to the top. Sverdrup had worked for 25 years to bring the Liberal party into power; it took him only five years to destroy his handiwork. The catastrophe was so complete that many Norwegians look upon it as an Ibsen drama, claiming that faults of character which ruined Sverdrup's career in the end had always been present, waiting for the moment to declare themselves. A fairer comment, perhaps, was that of the British envoy, Sir Horace Rumbold. After his first, not very satisfactory, interview with Sverdrup, conducted in German, he remarked that 'A long course of political agitation under adverse circumstances would not develop the more amiable sides of human nature.'[2]

The ministry which he formed in July 1884, began well. The suffrage was widened for the first time since 1814, so as to make an annual income of £40 the qualification in the towns and £25 in the country. The jury system was introduced at last. The principle of universal military service, which had been nominally extended to the towns in 1854, was made effective in a new army law. This met the old nationalist objection to any increase in its size by limiting service in the line to five years, with eight in the reserve, so as to reduce the proportion of line troops, which alone were placed at the king's disposal. An official grant was made at the same time to the rifle clubs, which had rallied so conspicuously to the support of the Storting and might almost be regarded as an equivalent for the

---

[1] The fourth volume, covering the union with Denmark, was not published until 1891; but the author's views were known earlier through his lectures.
[2] Confidential letter to Lord Granville, October 9, 1884 (Knaplund: *British Views of Norwegian-Swedish Problems*, pp. 99-101).

French National Guard. By the end of the century they had a membership of 30,000, two-thirds of whom were no longer liable to be called up for the army, and a stock of 15,000 army-pattern rifles.[1] But the change which most clearly registered the fact that the peasants were now the masters of the old official class was the language law. Since the death of Vinje in 1870 only one important writer, the novelist and poet Arne Garborg, had made use of *landsmaal*—and he used the other form as well. But for the peasantry, in the west at least, *landsmaal* had become a shibboleth by which to distinguish the true democrat from the adherents of the language of foreign snobbery—to which Ibsen and Björnson were at the moment giving new greatness. The new law placed the two forms in a position of absolute equality in the schools and in official usage. Thus democracy and the passion for egalitarianism triumphed over convenience, common sense, and (probably) the true interests of Norwegian culture.

So far, the Liberals had held together, even if Sverdrup's unwillingness to extend the franchise to the workers may be held partly responsible for the formation of a Labour Party, only three years after he had come into office as a democratic leader. But the new Labour Party almost by definition had no voice in the Storting. It was on the rock of religion that Sverdrup's majority foundered, for all the eloquence of Björnson could make no impression on the fundamentalist element along the west coast, where the spirit of Hauge brooded over a population which in its everyday life saw nature at its sternest and found it easy to believe in a god of vengeance. Trouble began with a grant, sponsored by both Ibsen and Björnson, to recognize the genius of Norway's great realist novelist, Alexander Kielland.[2] But Kielland's all too faithful picture of his native Stavanger had not spared the clergy, with the result that what we might call the evangelical wing of the Liberals combined with the Conservatives to refuse the money. Worse was to follow. Sverdrup, who was well read in English 17th-century history, believed that political self-government needed to be based on religious self-government. He therefore encouraged his nephew, who was minister for ecclesiastical affairs, to bring forward a bill for the institution of

[1] *Norway—Official Publication* (1900), p. 301.
[2] Two of his novels, *Garman and Worsé* and *Skipper Worsé*, had been translated into English in 1884 and 1885.

local church councils under lay control. The Conservatives made a counter-proposal for a different kind of council, with less localized authority and much more weight given to the clergy. But the decisive factor was the refusal of the intellectuals and many other younger members of Sverdrup's party to vote for a scheme which they believed would increase the power of the puritans. The councils would favour the appointment of puritanical clergy; the cultural work fostered by the Broad Church party would be banished from parochial activities; an old-fashioned piety, which the Radicals readily identified with hypocrisy, would reign supreme. The measure was defeated; the Liberal party was split; and at the election in 1888 the Moderate Liberals under Sverdrup secured only 25 seats as against 38 won by the Radicals and no less than 51 by the Conservatives. It did not help the reputation of Sverdrup with posterity that he tried hard to stave off the day of resignation, and hung on until June 1889 in a condition of dependence upon a demagogic cleric, who represented Stavanger in the Storting and had been mainly responsible for the shabby treatment meted out to Kielland under a supposedly Liberal government.

Sverdrup went out of office exactly five years after his triumphant arrival in the seat of power. When he died two and a half years later, he was already a 'back number'—this man who had created party politics out of nothing and almost single-handed had transformed a constitution. It is kindest to say that he aged early, and to point out that the political struggle had been made doubly wearing for him by a heavy load of debt, which he incurred when he forsook his practice as a solicitor to serve his country. But the fact that Norway's greatest politician is remembered, on the whole, with little respect and affection is due less to his responsibility for the party split than to the shortcomings, one might almost say tergiversations, of his policy towards Sweden. In this case the explanation advanced is a different one—his administrative inexperience, his complete lack of previous interest in foreign affairs (as distinct from the growth of democracy in foreign countries), and a certain deference to king Oscar's wishes. Sverdrup in his earlier years was a man who put no trust in princes. The change is so striking that it has been attributed to a natural affinity between two men of French antecedents and tastes; it may be more correct to suppose that Sverdrup fell victim to royal charm and a sympathy which the king showed (rather than felt) for a minister who had been thrust upon him from a new milieu.

As an Opposition leader, Sverdrup had played a large part in the rejection of the 'Scandinavian' proposals of 1867, with the result that foreign policy continued to be conducted nominally by the king in his capacity as king of Norway, in practice by the Swedish foreign minister in a council attended by one of the three Norwegian ministers in Stockholm and by one other Swedish minister. But in 1885 the Swedish Riksdag was influenced by the growth of parliamentary power in Norway to extend its own control over Swedish foreign policy, by requiring that it be conducted in a council attended by the foreign minister, prime minister, and one other Swedish minister. Since this would put the Norwegians in a minority of one against three when their affairs were discussed in the foreign policy council, an obvious injustice which the Swedes had not intended to perpetrate, the way was open for Sverdrup to negotiate a new arrangement in Stockholm. He accordingly agreed that the Norwegian representation on the council should be raised from one to three, and arranged for this to be formally incorporated by the two parliaments in the existing act of union. But the proposal, when it finally emanated from the cabinet in Stockholm, with the king presiding over his Swedish and his three resident Norwegian ministers, had a slightly different wording. 'Ministerial business shall be laid before the king by the minister of foreign affairs in the presence of two other member of the Swedish together with three members of the Norwegian government.'[1] Norway would be committed to the recognition in theory of what had been accepted for sixty years in continuous practice, namely, that their foreign minister was the Swedish foreign minister. A tremendous outcry arose, with Björnson's voice the loudest of all in condemnation of his former hero who now truckled to the Swedes. Sverdrup helped to demolish his own reputation by shuffling off responsibility on to the head of the Norwegian minister of state in Stockholm, who was eventually driven to commit suicide, just a year before Sverdrup fell from office.

But even more important than the disaster which overtook the Liberal leadership is the circumstance that the wedge had been inserted which took only two decades to split the union. The proposed revision of the act of union was summarily abandoned. Instead, the

[1] Protocol of May 15, 1885 (*Norges historie*, VI, Part 2, p. 59).

idea of a wholly separate Norwegian foreign minister began to be ventilated among Liberals. The leaders were still chary of pushing forward so dangerous and complicated a proposal, but they saw that hostility to the union was an attitude which helped them against the Conservatives with the bulk of the electorate. To many of the voters it seemed that the triumph over class rule in 1884 required to be completed by a further triumph over kingly rule, which they identified with Swedish rule.

N

CHAPTER X

A NEW MONARCHY

IN Europe as a whole, one era of national self-assertion closed with the union of the two Bulgarias in 1885 and the next did not open until the Young Turks made their revolution in 1908. For the year 1905, when the defeat of Russia by Japan produced a general unheaval throughout the multi-national empire of the Czars, resembled 1848 in that it proved in the end to be 'a turning-point at which European history failed to turn'. The position of Norway in this period is therefore quite exceptional, for the movement to make their independence complete, which began to monopolize the thoughts of Norwegians in the early 'nineties, was brought to success in 1905, giving the country nearly a decade in which to consolidate her new institutions before the outbreak of the first world war. The Norwegian monarchy is the youngest of those which still survive in Europe, by a margin of three-quarters of a century: it was fortunate in the moment of its establishment—on the eve of a time of unprecedented prosperity in Norway, while republicanism was still thought of as faintly unrespectable and quite probably bad for business.

The separation of Norway from the joint Swedish-Norwegian monarchy was, in one sense, a storm in a teacup. Throughout the period of the union, Norway had had full control of internal affairs, in accordance with the terms of the constitution of 1814. As regards external affairs, Swedish leadership had never involved Norway in war or even in a heavy military expenditure on account of a threat of war. The disputes between the two countries all turned upon semi-legal questions—the interpretation of the act of union, its relation to the antecedent Norwegian constitution, the nature of the best machinery for co-operation between the two governments. Considering their superiority in numbers and wealth, the Swedes were remarkably moderate in the ways in which they sought to defend their position as the naturally predominant partner in the union, which (in their view) had been intended by the powers to compensate them for the loss of a province, Finland, in the Napoleonic wars. In 1905, even the final crisis was solved without a drop of blood being shed: there were more sighs than scowls, more scowling than sabre-rattling, as the Swedes saw the Norwegians walk out of the 90-year-old union.

But for all Norwegians the event was, and is, the culminating point in their national renaissance. They had long suffered from an inferiority complex, which extended far beyond the field of politics: throughout most of the 19th century anything done by a Norwegian in the arts and sciences, commerce, and even sport had always to be vociferously acclaimed as the triumph of a specifically Norwegian culture. In 1905, however, they put a united national will behind the fulfilment of a political programme directed against Swedish interests. The risks, for the smaller nation, were obviously grave, even if they were not quite so grave as they seemed. When they won through, and the joys of complete independence were for the time being unclouded, the feelings of relief and of enhanced self-respect were comparable to those which other peoples associate with the winning of a major war. It would hardly be too much to say that many Norwegians thought of the whole of their history since 1319 as a wandering in the wilderness, from which they had now emerged into the Promised Land.

The fall of the Sverdrup ministry in July 1889 was followed by the first of two Conservative governments under Emil Stang, a competent administrator of the same type as his father, but dependent on the business interests rather than the civil service, whose prestige had suffered a fatal blow in the 1884 impeachments. His policy was to combine social reform with prudent finance, but little came of it. Within eighteen months he was involved in a new attempt to arrange a constitutional agreement with the Swedes, that diplomatic business should be 'transacted by the king in the presence of three members of the government of each kingdom'. So far, so good: but the Swedes inserted a reference to the participation of the 'Swedish minister who is head of the foreign office' — a statement of the existing practice which involved a denial of Norway's theoretical rights.

The ministry was promptly outvoted; the Radicals had a clear majority at the next election; and—what was more important—they came into power with a scheme for establishing a separate Norwegian foreign minister. One of its sponsors was the indefatigable Björnson, another, Ibsen's only son, Sigurd; he had been educated abroad, and made great play with the parallel of separate diplomatic representation in the south German states, which existed side by side with their membership of the German empire. The scheme showed the strength of feeling among their supporters, who had little idea of the difficulties which would be involved in any attempt to carry it out. As an easier course of action, which might achieve broadly similar results, ministers now proposed to institute a separate Norwegian consular service.

Since this was the issue which eventually broke the union, it may be well to note the nature of the Norwegian claim. Consuls were not mentioned in the act of union, and the special Storting of November 1814 rejected on grounds of economy a proposal that a separate service should be secured. Since 1836 consular appointments had been approved by the joint session of ministers, and since 1858 the Norwegian ministry of the Interior had contained an office for commercial and consular affairs: but the service lay under the unchallenged control of the Swedish minister of foreign affairs. But by 1891, when a Norwegian departmental inquiry favoured a change, Norway had solid, practical reasons for a new claim in the matter. On the one hand, a fresh shipping boom had restored her mercantile marine to third place among the world's fleets. As a matter of prestige, it seemed ludicrous that Norway's captains and shipping agents, unlike those who represented much smaller fleets, should be dependent upon services rendered by officials who were responsible to a foreign power. For the rank and file it was more than a prestige question, for it was not easy for a seaman who was penniless or had fallen foul of the police in a foreign port to get the help he needed from some Swedish aristocrat, who might have trouble even in understanding the gist of what he wished to say. On the other hand, there was the disquieting fact that Sweden, though her mercantile marine bore no comparison with the Norwegian, had an export trade which was twice as large. Even though a fair proportion of the principal posts in the consular service were held by Norwegians, might it not be the case that the siting of consulates and their general administration were related primarily to the needs of Swedish trade? This question was raised all the more urgently because in 1888 Sweden had begun to move over towards a high-tariff system to protect both agriculture and industry, with the result that the Norwegians had begun to lose their relatively free access to the Swedish market. They therefore needed the help of the consuls in finding new substitute markets.

The Radical ministry attempted to force their measure through by a specious plea that a Norwegian withdrawal from a joint service of such long standing, because it was not named in the act of union, should be treated as a purely internal Norwegian affair. King Oscar refused his sanction, whereupon they resigned. Stang returned to office in what we should call a Caretaker ministry, pending an election; failed to secure a majority; and therefore presented his resignation (January 1895). During the months of deadlock which followed, Swedish opinion rallied to the side of the king. The Norwegians, on the other hand, found that the Germans at least would not recognize any consuls they might appoint by unilateral action, and—what was much more serious—began to realize that long-continued Liberal opposition to defence expenditure had left the country completely open to a Swedish military action. The frontier had no protection, and lay within a day's ride of Oslo, where the Swedish cavalry might possess themselves of the main military depots. Trondheim was almost equally accessible to a similar and probably simultaneous coup. In May the Swedes finally terminated the free-trade treaty with Norway. On June 1 a new foreign minister was appointed, a friend of the crown prince named count Douglas, half-Prussian by birth and breeding and an exponent of the Bismarckian policy of 'blood and iron'. On the 7th the Norwegians gave in. They paid up their contributions to a consular service on the existing basis; agreed that a new Union Committee should negotiate a fresh settlement on equal terms with the Swedes; and eventually, in October, provided the Crown with a coalition ministry representing all parties.

The coalition gave place after the next election to a ministry drawn from the Radicals, but it is more significant of a temporary decline of domestic party controversy that in 1903 the coalition came back; and it remained in office until the eve of the final crisis of the union in 1905. Meanwhile, the third Union Committee had failed even more decidedly than its predecessors, since it produced four conflicting reports—two Swedish and two Norwegian—on none of which was any action taken. The only progress made with any union question was the removal at long last of the union emblem from the flag of the Norwegian mercantile marine, the measure being three times vetoed by the Crown but nevertheless allowed to take effect.[1] Count Douglas therefore resigned office. Boström, who had been prime minister of Sweden since 1891, also retired for a couple of years for quite other reasons, but came back into power in 1902, about the time when the great issue of the 1890's was being re-opened, under what seemed at first to be more favourable auspices.

In 1899 Sigurd Ibsen, ambitious, industrious, and well-informed, was given charge of an enlarged Norwegian Departmental Office for commercial, consular, and foreign business. He quickly elaborated a scheme to show how separate consular establishments could be combined in practice with the maintenance of a single diplomatic staff for the two kingdoms, an arrangement by which Swedish opinion still set much store. In 1903 agreement on these lines appeared to be in sight, and an election gave the second coalition ministry a definite mandate to persevere with the negotiations. Sigurd Ibsen became minister of state in Stockholm, where his father's international fame helped to make him most acceptable to king Oscar, and it looked as though identical laws on the proposed new set-up could quickly be drafted for the two parliaments. But the Swedish prime minister was an opportunist, who decided he had been unnecessarily conciliatory, and a materialist, who thought that in any case Norway could not resist the pressure of superior resources; he may in addition have calculated that the outbreak of the Russo-Japanese war had given him a good chance to settle the Norwegian issue without risk of outside interference. Whatever his motives, in November 1904 Boström slammed the door upon further negotiations by naming six 'dependency clauses' for inclusion in the projected identical laws. Two of these were matters of form, but the other four would firmly subordinate the Norwegian consuls to the Swedish foreign minister and his diplomatic staff.

The coalition government rejected the proposal as an insult, but would have allowed the argument to continue interminably. Sigurd Ibsen, for example, wanted to make the repeal of the act of union a

[1] This point had already been conceded in part from 1821 to 1838, and entirely during the short period 1838-44.

public issue at the next election—in the autumn of the following year. Thus 1905 might have repeated the fiasco of 1895. But in two vital respects the situation was different. Norway had learnt the lesson of her former defencelessness. The purchase of four modern ironclads (from the Armstrong Whitworth yard at Newcastle upon Tyne) and the construction of three coast defence works gave some security against attack from the sea. Two new forts on the eastern frontier were planned from observation of the operations at Santiago in the Spanish-American war of 1898, and the older ones at Halden and Kongsvinger brought up to date. The field army, due to mobilize behind the screen of these fortifications, was equipped with 140 quick-firing guns of a new German pattern, subsequently adopted in other armies, including the Swedish. Norway also contrived in the new emergency to remedy her former lack of strong leaders on either wing in politics. Björnson was an old man and a pacifist. Sigurd Ibsen (who was Björnson's son-in-law) was likewise pacifically-minded, and people unjustly suspected him of wishing to make a clever compromise with the Swedes. But two new stars had risen above the horizon.

Fridtjof Nansen represents the Norwegian ideal in the world of action, just as Björnson does in that of feeling. Born in 1861, he was a leading figure among marine scientists, but it was of course in the field of polar exploration that he had achieved fame, which newspapers could never cheapen. The Greenland expedition (already referred to) had verified at small cost, but at tremendous risk, his view as to the nature of the inland plateau. In 1893-6 the voyage of the *Fram* had verified a second hypothesis, about the westward drift of the polar pack-ice, but what the general public had been thrilled by was his heroic though unsuccessful dash for the Pole itself and the determination which brought him and his one companion alive through a winter of complete isolation and privation in Franz Josef Land. Nansen was never primarily interested in politics, but he was an ardent nationalist—on the *Fram* he used to worry about the Swedes—and in 1905 he was ready to rally opinion at home, and to create it abroad, in favour of a strong assertion of Norwegian claims.

But the man who saw precisely how to assert those claims, the pilot who weathered the storm, the national hero of Norway in 1905, was a Bergen shipowner named Christian Michelsen. Like most self-made men in western Norway, he belonged to the Radical party, though his point of view was sufficiently detached for him to have warned it of the impending debacle of 1895 two years in advance. Like most shipowners, he was keenly aware of the practical advantages of a separate consular service. Finally, like most successful shipowners, he was accustomed to measure risks and then to run them. Where Michelsen stood alone was in the ability he showed to transfer his powers of judgment from the world of contracts and freightages to that of kings and constitutions.

The surprise and shock of the 'dependency clauses' had, for the moment at least, completed a change which had been going on throughout the preceding ten years, namely the transformation of the Conservative party, so long the bulwark of the old order, into a party which vied with the Radicals in identifying patriotism with the will to resist. But how to use the moment of complete national unity? In March 1905 Michelsen formed a new inter-party ministry, pledged to make an unequivocal assertion of the Norwegian claims by means of a short bill, for introducing a wholly separate consular service within twelve months. It was passed unanimously, after great demonstrations on May 17, in which Nansen was to the fore as popular orator. On the 27th it was formally laid before the king by the three Norwegian ministers in Stockholm. In a tense scene, the aged sovereign pronounced his veto, which they refused to countersign. He in turn, on the express ground that 'no other ministry can now be formed', refused to accept their resignations. This situation gave Michelsen the opportunity he was looking for, to take quick, revolutionary action by quasi-constitutional means. On the night of June 6-7 communications with Stockholm were temporarily interrupted, so that king Oscar received only one hour's notice of two resolutions, secretly prepared and passed through the Storting, after previous debate in private, on the morning of the 7th.

> Whereas all the members of the ministry have resigned, and the king has declared himself unable to secure a new cabinet, and the royal power under the constitution has thus ceased to function, the Storting empowers the ministry to act as a temporary government for Norway and to exercise the powers granted to the king, subject to the changes made necessary by the fact that the union

between Sweden and Norway under the same king is dissolved and the king has ceased to function as king of Norway.[1]

In this way the first, unanimous resolution attributed the responsibility for a final rupture to a failure on the king's part. The second, which was opposed by half a dozen socialists, purported to soften the blow by inviting the ex-king to consent to the election of a prince of the House of Bernadotte to the vacant throne. Even if king Oscar proved irreconcilable, such a gesture would be sure to please the great European dynasties as an effort to keep the property, as it were, from going out of the family.

For throughout the period of crisis, which lasted until November, Michelsen had always three attitudes to consider and as far as possible to reconcile—the Norwegian, to be kept united; the Swedish, not to be unnecessarily antagonized; and the European, to be brought to Norway's side. The last was a tricky business, since the entire diplomatic service was under Swedish control and no Norwegian emissary had any official status. Important work was done by Fritz Wedel Jarlsberg, a scion of the formerly noble Dano-Norwegian family, who resigned from a diplomatic post so as to act for Michelsen in Denmark. But Nansen was the only Norwegian who had the ear of the whole world. By means of two visits to England, and by articles and letters which he addressed to the British, German, and French press, as well as by a short, explanatory book on *Norway and the Union with Sweden*,[2] he made Norway's case known. Some of the arguments appeared legalistic, and the Swedes were at pains to controvert them: but Nansen was received unofficially at the British foreign office, and the effect of his personality upon the public was at least to dispel the notion that Norway was in the hands of a band of irresponsible political adventurers. From an early date, too, opinion in England was gratified by reports that the favourite candidate for an independent Norwegian throne was not a Swede, but the husband of an English princess, the king of Denmark's grandson, prince Charles. This was in fact the project with which Wedel Jarlsberg was busy in Copenhagen. But if we ask, what chiefly gave

[1] Resolution moved by the President of the Storting (*Norges historie*, VI, Part 2, p. 256).

[2] Published in London in June, and reprinted in November, 1905. This seems to have been the most successful of the seven or more attempts to present either the Norwegian or the Swedish point of view in English.

weight to the Norwegian case, not only in London but in all the capitals of Europe and in America, the answer may well be, the respect inspired by the mercantile marine. Michelsen the shipowner and his associates counted for something in City circles: at the outset of the crisis he had negotiated a £2,000,000 loan, and throughout the period of secret and expensive military preparations a government which had no official international status never lacked financial support.

The Swedish reaction to the *coup* of June 7 was hostile and threatening though never positively bellicose. At first, indeed, it was only the Socialist party in Sweden which withstood the surge of indignant sympathy with their king, whom the Norwegians were deposing by brusque employment of a mere subterfuge. But king Oscar was too old, the crown prince too wary, deliberately to embark upon a war which might eventually bring back the Norwegians to allegiance, but never to loyalty. Accordingly, the Swedish policy was to impose conditions, pending acceptance of which there was no recognition of Norwegian independence, no settlement of the throne question, and a state of uncertainty which might wear the Norwegians down. Count Douglas and his friends in the First Chamber of the Swedish parliament, though not in office, stood for a possible strategy of prolonged mobilization on the frontier, which was regarded by Michelsen as a formidable prospect. He therefore chose the path of conciliation, and even anticipated the first Swedish demand by making arrangements for a plebiscite, which on August 13 endorsed the Government's action by a vote of almost exactly 2,000 to 1 in a poll of over eighty-five per cent of the electorate. The second main demand was more difficult to meet, since it concerned the frontier fortifications, built recently at considerable cost and providing the only valid line of defence for the Norwegian capital. When negotiations were opened at Karlstad on August 31, the Swedes required their demolition as part of an agreement to set up a neutral zone on both sides of the frontier between the 61st parallel and the sea. The Norwegians resisted bitterly on what they regarded as a point of honour, and a good many seemingly ominous preparations were made for possible hostilities.[1] But the great powers—in the year of the Kaiser's

---

[1] According to *Det norske folks liv og historie*, X, 468, the Norwegians had 22,500 men under arms—about one quarter of their full strength as stated in *Norway—Official Publication* (1900), p. 301.

challenge to the Entente at Tangier and the Russian catastrophe at Tsushima—exercised a restraining, commonsense influence on their smaller neighbours, whom they wished to deter from introducing further complications on the European scene. Wedel Jarlsberg and Nansen made themselves active in Copenhagen (the latter also in London), and on the motion of Isvolsky, then Russian minister in Denmark, Russia and France urged moderation upon the Swedes. The result was a compromise. The neutral zone—which only the Germans have ever violated—was duly established, but Kongsvinger was excluded (subject to a ban on any further development) and Halden, though included, was allowed to retain its ancient fortifications, which had only historical significance.

The Karlstad Conventions, which also included an arbitration treaty and measures for safeguarding the interests of the nomadic Lapps and the transit trades (such as Narvik iron), were signed on September 23. After that the Swedes repealed the act of union and the way was clear for king Oscar to renounce the Norwegian throne by a proclamation, dated October 26, in which he also declined the offer to elect a prince of his house. That offer had played an important part in the events of the summer by making it more difficult for the Norwegian government to place an alternative candidate at the head of their state, so as to secure an easier recognition by the powers. The Czar and the Kaiser, when they met at Björkö in early July, had had their own nominee, prince Waldemar of Denmark; but he had some personal drawbacks—a Catholic wife, and children who were too old to be Norwegianized—and made no headway against king Edward VII's ardent advocacy of the choice of prince Charles. His arrival in Norway during the summer, whether accompanied or not by princess Maud and king Edward's infant grandson, would have made it virtually impossible for any English government to refuse support to Michelsen in a trial of strength with the Swedish negotiators. But Danish policy, which wished at all costs to avoid any embroilment with Sweden, held him back, pending Swedish agreement that there really was a vacant throne. Thus it was not until the end of October that any practical steps could be taken.

The situation was now different, for the prince's coming was no longer a matter of securing some foreign support in an expected emergency but a deliberate political action: full account must therefore be taken of the republican opposition. The Radicals had always had a republican tradition, fostered by Björnson, though it is note-worthy that as soon as it became more than a sentimental issue, Sigurd Ibsen had expressed himself against it as being inexpedient: 'The republic means external isolation and internal dissension'. But in the autumn of 1905 there was still a definite extremist group in the Storting, which mustered 16 votes against acceptance of the humiliating but inevitable Karlstad Conventions, and had the same doctrinaire attitude towards the argument that monarchy was more respectable and that the existing constitution provided for a king. What might be the strength of republican feeling in the country as a whole it was hard to say. Prince Charles urged the desirability of a plebiscite, to which the Storting agreed with some reluctance, on the ground that it was their constitutional prerogative to choose a king. In the end, the plebiscite took the form of an invitation to the voters to endorse the proposed choice of prince Charles. The only repub-lican member of the Michelsen cabinet, Gunnar Knudsen, resigned in protest; but the republicans had no clearcut alternative constitu-tion in readiness, and were seriously weakened by the fact that Björnson deserted their cause. Many voters were also influenced by a very proper sense of indebtedness to Michelsen, who was morally committed to the prince. The poll on November 12-13 gave a majo-rity of almost 4:1, with seventy-five per cent of the electorate voting. The Storting then dispatched a unanimous invitation to prince Charles, who before the end of the month had made his official entry into Oslo, fulfilling the dream of many generations of ardent patriots.

In choosing the style of Haakon VII, the young king is said to have been influenced by Wergeland's words, addressed to the Akershus fortress, symbol of past glories:

> With what joy thy towers would shine,
> Saw they Haakon's age again!

The first nine years of the new reign, up to the outbreak of the first world war, have about them the atmosphere of a national idyll. The well-intentioned, intermittent control is no longer exercised from Stockholm; the iron pressure of international conflicts has not yet taken its place. The Norwegian people is left free to concentrate upon managing its own affairs without let or hindrance — which was what the less imaginative at least believed had been their way of life in the spacious mediaeval age. Party politics may be said to have returned with the departure of Michelsen to his shipping business in 1907. The following year the ex-republican Gunnar Knudsen, who was now the leader of a new Consolidated Liberal Party, became the head of king Haakon's government: with one interval, he was to occupy that position for a period of nine years. The powers of the Crown were being exercised with a circumspection which made it impossible for the most hardened republican to find fault; but a special constitutional amendment made it doubly certain that no future king should challenge the supremacy of the Storting by attempting to apply a suspensive veto to constitutional changes. Democracy now reaped the fruits which it had had no time to gather during the later stages of the long struggle with the king.

Manhood suffrage had been established in 1898, subject to five years' residence in the country and freedom from the acceptance of poor relief. By 1913, women, who had obtained a local government vote (subject to an income qualification) as recently as 1901, were in possession of exactly the same suffrage rights as men: in this respect, Norway was the most advanced sovereign state in Europe. Other refinements in political technique after 1905 were the introduction of direct elections to the Storting and eventually of proportional representation. Another characteristic feature of the period is the success of causes which had long enlisted support from the small-farmer class, especially in the west. In the Church they combated Liberal thought by the foundation of a special fundamentalist theological school within the university, based on the outlook of the rural congregations. In the matter of temperance a system of local option was administered with such zeal that all country districts except six, together with thirty-six of the town areas, had gone 'dry' before the war began in 1914; the per caput consumption of alcohol was about one-third the British. But the most significant advance was that of the language reforms. In 1907 *landsmaal* was made a compulsory subject in the matriculation examination. A few years later a prime minister from Bergen, the headquarters of the *landsmaal* movement, spoke of it with such indiscreet enthusiasm that his Conservative partners in a coalition ministry drove him from office, only to find that the reconstructed cabinet had another language enthusiast in charge of the Church and Education Department.

The wishes of the countryside could not be ignored at a time when small farms (those with less than ten acres of arable land) were rapidly increasing, as were also smallholdings, while the main decline was in the number of the depressed cottar class, which fell by nearly two-thirds during the half-century up to 1907. Improved methods were spreading rapidly from the State Agricultural College and the Department of Agriculture, both established at the turn of the century. For better or worse, the farmer now felt (as he had begun to feel a generation earlier) that he must keep on a level with townspeople by possessing the clothes and furniture produced in town workshops; and to pay for them he was prepared to study new methods at night by the light of his paraffin lamp. There were, of course, many backward areas, even after the completion of the Oslo-Bergen railway in 1909 (summit height over 4,000 feet) opened up the hinterland of the two main towns as never before. But corn prices in Norway had not fallen as catastrophically as, for instance, in Sweden; and it was now possible to make good profits from stock-raising and dairy-farming and even market-gardening. For industrial wage-earners were becoming a numerous class with a considerable purchasing-power.

We have now reached the central fact about the fortunate era of 1905-14: by a remarkable coincidence, the political and the industrial revolution were simultaneous. If political development had been cramped by the joint monarchy, industrial development had been seriously hampered by the absence of coal. The textile factories, for instance, depended entirely on imports from Tyneside, and worked exclusively for the home market, with the result that, as late as 1900, factory work occupied not more than three per cent of the population. But with the dawn of the age of electric power Norway's handicap was gone. She had been quick to develop a complete network of telegraphs; by 1886 women operators were at work in a modern telephone exchange in Oslo; and at the same date electricity was in use for lighting up the Polar darkness in the streets of far-away Hammerfest, opportunely under reconstruction after a fire. Gas had been an urban luxury, dependent upon the accessibility of a coal supply from England, whereas this new form of lighting could be employed wherever there was a waterfall. By the 1930's it had made the paraffin lamp more of a rarity in Norway than in rural England. It was, however, the industrial use of hydro-electricity which reshaped the economic life of the country.

The ubiquitousness of the old, water-driven sawmills is a reminder, if any were needed, that terrain and climate combined to make Norway a land of waterfalls. A few of the largest, with a perpendicular drop of 500 feet or more, were among the best-known tourist attractions; but in fact almost every one of the main rivers has by English standards a tumultuous course between the snowline and the sea. The falls were not only numerous but convenient — usually cheap to build from, and with good access to ice-free ports. The rapidity of the change can be illustrated statistically. In 1900 Norwegian industry used a total of rather less than 200,000 h.p., in 1915 rather more than 1,200,000 h.p. — the steam engine contributed about 60,000 of the increased h.p., all the rest came from harnessing the water. Part of this huge increase went to serve existing industries, particularly the pulp and cellulose exports which grew out of the original timber trade. Another large part was used in processing raw materials which the cheapness of the electricity supply made it profitable to import, such as alumina for aluminium. By 1913 more than half the total importation (by value) was of this kind. There was yet a third possibility. In the year of king Haakon's accession an important corporation was founded to exploit the Norwegian scientist Kristian Birkeland's solution of the problem propounded by Henry Cavendish in 1785 — how to extract a nitrogenous fertilizer from the atmosphere. The interested parties already owned what at that time was the biggest power station in Europe, but needed far more capital than they could secure in Norway: the City was sceptical, with the result that Norsk Hydro, which is still the biggest concern in the country, was based mainly on French, with some Swedish, participation. By 1914 it had a mammoth installation at Rjukan, in a precipitous valley which for five months a year completely shuts out the sun; one of its by-products was the heavy water which had such strategic importance in the second world war.

In other respects, too, this was a period when the stream of industrial progress no longer passed Norway by. The mercantile marine was successfully converted from sail to steam — five-sevenths of it before the outbreak of the war of 1914-18 temporarily checked the process of change — and began to develop the big Lines, without which it would have been impossible to compete on the world market in an age of steamships and, later, motorships. The whalers, having been excluded from the waters of North Norway on the ground that they spoilt the fishing, experimented with a floating 'boiler' based on the British possessions in the Antarctic. This was in 1905: for the next nine years no other Norwegian enterprise yielded such rich dividends. Even the fishermen of the far north, whose chronic indebtedness to the local small capitalist had caused them in 1903 to return the first socialist representatives to the Storting, suffered less by the dreaded inroads of the steam trawler than they gained—round about 1910—by the introduction of the cheap petrol engine, still to be heard chugging its peaceful way from fiord to fiord.

❀

Nearly a decade of uninterrupted and unparalleled prosperity culminated in a centennial exhibition, held at Oslo in May 1914. The people looked back upon a hundred years of progress, of which the best part was clearly the last, when the satisfaction of their political ambitions had released so much energy for other objects of interest. But economic change and growth of course presented the politicians with new problems of reconciling the public and the private interest —difficult problems, whose attempted solution had cast whatever shadow there was to mar the average man's appreciation of the happy scene.

Belief in the future supremacy of hydro-electricity, which enthusiasts expected to outmode both coal and oil in no time, led to an unedifying struggle for waterfall concessions. A half-share in the great Rjukan fall had been sold by its peasant owner in 1890 for £30: what fortune might not await the bold speculator? And even when these great natural resources changed hands at prices not tantamount to robbery, their development more often than not was the work primarily of foreign capital. Feelings of wounded national pride among the many combined with the desire of an intellectual minority to experiment with the ideas of Henry George, whose *Progress and Poverty* had been available in a Norwegian translation since the 'eighties. In 1906 rumours of an impending large-scale incursion of English capital to buy up the waterfalls led to the passing of a so-called panic law, which gave the government a veto on all developments. Three years later, the first Knudsen ministry passed two permanent and comprehensive Concession Laws. The main law, which applied equally to all companies of domestic and foreign origin alike, and took in the development of mines and other real property as well as waterfalls, gave the state a right of purchase. Intending concessionaries must face the prospect that, after an interval ranging between sixty and eighty years, their power station and its machinery—though not the factories for which they might be using the power—reverted to the Norwegian government without compensation. The second law concerned woodland only, laying a direct ban on any purchase by foreigners and imposing minor but significant restrictions on purchase by native interests other than local residents. The laws were passed by a very narrow majority, but later governments did not venture to attempt their repeal.

It was in accordance with the ardent nationalism of the day that the state should figure as the protector of national values and of the localized, individual interest. The effect was certainly to slow down development. Half a dozen schemes, including at least one big British venture, were abandoned at once, and right up to the 1930's Sweden, which had no comparable restrictions, sometimes provoked envious comparisons. One historian notes with regret that 'Norway lost its natural position as the world supplier in the field of electro-chemicals'. Others may prefer the line of argument by which Michelsen defended the restrictive system, first introduced while he was prime minister:

> I for my part hold the view that our country will be better served in the long run by having its two million inhabitants, or thereabouts, whose circumstances allow them to live at an approximately equal level of well-being—than to see that population in a short time greatly increased or perhaps doubled by a numerous and unfortunate proletariat. . . . For a small people like ours I think it is best first to find out whether such a development is for the good of the country, and if it is not, whether it can be checked or counter-balanced.[1]

Nevertheless, there was a proletariat of limited dimensions already in existence, and the minister who was chiefly responsible for formulating the Concession Laws also made it his business to elaborate a social code to meet the situation. Johan Castberg was a solicitor, like Sverdrup, and about the time of the latter's fall from power he had made a comprehensive study both of Bismarckian state

[1] W. Keilhau: *Det norske folks liv og historie i vaar egen tid*, Oslo, 1938, p. 121.

o

socialism and of the more empirical reforms in England. But the so-called Radical People's Party or Labour Democrats which he founded did not secure a large following outside his home district of the Uplands, and in 1905 he had been the supporter of an extreme nationalism against the acceptance both of the Karlstad Conventions and of the monarchy. Only for one brief period did he hold the office he really wanted, when in 1913-14 he was the first Minister of Social Affairs. Nevertheless, Castberg's legislative record is impressive. In 1903 he got a special bank established to help cottars and others of the rural poor to buy farms. He developed the principle of accident insurance, begun in a small way in the 'nineties, so that it covered seamen and fishermen, the two classes that needed it most; and he introduced sickness insurance for wage-earners in 1909 — two years ahead of Lloyd George. In 1915 he crowned his work by making improvements to his bank and by a measure designed to bring Norwegian factory law abreast of the best practice abroad. In another field, he was a divorce law reformer and the author of an act which, in defiance of custom and convention, gave illegitimate children an equal right with others to the father's name and property.

Castberg had a high sense of social responsibility, which did much to prevent the industrial revolution from producing in Norway its characteristic accompaniments of crude exploitation, slum conditions, and deterioration of the race. But Norway also had at least three other advantages. She could profit by our bitter experience; the use of electricity was as clean as that of coal was dirty; and, less obvious but equally important, whereas steam tends to concentrate population, electricity encourages its dispersion. The new industries produced mainly for export, so they did not need to be located close to some domestic market in the towns. Any waterfall within easy reach of the seaboard could provide the necessary power; suburban and rural sites had a natural attraction for the *entrepreneur*, because there the land was cheaper and the price of labour less likely to be enhanced by competition with other employers. Hence the striking fact that, in the first decade of the new century, people living in the more concentrated rural areas (as distinct from isolated farms) increased by one-third, to a figure of nearly a quarter of a million. Very many of these belonged to that fortunate group to whom industrial employment gave higher real wages, lighter work, and considerably shorter hours than life on the farm had done, while their homes and environment continued to be what we should call typically rural. In addition, this dispersion of industry made it possible for many of the more active and enterprising workers to combine part-time employment in the factory (particularly, a seasonal occupation like fish-canning) with small-scale farming on their own property—a proletariat with a difference.

Nevertheless, the growth of a Labour movement in Norway, which was a natural accompaniment of the industrial changes, jarred at times upon the general harmony. Mention has already been made of the first Social Democrats, sent to the Storting of 1903 by the distressed fishermen of the far north under the leadership of a local clergyman of unusually advanced views. By 1912 the Party was returning twenty-three members to the Storting, a total only one below that of the Conservative opposition: but they had no outstanding leader and, while acting as a pressure group for Castberg's social reforms, lacked a distinctive programme of their own, apart from a short-sighted outcry against compulsory service for national defence. Trade unionism had a greater impact on the life of the people. The earliest of the modern unions was founded by the typographers, a relatively well-paid group of skilled workers, as early as 1872; but the National Federation (equivalent to the T.U.C.) did not come into existence until 1899 and had no more than 15,600 affiliated supporters in 1905. At that juncture a leader emerged to take advantage of the new opportunities.

Martin Tranmael was a peasant's son, a painter by trade, and an emigrant to America, who returned to Norway in the winter of 1905-6 imbued with the syndicalist creed of the then notorious I.W.W. (Industrial Workers of the World). In the next few years there were important strikes of paper-workers, metal-workers, and miners, and in January 1912 Tranmael gave a direct incitation to sabotage.

> Sabotage is objected to as being 'immoral'. My view is that the most immoral thing of all is to fail to use the strongest means. Sabotage can be practised in many ways, both active and passive. Is it not ridiculous to leave a well-polished machine when one goes to war? Is it not disgraceful to make conditions of work safe for strike-breakers in the mining industry? Or suppose there were a few shots of dynamite left in the holes, which only the strikers

knew about, don't you think strike-breakers would think twice before taking up the work?[1]

One consequence was a split, both in the Social Democratic Party and the trade unions. But the Federation continued to grow, and when the government tried to blunt the strike weapon by a compulsory arbitration law (1913), the unions were sufficiently determined and united to cause its abandonment within two years, leaving behind only a labour court and conciliation system. At the outbreak of the war, the Federation's total membership of 68,000 was still insignificant by European standards, but what reputation it had was gained by left wing extremism. For Tranmael's strength lay in his organization of the constructional workers and floating labour force of the big new industrial installations, who like the English railway 'navvies' moved from place to place, carrying with them the atmosphere of an American 'boom town'. These rootless proletarians had no part in the national idyll of these years, but their role in later developments was (as we shall see) an important one: for the unusual speed with which the industrial revolution took its course in Norway made them a relatively numerous and dangerously impressionable social group.

The outside world as a whole knew little of these stresses. The new Norwegian monarchy had lent a certain personal and topical interest to a small country which was chiefly remarkable for its huge mercantile marine and its attractions for tourists. Kaiser Wilhelm II, in spite of some disappointment at the turn of events in 1905, continued to display a romantic enthusiasm for the fiords and visited them almost annually: his subjects followed. The English, perhaps taking their cue from the leisured class of salmon fishers and mountaineers, who had written innumerable books about the country, found Norway almost as accessible as Switzerland and possessed of a rather similar appeal. But it is easy to attach too much importance to fleeting impressions formed by holiday-makers, who saw chiefly the picturesque but very thinly inhabited districts of the west coast. Apart from the king and his English queen, Nansen, who served for a couple of years as Nor-

[1] From a lecture given in Oslo, January 4, 1912 (Keilhau, p. 199). A different version with no precise date is given by Edvard Bull: *Arbeiderklassen i norsk historie*, Oslo, 1947, p. 224.

way's first minister in London before returning to his scientific studies, was the only internationally known personality. We might perhaps add the name of his fellow-explorer, Roald Amundsen, who emulated the voyage of the *Fram* by navigating a 47-tonner through the North-West Passage in 1903-5, and on December 15, 1911 planted the Norwegian flag at the South Pole. But the circumstances of his successful rivalry with Scott, and the death of the latter on his disconsolate return journey from the Pole, diminished English appreciation of the deed. Another remarkable achievement, when a Norwegian piloted the first aircraft across the North Sea in July 1914, was completely lost to view in the hurrying tide of world events.

In the field of the arts, the Norwegian accomplishment made less stir than it had done in the 1890's, when the last phase in Ibsen's stupendous dramatic creation coincided with the main work of a group of remarkable painters, headed by Edvard Munch, who had no equals outside France. Ibsen died in 1906 after long illness, Björnson not until 1910: but although the latter remained active until the last, what the world saw in him was not so much the Norwegian literary genius as the champion of Dreyfus against the clericals, of the oppressed Finns against the Czar, of the peace movement against the warmongers. By contrast, the only new writer with a big international following was one who, if he preached any gospel, preached the worship of strength. Knut Hamsun in 1905 was an advocate of extreme measures against the Swedes, and his intense admiration of German 'virility' outlasted the experiences of two world wars. But for the present purpose what matters is that Norway had this one novelist who was read the world over, extolling youth, inveighing against industrialism, and rendering unforgettable the struggle to win a living from the scanty soil of his native land.

Concrete evidence that the struggle was still, in the poorer and less accessible districts, a desperate one was provided by the continued high rate of emigration. Norway at the turn of the century had one of the highest net reproduction rates in western Europe, and throughout the following decade only Ireland and Italy surpassed Norway in the proportion of their population which went to the building up of the new world. One consequence of the surging nationalism of 1905 was the attempt to combat this drain upon the national strength by forming an official Society for the Limitation of Emigration. In 1912 this turned from mere propaganda to the practical task of 'internal colonization' — financial support for pioneers who would try to clear the land for new farms on ground in Norway which previous generations had deemed unusable. When the war stopped emigration, this became important. But it was perhaps a more farsighted policy which founded a Norwegian Association among the emigrants overseas, so as to foster the interest in Norwegian affairs which had been roused during the years of crisis. This was the more desirable as the latest wave of immigrants did not make their new homes entirely in the middle west and would be more easily lost to Norwegian influences, though in 1910 the U.S. census returns showed that they were still the most closely concentrated nationality in the Union. As a consequence, Norwegian, the language of the smallest independent people in Europe, ranked ninth in the number of its users in America. The same impartial source reckoned the total of Norwegians in the country at just under one million — 400,000 born in Norway and nearly 600,000 children of immigrated Norwegian parents. When allowance is made for the influence of the Church, the language press, and Associations upon second and third generation immigrants, it may be claimed that the day was fast approaching when Norwegian-Americans in the widest sense of the term would outnumber the Norwegians of Norway.[1] The emigrant ships therefore gave Norwegian culture and political ideas an influence in the New World which cannot be accurately assessed but should not be ignored.

The new kingdom inherited no tradition of foreign policy, and was disinclined to make one: the uninterrupted prosperity could even be attributed to the fact that it stood aloof from international crises and the armaments race. It was also, however, a question of inexperience. In November 1907 the 52-year-old guarantee of integrity, which the western powers had given to Sweden-Norway, was replaced by a guarantee for Norway alone, to which Russia and Germany were also parties. This ensured the integrity of her territory, inclusive of the neutral zone, but not her permanent neutralization. The Swedes felt that the treaty was aimed against them, or at best closed the door to any common defence policy for the future. Many Norwegians, on the other hand, thought that its terms reduced their country to an inferior international status, especially when the

[1] Stated to have arrived by F. D. Scott in *The Journal of Modern History*, Chicago, XVIII (1946), p. 38.

Germans next year used it as a reason for excluding Norway from a six-power treaty, by which the other states directly concerned (with the significant exception of Belgium) guaranteed the maintenance of the status quo along the coasts of the North Sea. When Norway finally decided to apply for inclusion, the negotiations were already virtually completed. But even to the inexperienced eye Norway's position in relation to the rival European blocs began to seem serious, when at the height of the July crisis in 1911 the Germans sent sixteen capital ships to exercise in the west Norwegian fiords, while a dozen of their destroyers anchored off Drammen, within easy sailing distance of the capital.

The Norwegian government attempted to provide for the situation by an additional appropriation of £1,000,000 for naval defence, a revision of mobilization arrangements, and an effort to accumulate reserve stocks of corn. But Norway was now far less self-supporting than in the time of the Napoleonic wars; and in the growth of her mercantile marine, which she could in no circumstances afford to lay up, she had given other hostages to fortune.

CHAPTER XI

THE IMPACT OF WORLD AFFAIRS,
1914-39

IN the first week of the war of 1914-18, Norway was in a condition of uncertainty and alarm. Although the navy and the coastal defences were promptly mobilized for the safeguarding of neutrality, the fact that the German battle cruisers had been manoeuvring between Bergen and Trondheim as late as July 26 suggested the probability of great naval battles off the coast. How they would affect the fate of Norway, no one could tell: there was therefore a great drain of gold from the banks, buying-up and hoarding of foodstuffs, and a creation of acute local shortages, especially in the far north. Yet the most real danger was at once averted. The Swedes buried the recent past and adhered to the first Bernadotte's policy of holding the Scandinavian peninsula united in the face of Great Power conflicts. On their initiative, the two governments bound themselves on August 8 'to exclude the possibility that the state of war in Europe shall under any circumstances lead to the taking of hostile measures by either kingdom against the other'.[1] In December, a meeting of the three kings at Malmö advertised Denmark's support for the common neutral line. There was a second royal gathering at Oslo three years later, and though their very different strategic and economic situations prevented the growth of any Scandinavian policy, there was certainly a growth of sympathy among the three countries and much exchange of information about practical question arising out of the war, from ration systems to methods of disarming mines.

One less fortunate result of the improved relations with Sweden was a tendency to follow the Swedish view as to the assertion of maritime rights. Sweden traded largely across the Baltic, remote from British naval power; Norway westwards, partly through the Chan-

[1] W. Keilhau: *Det norske folks liv og historie i vaar egen tid*, p. 150.

nel, mainly north of Scotland—in either case under British control. Norwegian ships with any doubtful cargo were brought into Kirkwall for clearance, and it was useless to protest. But the Swedish prime minister of the day, the elder Hammarskjöld, was an ardent international lawyer, who secured the signature of the Norwegian government to many sharply-worded common protests against British definitions of contraband and so forth. The Norwegian prime minister, Gunnar Knudsen, was a Liberal businessman; his foreign minister, Ihlen, shared his ignorance of foreign affairs, in which their country had virtually no experience; and, in so far as they had any policy of their own, it was purely opportunistic. For a hundred years Norway had had closer cultural ties with Germany than with Britain. The arts and sciences, to say nothing of religion, had their roots in German soil. The commercial and shipping interests, on the other hand, looked towards Britain: but even they were not altogether free from the unjust suspicion that the irksome British contraband control was designed to ruin the Norwegian carrying trade. Therefore we must think of Norway in the two first years of the war as relatively unconcerned about the rights and wrongs of it, but very much concerned to make money while the opportunity lasted. The government was so sure that it would be a short affair that they did not even attempt to recover the cost of the neutrality defence and other emergency expenditure by imposing any immediate new taxes.

They were two halcyon years. The British, it is true, watched the trend of Norwegian trade very closely through an army of agents (said to have numbered 200 by 1916) and negotiated detailed 'branch agreements', so as to prevent imports from reaching those branches and those individual businesses which were known to export to Germany. To take a simple example, the fish canners could get no tinplate for their cans unless they undertook to divert elsewhere the twelve per cent which, on the basis of pre-war figures, would naturally have found its way to our enemies. But the result was a political and moral, rather than a commercial, grievance: for Norway (unlike the other European neutrals) had her biggest trade outlet to the Allies, and what she was prevented from selling to their enemies could be sold to them on profitable terms. In any case, as in previous war periods, Norway's greatest gains came from the carrying trade. Freight charges rose to nine and ten times the pre-war level, which had the incidental effect of making Norway's own imports very dear; but mainly it meant golden opportunities for her innumerable tramp steamers, which flocked into the best-paid employments, such as the carriage of English coal to France. Shipping shares became the object of feverish speculation, and the losses due to German mines and submarines were made up by purchases in the United States and elsewhere. At the end of the second war year the fleet was larger than ever; the quarrels of the nations still seemed a purely external affair—except for one small minority, the seamen, some of whom had already known their ship sink beneath their feet; and only the fixed-income group was seriously affected as yet by scarcities and rising prices. In 1915 there had been leisure for Castberg, though no longer a member of the government, to complete his edifice of social reforms, which the country could now clearly afford.

Norway then became for a few months the unhappy subject of a kind of tug-of-war between the combatants. In 1915 the Germans sent numerous small craft up through the Leads to buy fish in Norwegian coastal waters from the actual fishermen. As an immediate reply the British government employed a Bergen wholesaler to make secret purchases on their behalf up to a value of £10,000,000. This action clearly benefited the Norwegian fish trade, which acquired a substitute for its normal market in the south of Europe (lost through the wartime rise in the cost of transport) and also, thanks to this private arrangement with the British authorities, could count on importing the coal, salt, hemp, and petrol without which the fisheries would come to a standstill. But the consequent enormous rise in the price of fish led the British, in August 1916, to use their power of withholding the imports so as to impose a more onerous agreement.

This gave Britain the right, but not the obligation, to buy at a price fixed for the duration of the war all except fifteen per cent of all Norwegian fish available for export. No allowance was made for the fact that the cost of the coal and petrol used in the fisheries continued to rise, and when the British government twelve months before the end of the war decided to stop buying, the Norwegian authorities had to fill the gap with a subsidy of £8,000,000. But the immediate political effect was the most serious, for the German counter-measure took the form of a special submarine campaign off the North Norway coast. Eleven small ships were sunk in eight days; some members of their crews died of exposure to the rigours of the Arctic sea. The Norwegians tried to retaliate by announcing that submarines in territorial waters would be liable to attack, to which the Germans replied by a Note (October 20, 1916) worded as an ultimatum, except for the absence of a time-limit. The Allies promised military support, if need be, but made it clear that they did not wish to add to their military commitments. The Germans were eventually pacified, partly by a modification of the ban on submarines entering Norwegian waters—which in any case could not be prevented as long as they remained submerged—but chiefly by an offer to let Germany have fifteen per cent of a rather indeterminate 'average catch' of fish and to negotiate a new general trade agreement.

But Norway had also simultaneously fallen foul of the Allies. By an arrangement with the Americans the British government stopped the supply of electrolytic copper for the Norwegian hydro-electric industries, pending an agreement to cease supplying copper pyrites (non-electrolytic) from Norway to Germany. An admonitory British communication pointed out that the copper went to the manufacture of shells and submarines: hence the high price the Germans were willing to pay.

> The inflated price of Norwegian copper is, in fact, the price of blood—the blood of a friendly people to whom Norway would necessarily look for assistance in time of need, and on whom she depends, not only for the continuance of her present prosperity and independence, but for her existence as one of the foremost seafaring nations of the world.[1]

An agreement was accordingly fixed up, after interviews conducted with Ihlen in French, on the basis of an English translation which imperfectly rendered the original Norwegian proposal. One of several hitches in carrying out the agreement arose from the fact that the Norwegians believed that its wording did not preclude them from supplying the Germans with a low-grade ore, not generally regarded as 'copper pyrites' but which the Germans were nevertheless able to use. When these hitches were found to coincide with difficulties about the fulfilment of the fish agreement, the British lost patience. At Christmas 1916 an embargo was laid upon all export of coal to Norway. A period of severe weather followed, with the result that domestic supplies were exhausted, gas was running low, and even.

[1] W. Keilhau: *Norway and the World War*, p. 335.

the icebreakers could not get up steam to keep the fiords open. But Ihlen was to some extent only playing for time. When the trade agreement with Germany had been duly signed on January 23, it became easier to withhold the pyrites, as Britain demanded. This was done, and both pyrites and fish were sold, not only to destinations, but at prices fixed by Britain. In all the circumstances, it is hard to disagree with the comment passed in the Storting by the rising Liberal leader, J. L. Mowinckel: 'The English coal prohibition was an unnecessarily strong measure and undeservedly severe punishment.'[1]

It was perhaps fortunate for Britain's reputation in Norway that, before the end of the eight-week ban on coal, Germany had announced the introduction of unrestricted submarine warfare. This not only lent point to the British arguments about the use to which copper was being put, but it showed the Germans in their true colours as worshippers of Might is Right. At the same time as the Norwegians were rendered more sympathetic to the cause for which Britain was fighting, the fact that they were the only neutrals whom the German threats did not for a moment dismay gave the British an increased regard for a nation of brave seamen who shared our risks. Thus the scheme by which certain vessels belonging to neutral powers were held in British ports as security, until another vessel of the same nationality was known to have sailed for Britain, was never applied to the Norwegians. On the other hand, they were awarded a most advantageous settlement, under which their ships were hired to serve under the British flag on the North Sea and other dangerous routes, while an equal amount of shipping was allocated to Norwegian use elsewhere. Ships serving under the red ensign could of course be armed, whereas it was the peculiar bitterness of their situation that they themselves as neutrals could not retaliate against the submarines which sank their ships at sight. And not only submarines: within a few months the seizure of a German diplomatic bag at Oslo brought to light 15 cwt. of explosives, made up into suitable form for the destruction of ships at sea. This particular consignment was probably intended for use in American harbours; but the reason for some hitherto unexplained disappearances of Norwegian ships was now obvious. This was the second occasion on which Norway might have been brought into the war. However, by this time the submarine menace was slowly beginning to recede, one

[1] P. G. Vigness: The Neutrality of Norway, p. 69.

main reason being the institution of the convoy system, which again helped to establish relations of mutual sympathy between convoyer and convoyed.

But another factor in the fight against the submarine was of course the entry of America into the war in April 1917. From that date onwards British-Norwegian relations tended to fall into the background: supplies, if any, were to be obtained by direct negotiation on the other side of the Atlantic. Ihlen, who two years before could have had a lasting trade agreement with the British government if he had thought it worth while, was faced by the termination of all branch agreements in October. Meanwhile, he had sent Nansen as his most persuasive representative to America, where he was faced with cold inquiries as to why Norway and the other European neutrals did not take the field against Germany. If they could not fight, then they could at least break off all trade relations with the Germans; or, as an absolute minimum, prove by means of a thoroughgoing rationing system that what they asked for was needed to save them from starvation. Norway, which had begun the war period secure in the comforting reflection, 'We have America to fall back upon',[1] now for the first time experienced serious distress. At the beginning of 1918, when rationing was belatedly introduced, stocks were already running out. But Ihlen and Mowinckel, according to American reports, were still advising the Storting that Germany would win the war, and the former demanded of the Americans greater freedom to export fish and metals to Germany than they were prepared to concede. British influence made the American terms stiffer rather than easier. Finally Nansen, who had gained great advantages for Norway by his resolute conduct of business with the Americans, tired of Ihlen's procrastinations and signed the agreement on April 30 on his own responsibility. Exports to Germany were heavily reduced, and Norway received her essential requirements in grain, sugar, fats, and industrial raw materials. In the last two months of the war Norway did, indeed, sign a further abortive trade agreement with Germany. But what is more indicative of the position she had now taken up is her consenting at long last to mine the Leads, so that German submarines might not escape round the far edge of the mine barrage which the Allies had by then stretched right across the North Sea.

[1] *Aftenposten*, Oslo, August 1, 1914.

When the war ended, what was most memorable in Norway's experience of Armageddon was the sacrifice of one-half of her mercantile marine and of 2,000 lives from among the crews who manned it. Norway had had to suffer this with neutral forbearance, although she had lost a greater tonnage than any of the combatant powers except Britain, which could so much more easily afford the loss, and was (by 1923) brought down from fourth to eighth place among seafaring nations. Undoubtedly, this sombre experience coloured the future, making it harder for Norwegians to ignore international relations as not being their concern, and also giving them an increased sympathy with Britain as compared with Germany. At the same time, the war had, for the moment at least, raised Norway through the earnings of her fleet to a higher economic status. From 1915 onwards her currency stood above its gold value, not to speak of its appreciation in terms of sterling. By the end of the war a foreign debt of £40,000,000 had been turned into a credit of nearly twice the figure—approximately what the fleet had earned. Many industrial undertakings, including the largest paper and pulp business and to some extent the wealthy Norsk Hydro, replaced foreign by native capital. In 1917 the Storting viewed the future with such confidence that a new law made absolute the exclusion of foreign capital from any share in new hydro-electric development.

Internally, the effect of the war, in Norway as elsewhere, was to encourage the growth of a class of *nouveaux riches*, stock exchange gamblers and persons who 'cornered' stocks in a constantly rising market. Their unbridled expenditure on riotous living accorded ill with a tripling of the national debt, owing to inadequate taxation of war wealth, and a rather firm attitude towards the claims of the workers: in 1916 compulsory arbitration in labour disputes was introduced for the duration of the war.[1] As there was no unemployment, wages naturally rose, though only a few special groups, such as seamen, gained more than the 240 per cent rise in the cost of living. When the Americans pressed for rationing, the responsible minister made out that it would not achieve any economy, since a considerable part of the population, especially in the fishing districts, already consumed quantities of meal and sugar smaller than he dare

[1] A bone of much contention, the system was abandoned in 1920, but restored in 1922-3 and 1927-9, and again under different auspices after the second world war, for the period 1945-52.

propose as a general ration. The distress, as we have seen, was most acute about the turn of the year 1917-18, that is to say, at the time when news from Russia suggested that one possible result of the war might be the establishment of workers' governments upon the ruins of the old order of society. Councils of Workers and of Soldiers began to be formed, and in March 1918 these embryo soviets held a meeting of 170 delegates in Oslo under the leadership of Tranmael, who also secured a majority in the Social Democratic party for a declared policy of revolution. Nothing more came of the Norwegian soviets, whose representatives were very politely received by the prime minister. But when the war ended the Norwegian Social Democrats, with Tranmael now established as secretary, had already through the so-called Zimmerwald movement made important contacts with the nascent Soviet Union.

In 1919, however, the masters of the world met, not in the Kremlin but at the Quai d'Orsai, where the Norwegian minister in Paris, Wedel Jarlsberg, based wide claims on the shipping losses incurred by his country in serving the Allied cause. Russia was so lightly regarded that a rectification of the frontier in North Norway was one of the forms of compensation discussed. Probably it was just as well that Norway did not get either this or a German colony in East Africa, but a territory which, if of uncertain value, had hitherto been a virtual no man's land. The international status of Spitsbergen had actually been under consideration by the powers in July 1914; the Norwegians were probably its first discoverers; they were willing to administer it on the basis of an 'open door' for the economic interests of other powers; and, when Curzon nevertheless hankered after its inclusion in the sphere of British interests, Wedel Jarlsberg was clever enough to secure the support of Balfour for his case. The upshot was that the bounds of Norway were extended, for the first time since the central middle ages. Spitsbergen produced coal, of which Norway had no native supply at all, and its annexation provided a precedent.[1] Jan Mayen island, useful only for weather forecasting, was likewise incorporated in the kingdom in 1929; and the spread of Norway's whaling interests in the Antarctic led to the

---

[1] Approved by the Powers generally in 1920 and by the USSR in 1924, annexation became effective on August 14, 1925. In 1955, the quantity of coal exported to Norway was 322,000 tons.

creation of a new category of dependencies—Bouvet and Peter I Islands, both uninhabited, and Queen Maud's Land, a section of the Antarctic continent nine times as big as Norway, of which the potentialities are still unknown.

But what Norway chiefly hoped for as a result of the war was the growth of a new international system, in which a small state might make an effective contribution to the management of the world's affairs. When Nansen had been challenged in America as to why Norway did not enter the war, he had proclaimed a higher mission.

> Small states have, in some respects, an advantage over the larger. Their culture is more homogeneous. An idea can more quickly penetrate to all the people within their borders, and set its stamp upon them. . . . Small states have a peculiar mission to seek out and find the new paths that humanity must tread in order to abolish war altogether.[1]

Accordingly, in January 1919 the Norwegians had ready their own plan for a league of nations—more democratic, more absolute in its denunciation of any resort to war, more positive in its attitude to disarmament, and more concerned with the protection of national minorities than the plan which the great powers actually adopted. When those powers furthermore arranged matters so that the Council, in which they predominated, should mainly conduct the business, Nansen proved indefatigable in maximizing the influence of the Assembly and using its short annual sessions to create a world public opinion. Right up to his death in 1930 he was the spokesman of humanity, the embodiment of a world conscience. He arranged the repatriation of 380,000 prisoners of war at an average cost of less than £2 per head. He worked for the resettlement of about one and a half million White Russians, whom the civil war had left scattered almost to the ends of the earth, and for the survival of five times that number of Red Russians, mostly children, in the Volga-Ukraine famine of 1921-2. He organized a large-scale exchange of populations between Greece and Turkey, then recently at war with each other. He took up the cause of the long-persecuted Armenians, for whom he tried to develop a national home in the Soviet region of Erivan: but Baldwin condemned the cause which Gladstone had once cherished. Thus Nansen brilliantly vindicated the claim he had made

[1] *The American-Scandinavian Review*, VI, p. 9 (report of interview).

on behalf of small nations as regards their capacity to lead, though the withholding of funds for his ventures inside Russia is a reminder that he was less successful in inducing the great powers to follow the small.

From the point of view of Norwegian history, the fact that he remained their principal delegate, even when their prime minister attended at Geneva, is sufficient indication that his humanitarian actions commanded national support. His work abroad engendered a feeling of pride, which the domestic policies of the day did not. In the sphere of practical affairs, no Scandinavian had had so much influence in the world since the time of Charles XII of Sweden. Lord Curzon, with whom the spokesmen of small democracies were not usually popular, once described Nansen as 'the only living man to whom the doors of every Chancery in Europe were flung wide open.'[1] The early years of the League of Nations are inevitably associated with the prestige which Nansen attained, and the lustre which this shed on Norway was an important factor in national growth. But it should not be forgotten that Norway made other contributions to the work of the League. For a quarter of a century the secretary of the inter-parliamentary union was a Norwegian, Christian Lange, whose studies on the legal side of the post-war developments brought him a half-share of the Nobel peace prize in 1921. Mowinckel, who was three times prime and foreign minister during the inter-war period, was another ardent supporter of League principles; and a Norwegian Conservative leader, C. J. Hambro, was destined to preside over the last sad phase in the League's fortunes.

The League held the same central position in Swedish and Danish as it did in Norwegian thoughts about foreign policy. They welcomed the advent of the rule of law in international affairs and the intended banishment of the appeal to force. Their sympathies were all with Nansen when, with prophetic insight, he denounced the failure of the powers to apply these principles in the first test case, when Mussolini challenged their intentions by his punitive bombardment of the Greek island of Corfu. Throughout the 'twenties, the Scandinavian countries set the example in their dealings with each other, which were made more cordial by their habitual collaboration in the work of the League. Iin 1919 a Northern Society was founded, which fostered common cultural interests as a basis from which common

[1] Vigness: *The Neutrality of Norway*, p. 129.

P

economic or political ventures might be able to grow. This went sufficiently well in the three Scandinavian kingdoms for Finland and Iceland to wish to join. A more concrete achievement was the signature of a series of arbitration treaties, by which the Northern states excluded the use of force in the settlement of their mutual disputes. This was the more remarkable because in 1927, when the Storting ratified the agreement with Denmark against a minority vote of fifty-three from the Conservative and Agrarian parties, a serious dispute was already in being.

The annexation of Spitsbergen, which (as we have seen) was the main nationalist success in this period, could hardly fail to remind the Norwegian of his lost colonial heritage—the ancient possessions of the Crown which had passed to Denmark in 1814, almost through inadvertence. West Greenland had since been administered as a Danish colony, but East Greenland was hardly of interest to anybody except a handful of native Eskimos until after the first world war. The Danes then formally asserted their sovereignty over Greenland as a whole, which proved to mean the extension of the trade monopoly already enforced in the west and the exclusion of Norwegian whalers and other hunters. The Norwegians protested, and in 1924 a compromise was made, in which the question of sovereignty was ignored but Norwegians were given free access to most parts of East Greenland territory. Ardent nationalists were dissatisfied by a compromise, and public opinion secured government backing for some adventurers who, in 1931 and 1932, raised the Norwegian flag in districts of the east coast to which they gave the name of Eric the Red's Land. Denmark referred the matter to the international court at The Hague, which decided in its favour. The Norwegians considered the judgment to be historically ill-found and in practice unfair to their needs. But they accepted it (and have acted upon it ever since) in the spirit appropriate to a law-abiding people in a law-abiding age. This was in April 1933, three months after the accession of Hitler to power had made the spirit of Nansen an anachronism in world politics.

It is probably significant of the contrast between the foreign and the domestic policies of Norway in the post-war era that Nansen never became a party leader or accepted political office. Lesser men presided over a scene of almost unlimited confusion. Knudsen's

Liberal ministry had lost its majority at the 1918 election, but held on for two more years; its ten successors averaged no more than eighteen months apiece. A little of the uncertainty may be attributed to the introduction of proportional representation in 1919; but the main factor was the failure of the traditional parties to lead the nation convincingly in the face of grave post-war problems of inflation and unemployment. To make this criticism is not to disparage Norway, for Britain and others of the ex-belligerent states found a similar difficulty in facing up to rather similar problems. But it helps to explain the emergence of a new Agrarian Party and of a transformed Labour Party, and the fact that the latter eventually held office for a period of quite unprecedented length.

In 1919 there was a brief spending spree, in which imports were five times their normal size. Labour was conciliated to some extent by the enactment of an 8-hour day and a 48-hour week. The Liberal idealists turned their attention from the language question — they had been busy at the end of the war renaming 15 counties, 5 bishoprics, and 189 districts in conformity with ancient rural usages — to the promotion of temperance. Prohibition, which had been instituted as a temporary measure in wartime, was endorsed by a plebiscite (489,000 — 305,000). In the following summer conditions were still such that, after resort to compulsory arbitration, the workers were accorded a higher wage level. But in the autumn, to quote the words of a shipowner, 'the bottom fell out of the barrel': the laying-up of ships was in fact the most ominous sign that Norway was in the grip of a depression of world dimensions. By 1926 shipping, indeed, had entered upon a new period of expansion, in which a bold expenditure on motorships and specialization in tankers brought the Norwegian fleet back to its pre-war position of fourth in the world. There was also a remarkable growth of whaling, which from 1923 onwards was conducted from a new kind of vessel, the 'floating factory': this enabled the processing of the catch to take place entirely at sea and six times as fast as before, with a voyage of less than eight weeks direct from Norway to the Antarctic. But in spite of these redeeming features, the depression which began in the autumn of 1920 continued to affect both industry and agriculture until the middle of the 1930's.

Norway's position was peculiarly vulnerable. Her mercantile marine depended for its profits both upon the continuance of world trade expansion and upon the continuance of the liberal attitude which had set the carrying trade open to free competition. Her export trade—the largest in Europe per head of population—represented a way of disposing of vast quantities of fish, wood products, and hydro-electric manufactures which, in the absence of foreign customers, could not possibly be consumed at home. Her agriculture could not be made self-sufficient: its most promising new development was the breeding of silver foxes, but the furs had to be marketed abroad. Moreover, Norway in the 1920's could no longer choose the alternative in hard times of exporting population, for the American immigration restrictions were now coming into force. But in an admittedly difficult situation, the policy of successive Liberal and Conservative governments made things worse.

One clear example is the prohibition law of 1921-7. Outside religious circles, this roused the national feeling for individual independence and self-assertion. Evasion at first took the form of fictitious medical prescriptions for alcohol; then smuggling set in; finally, there was a widespread practice of home-distilling. By 1926, when a second plebiscite showed a majority of 531,000 to 423,000 against prohibition, something like half the population had become involved in the epidemic of lawlessness. In addition, the country had become involved in a tariff war with Spain and Portugal, which refused to buy from a people to whom they could no longer sell their wine. In 1927 a system of state monopoly was set up, which imposed high prices and severely restricted the opportunities of sale; but a part of the fish trade was lost permanently to the Icelanders.

Another way in which the government showed lack of foresight was in its attitude to the banks, which had enjoyed a mushroom growth during the war years and in very many cases lacked any substantial resources to enable them to weather hard times. Reconstruction was inevitable, with losses for investors and a recession in industry creating unemployment. But the government tried to put off the evil day by bolstering up the banks with deposits from public funds, a risky and compromising course of action, for which one finance minister was unsuccessfully impeached. Its only result was to prolong the credit crisis far beyond the period of similar troubles elsewhere. Meanwhile, the Norwegian Krone fell rapidly from its high estate. By 1925 it stood at one half of its pre-war value in gold, and to have stabilized it at three-quarters of the old value might have represented a fair compromise between the opposing claims of creditors and debtors. But the government, influenced no doubt by British example, determined to restore the pre-war gold value in full. This was done in 1928, to the profit of foreign speculators (chiefly Americans) who had been buying for the rise, and to the misfortune of debtors, such as the numerous class of farm mortgagees.

A feature of the period had been the growth of a new Agrarian or Peasant Party, which had made its debut with seventeen seats in the Storting of 1921. This represented the big farmers of eastern Norway rather than the small farmers of the west, who continued to be the mainstay of the declining forces of Norwegian Liberalism. The Agrarians were the enemies of free trade, and were largely responsible for the nature of the state corn monopoly, established on a permanent basis in 1928. This institution was to hold a year's supply as protection against war; import the necessary quantities from abroad; and purchase the whole of the home-grown crops at prices which need not bear any relation to the world market. They were also the enemies of trade unionism and high wages, especially for the woodsmen who were often their employees. An Agrarian was prime minister in 1931, when the minister of defence, a certain Major Quisling, earned notoriety by his use of troops against strikers at one of the Norsk Hydro plants. But deflation hurt the peasant as much as the industrial worker, and necessity makes strange bedfellows. In March 1935 it was the co-operation of the Agrarians which gave the Labour Party at long last a majority in the Storting.

Their history since the end of the war had been a chequered one, the struggle to wrest power from the middle-class parties being complicated by an internal struggle to decide what complexion of Labour Party should eventually exercise that power. In 1920 the trade union federation accepted the line which the majority in the political Labour movement had accepted in the early days of the Russian soviet revolution, and Norway duly became a member of the Russian organization for world revolution, the Third International. But as early as March of the following year the Right Wing of Norwegian Labour demurred to the 'Moscow theses', the revolutionary tactics which members of the International agreed to employ inside their various countries, and formed a separate Social Democratic Labour Party to work exclusively within the parliamentary framework.

Two years later Tranmael likewise became impatient of the shackles imposed by the theses; got the support of many younger men, such as the influential trade unionist, Nygaardsvold, in resisting Russian pressure to conform; and broke away from the Third International. The Norwegian Labour Party under his influence remained the most revolutionary in western Europe, with a firm belief in the dictatorship of the proletariat; but his action meant that there was now a Norwegian Communist Party as well. At the next election Labour won 24 seats, Social Democratic Labour 8, and Communism 6. Not until 1927 did a reunited Labour Party make its appearance, to rally new classes of voters, reduce the Communist group to insignificance, and present the middle-class parties with a serious challenge.

Labour, with 59 seats, then became the largest party in the Storting. Due consideration of this led king Haakon to make one of his very few personal interventions in domestic politics, when in January 1928, against the advice of an outgoing Conservative prime minister, he entrusted the formation of a new ministry to a moderate Labour, rather than to an Agrarian, leader. But a disagreement with the Bank of Norway about credit policy, a matter which touched the bourgeois parties closely, occasioned the fall of the first Labour government after only eighteen days.[1] Trade at that time showed signs of recovery, but the deepening world crisis, which began to spread outwards after the collapse of the American stock market in October 1929, and two years later drove Norway off the gold standard a week after Britain, soon made the demand for some positive social action more pressing. By December 1932 Norway had reached the astonishing position that forty-two per cent of trade unionists were without employment. As for the independent peasant, his plight was almost worse, for the value of primary produce—his crops, his timber, or his fish—fell faster than that of industrial commodities. Peasants and fishermen were now attracted by a Labour party programme of extensive state intervention in the economic life of the country, entitled *Work for All!* They were also attracted by the faith which even extremist Labour leaders—on tactical grounds—began to profess in parliamentary democracy, as a framework within which they could carry out their immediate pro-

[1] 'A victim to the nervousness which had seized our financial centres' (C. A. R. Christensen: *Det hendte igaar*, Oslo, 1933, p. 191).

gramme. Moreover, the shadow of German Nazism had begun to fall across the scene, which caused a few of the most reactionary Agrarians to follow Quisling's lead into an imitation Nazi Party, but reconciled others to the idea of co-operating with Labour to end the crisis. The last Liberal government fell in March 1935 on a motion for restricting public expenditure, rejected by the Labour Party with the help of the Agrarians. The shipowner Mowinckel relinquished control of the country to the ex-navvy Johan Nygaardsvold — the end of a class struggle for power which began in earnest with the workers' and soldiers' councils of 1918.

The Labour movement in Norway was extremely fortunate in obtaining power at a time when the conditions from which it aspired to rescue the people were already being alleviated by the improvement of world trade. Shipping provides an index of the change: in the two years preceding the formation of the Labour government the tonnage laid up had declined from 1,600,000 to 313,000, and feverish rearmament was to make 1937 its best year since the war. At the same time industrial production in Norway was also recovering; by 1937 it stood thirty per cent higher than before the American collapse. The recovery of agriculture was in the nature of things slower; but here, too, we mark the beginning in 1933 of a development which trebled the wheat crop in four years. The government also enjoyed another advantage, in that the Liberals, who had once championed the social reform policies of Johan Castberg, had prepared the way for them by measures passed during the difficult years of crisis and had themselves planned others of far-reaching importance. These could now be passed by Labour with the assurance of Liberal support. Nevertheless, the new social reform era was doubly significant. It showed what immediate benefits a Labour government, even though it lacked an independent majority in parliament, could confer on the classes it claimed to represent; and it gave to Norwegian life a general stamp of social egalitarianism — 'fair shares for all' — which was important for its later development, during and after the coming war. For, although Nygaardsvold held office for the record period of ten years, five of them were spent in exile.

Two of the main reforms followed lines which were already well established in Britain. Old age pensions were provided at the age of seventy for all persons in need, and special pensions were given to the disabled and the blind. A scheme of unemployment insurance was set up for the bulk of the workers who had been covered by the health insurance legislation of 1909. But the institution of a statutory nine-days annual holiday with pay went far beyond British practice. The Workers' Protection Act, concerned primarily with the enforcement of conditions of health and safety in all places of employment, like-wise included some novel provisions. Rules of employment must be drawn up in consultation with five workers' representatives. Every local council must establish a Labour Inspectorate, which must in-clude at least one employee in its minimum membership of three. After three years' employment a worker became entitled to compen-sation for dismissal up to a maximum of six months' wages, unless his employer could plead 'extraneous circumstances', such as decline of trade, or 'pressure exercised by the other employees of the estab-lishment or by an organization'.[1] Government influence, in other words, was now unmistakably on the side of the trade unions; their membership grew during the 'thirties by 157 per cent. The wide-spread introduction of labour-saving machinery kept the unemploy-ment rate high—about half of what it had been at its worst—but by 1938 wages per hour had bigger purchasing power than at any pre-vious time and almost exactly two-and-a-half times their value at the beginning of the century.

Another popular movement with which the Labour government was naturally allied was that of the co-operatives. The first co-operative shops had been established by Marcus Thrane, but con-tinuous development began with the foundation of the Wholesale Society in 1906. Turn-over doubled during the 1930's, evidence both of working-class prosperity and of growing adhesion to the Labour Party's attack on private enterprise. Co-operative marketing of pro-duce and purchasing of materials and equipment also have a long record of development in Norwegian agriculture. Co-operative dairies, in particular, are a century old, and by 1931 the sale of milk had been made their legal monopoly in every district where a majority of producers so desired. The fall of prices during the crisis likewise produced legislative encouragement for the co-operative marketing of meat. There remained, however, one field which had

---

[1] Workers' Protection Act, Sections 34, 42, and 33, translated as part of a collection of thirty-three Acts in *Norwegian Social and Labour Legislation*, 2nd edition, Oslo, January 1953.

been largely neglected. In the words of an American enthusiast, written about the end of 1936:

> The government has given notice that the next great work, which lies before it, is the thorough and effective co-operative organization of all the fishermen and fisheries of Norway. The Norwegian fishermen are standing before the portals of a new era. The men on the farm and in the factory have already shown the way.[1]

By the time the war came the Fresh Fish Law of 1938 had resulted in fishermen having—for the first time in Norwegian history—an effective collective control of the prices at which they sold the national staple of cod. The government had also greatly increased the efficiency of a scheme for marketing the winter herring, which had been started rather earlier, and encouraged the fishermen's trade union (founded in 1926) in an ambitious plan for supplying their own equipment.

Norway is a country in which many fishermen have always eked out their scanty livelihood by small-scale farming, and the industrial worker is also in very many cases the proprietor of a smallholding. It was therefore of interest, not merely to the type which would formerly have emigrated, but to the mass of the population, that new farms were now being established more rapidly. Increased loans were the main factor in bringing the rate up from 500 to 2,000 a year; but marginal land was also made usable through the growth of the roads and railways. With a view to reducing the burden of unemployment the Labour government spent two-and-a-half times as much as its predecessor on schemes which included a railway to Stavanger, completed in 1944, and one to Bodö, which still comes to a halt in the mountains just north of the Polar Circle. As expenditure on social services was three times as great as before, it might seem remarkable that, when Budgets were rising rapidly elsewhere, the total of the Norwegian Budget rose only from £19,000,000 in 1934-5 to £31,000,000 in 1938-9, while the public debt actually decreased.

The explanation lies in the sphere of foreign policy. Norway's basic interest was in the free and undisturbed development of international trade. Her only departure from a strictly liberal attitude, the attempt to assert her claims by direct action in East Greenland,

[1] O. B. Grimley: *The New Norway*, p. 100.

had brought discredit upon the Agrarian nationalists who promoted it. The Labour government inherited from its predecessors a grouping of Scandinavia with Belgium, Holland, and Luxemburg, which sought to check the movement towards ever-higher trade barriers by a mutual agreement to make no increase without prior consultation. The signatories to this Oslo Convention of December 1930 controlled ten per cent. of world trade, but that was not enough to alter world trends, and they made little headway against the system of bilateral commercial agreements. Norway, for instance, depended for access to the British market, which mattered most to her, upon a treaty of 1933, binding her government to take seventy per cent of British coal. Nygaardsvold left the conduct of foreign affairs very largely in the hands of his colleague, the distinguished historian, Professor Koht, who thought that, if the Oslo group had failed over trade, a separate position might still be asserted successfully over politics. The Scandinavian states were deeply disappointed at what they deemed to be the tergiversation of the powers regarding the application of sanctions to the Italo-Abyssinian conflict. They therefore joined with the other European neutrals of the first world war to give notice, on July 1, 1936, that they no longer accepted the obligation to impose sanctions at the request of the League of Nations. Two years later, when the threat of a second world war had drawn appreciably closer, the Scandinavians further asserted their separate position by an agreement to adopt similar rules of neutrality.

When nations arm, however, it does not take two to make a quarrel. In retrospect, the rules of neutrality matter less than the fact that the Nygaardsvold government did also make some modest preparations for the eventuality of Norwegian participation in a war. By 1938 military expenditure, which had been pared away year by year down to 1933, had risen in the annual Budget to a figure of £1 per head of population. Little as this was, it represented a remarkable change in a party which had fought against conscription since 1906, contained influential leaders—including Tranmael and at least one future prime minister—who had been imprisoned for subversive activities in this connection, and still regarded Norway's small cadre of professional officers as reactionaries pure and simple. In the advance of Nazism and Fascism they now saw a threat to their class as well as to their country, and a few of the boldest spirits even thought in terms of a possible need to give positive support to Russia. But the general attitude towards defence was still a grudging one, as witness Koht's remarks at the Labour Party congress of 1936:

> So far as I understand, everybody is agreed that we cannot and will not have in this country any 'strong military organization'. And if we cannot create a strong military organization to defend ourselves, neither can we go to war for other people.[1]

Nevertheless, it would be wrong to suppose that the world expected more from Norway or resented — if, indeed, it knew — the attitude of its new foreign minister. As late as April 1939, when president Roosevelt listed Norway among a number of countries which might feel themselves threatened by Hitler, Norway (unlike Denmark) felt strong enough to refuse the non-aggression pact offered by Hitler in consequence. Not only so, but Hambro, whose League of Nations activities made him something of a national spokesman, though not in office, declared in an article published on the very eve of war that Norway did not desire to have any guarantee from the western powers. Were not tourists still flocking to Norway, now often advertised as 'the peaceful corner of Europe', a land which in 1939 could look back upon one-and-a-quarter centuries of undisturbed tranquillity?

❈

A peace brooded over Norway which can never return, for it was the peace peculiar to a country where deeds of violence were only dimly remembered as 'old, unhappy, far-off things'. The foreigner came to see nature at its most majestic and man at his most rational, in a land where there was not one memorable scene of human conflict to be visited more recent than the deathplace of Charles XII. In the 1920's, indeed, the genius of Sigrid Undset in a series of great historical romances had called back mediaeval Norway from the dead, but her evocation of Catholic Christendom seemed only to intensify the associations of peace. But it is important to notice a partial change of attitude towards Norway, which occurred during the inter-war period and especially in the years of Labour rule. Neither the aristocratic salmon-fisher, who lingered by the same river season after season, nor the middle-class tourist, pursuing the picturesque in his carriole, had commonly regarded the people themselves except as necessary background figures — the gillies, boatmen,

[1] E. Bull: *Arbeiderklassen i norsk historie*, Oslo, 1947, p. 336.

hotelkeepers, and guides—who appeared to him to live in an honest but not particularly interesting frugality. But an increasingly democratic Britain found new points of contact: Oslo, for instance, was not just the starting-place for tours in east Norway but the venue of some fascinating social experiments—the schoolchildren's 'Oslo breakfast', municipally owned cinemas, and great functional blocks of working-class housing. As social and economic prospects in many parts of Europe grew darker, the Americans also discovered in Norway a small country which, through co-operation and enlightenment, had found a way of avoiding both dictatorship and class conflict. Finally, when war among the great powers began to loom up as the almost unavoidable catastrophe, Norway's success in having kept out of war for so long began to attract attention as an achievement deserving of closer study. Nobel in the 'nineties had chosen the Storting to be the awarders of his annual peace prize: had the Norwegians perhaps found a permanent solution to the problem which was vexing much larger nations, of how to reconcile isolationism and self-respect?

CHAPTER XII

THE WAR OF 1940-45 AND SOME CONSEQUENCES

IN September 1939 the Norwegian people had no intention of deviating from their traditional neutrality. They had stayed out of the first world war, although a cause which was sponsored by men like Asquith and Grey had more to commend it to Knudsen and his fellow-Liberals than any appeal which Chamberlain could make to a Norwegian Labour government. Hitler had very few admirers in Norway, but the Anglo-French policy which had sacrificed Czechoslovakia at Munich in 1938 created very reasonable doubt as to our intention of saving Poland, when we obviously lacked the means to defend its territory from being immediately overrun. The League of Nations had disappointed the hopes of the idealists: hence the policy of withdrawal from League commitments, begun (as we have seen) in 1936, from which Norway in common with the other Scandinavian powers saw now no reason to depart. As for Norway's ability — as distinct from her inclination — to stay out of war, the supply situation was considerably better than in 1914; but the trend towards complete disarmament, belatedly reversed, meant that her Navy this time could mobilize only a neutrality watch, not a neutrality defence. When Russia, after dividing the Polish spoils with Germany, launched her invasion of Finland on November 30, this so far brought the war home to the rest of Scandinavia that Norway mobilized one of her six field brigades to guard, or try to guard, the Finnish-Norwegian frontier. Meanwhile, trade agreements were being negotiated both with Germany and with the Allies; the latter also chartered rather more than half the Norwegian mercantile marine, including nearly the whole of the tanker tonnage.

In 1939, as in 1914, Norway's primary interest for the contending parties was in relation to the blockade; but her position was more precarious than before. On the one hand, the Allies were acutely conscious of their weakness: they were notoriously unready for war in the air, needed a long respite in which to build up their land forces for victory on the Franco-German frontier, and were bitterly aware of the limitation imposed upon the effectiveness of the naval block-ade by the suddenly established friendship between Germany and Soviet Russia. On the other hand, Germany had a ruler who had risen by strategic strokes of calculated daring, and he was well aware of the school of thought which claimed that Germany could have derived greater benefit from her navy in 1914-18 if she had used it to win a foothold along the east side of the North Sea, instead of re-maining cooped up in the 'wet triangle'. The Allies, accordingly, jumped at the idea that the supply of Swedish iron ore, which, during the annual freeze-up of the north Baltic, reached the enemy via Narvik and the Leads, was so essential to German war industry that to deprive her of it would end the war in a twelvemonth. The free passage through the Leads was in any case open to abuse, as the British demonstrated to their own satisfaction when they unlawfully released in Norwegian waters the 299 prisoners whom the *Altmark* was carrying through to Germany.[1] This was in February 1940, the month which marks the climax of a series of vain efforts to induce the Norwegian and Swedish governments to admit Allied troops in transit, to save the Finns from the Russians: if those troops were to succeed in establishing a firm front against Russia in the far north, the Swedish iron ore would be securely held by their lines of com-munication. It was such a big 'if' that we may be glad the Finns instead made peace (March 13), leaving the Allies to adopt the less ambitious policy of mining the Leads. If the Germans submitted to this demonstration of British naval strength and determination, well and good. If not, we held forces in readiness to help the Norwegians to resist such action as would be open to the Germans—surprised, discomfited, and held in check by the Royal Navy.

Hitler, however, preferred to give, rather than to receive, sur-prises; chose to risk his hopelessly outnumbered fleet, instead of

[1] In British eyes the justification for the boarding of the *Altmark* depends, partly at least, upon Norwegian rejection of the compromise—the return of the ship under joint guard and escort to Bergen—proposed in Churchill's in-structions to Captain Vian. The commander of the Norwegian torpedo boat, however, 'definitely cannot remember' that this compromise was offered to him (W. S. Churchill: *Second World War*, I, 444; Commander E. A. Steen: *Norges Sjökrig 1940-1945*, I, 79).

awaiting its discomfiture, which had been the general policy in 1914-18; and foresaw what air power could do to loosen the hold of the British Navy upon the approaches to southern Norway. His expedition, which completed the conquest of Norway in two months, took scarcely longer to prepare. Quisling visited Hitler in December, to feed his fears that he might be over-reached by the British and to inflame his ambitions for another politico-military triumph by putting at his service a native Nazi party, obviously weak and unreliable, but good enough to spread confusion invaluably at a crisis. But it was not until after the *Altmark* incident on February 16 that Hitler became fully committed to the plan then under preparation. Besides securing the iron ore and (*ex hypothesi*) ousting the British, it was designed 'to give our navy and air force a wider start-line against Britain': it would be interesting to know whether a start-line against Russia also entered into the private calculations of the ambivalent Führer.

By coincidence the German expedition was already approaching the coast of Norway at the moment when the British carried out their intended operation of mining the Leads, at a point just north of Bodö. This fact had two important results. It confused Norwegian counsels, for Koht was busy drafting protests against the admittedly outrageous infringement of territorial waters by the British and failed to pay due attention to the evidences of immediately impending German action of an infinitely more outrageous character, which came in on the day of the mining — April 8. It also confused British counsels, for the first reaction to the news that the Germans were at sea was to throw overboard (almost literally) the arrangements for landing in support of the defence of Norway against German aggression. A naval battle was to be preferred. But, when the Royal Navy unfortunately failed in the very thick weather to find the Germans while they were still at sea, troops who had been disembarked without their equipment could not be made available for a counter-thrust before the Germans were properly established on Norwegian soil. Nevertheless, it would be quite wrong to attribute the staggering success of the German *coup* to luck. The synchronized approach of six different forces at widely separated points on the Norwegian coast was a work of brilliant organization, based on two sound concepts — the ability of air power to remedy an otherwise weak general position, and the advantage which a completely unscrupulous aggressor has in the first critical hours when his victim is not psychologically conditioned to resist.

At breakfast-time on April 9 the Germans had taken possession, virtually without loss, of Narvik, Trondheim, Bergen and Stavanger. The coast defences at Kristiansand surrendered at about 11 a.m., at which time troops had begun to arrive by air in Oslo: apart from anti-aircraft guns, no effective resistance was offered in the capital. But ten miles away, a small fort well placed at the narrowest point in the Oslofiord had shown what a handful of resolute men could do. By torpedoing Germany's newest cruiser, the *Blücher*, they had delayed the occupation of Oslo, and so enabled the king, government, and parliament to make their escape inland. What was to be done? The decision to mobilize had been left too late: the Germans were now in possession of the main military centres, and Quisling as head of a self-proclaimed government was busy countermanding the mobilization orders which had been issued in a rather uncertain way overnight. Even before the national authorities left Oslo at 7.30 a.m., it had been evident that the German air force, to which Norway could offer no challenge, could spread panic wherever it chose. In the circumstances, it showed great courage that the terms of 'peaceful co-operation' with the Germans, which their minister had laid before Koht in the small hours, were still rejected, and that the Storting gave plenary powers to the government, enabling it to function even if driven into exile. On the 10th, there was a further meeting between the king and Koht and the German minister, when the will to resist was stiffened by insistence upon the formation of a new government headed by Quisling—a direct affront, not merely to democratic ideas of procedure, but to the much older tradition of national independence in internal affairs, even when the foreign relations of the country had passed into foreign guardianship. Meanwhile, there had been immediate offers of Allied help. A message from Chamberlain read, 'We are coming at once, and in great force'; and before the day was out, the news of Captain Warburton-Lee's gallant destroyer attack on the much larger German force in Narvik harbour came to distract attention from the bitter truth, that the Norwegians had relied in vain upon the British Navy to keep the Germans out.

❋

The events of the campaign which followed have left surprisingly little direct impression on the Norwegian mind, and can therefore command little space in this history. Owing to the difficulties already referred to, only a small minority of able-bodied Norwegians had any chance to take part. In the south-east, by far the most populous part of the country, the only effective resistance was that of one division, to which the new commander-in-chief, General Otto Ruge, linked his headquarters. This made a fighting withdrawal from the outskirts of Oslo to the mouth of the Gudbrandsdal, where the British made contact twelve days after the invasion began. Another field brigade came over from the west to prevent the position in the Gudbrandsdal from being outflanked on that side. A smaller force co-operated with the British and French when they landed to the north of Tróndheim. Otherwise, the Norwegian sphere of activity was in the far north, where they were properly mobilized in advance and were able to bear the brunt of the bitter fighting in the snowclad mountains which led to the recapture of Narvik. But — and it is a very big 'but' — Narvik was extremely remote from the interests of the average Norwegian, and the news of its recapture was in any case quickly drowned in that of its second loss. Two other splendid Norwegian achievements, the defence of the disused fort at Hegra, east of Trondheim, and the establishment of a 'pocket' in the mountains of Telemark under a second lieutenant who did not accept superior orders to capitulate, deserved to be known, if only because they were continued after the entire withdrawal of Allied support from central Norway. These were, however, in both cases the work of about 300 men. It is significant both of the small scale and of the hopeless odds of Norway's fight that her heaviest single loss was that of 286 men in the two obsolete ironclads posted for the defence of Narvik on the morning of April 9. One was tricked into a parley and then blown to pieces without warning; the other had time to fire seventeen rounds before the torpedoes went into her sides.

General Ruge had only accepted command of the Norwegian forces from the government on April 10 — when his predecessor, who thought the situation hopeless, retired conveniently through old age — in the express belief that the promised Allied support would counterbalance the advantages of the Germans in numbers of properly trained men and modern military equipment. The sequel was a series of disappointments and disillusionments both for the general and for the government which he advised; and these were the more hurtful because the Allies were too alarmed about the supposed influence of Quisling (who they knew had been an army officer and minister of defence) to give the Norwegians the advance information of their intentions which might often have softened the blow. From the Norwegian standpoint, it might be possible to distinguish four phases.

To begin with, it was possible to suppose that the success of the German invasion could be checked by a mere reassertion of Britain's traditional naval control off the coasts of Norway. When the expected attack on Bergen was called off by the British Admiralty in the early afternoon of the 9th; when German seaborne supplies, impeded only by submarine attack, began to arrive in Oslo; and when the German heavy ships which had accompanied the invasion fleet got back to their home ports without destruction, it became clear that British seapower, in spite of two victories at Narvik, could not by itself redress the balance in Norway. But it could bring Allied troops to the scene of action. It was unfortunate for British prestige that the first units to be engaged were imperfectly trained and under-equipped Territorials, who were no sooner landed than defeated—both in the key position (as Norwegians saw it) at the mouth of the Gudbrandsdal and in an attempted advance on the other side of Trondheim, from Namsos. This ended the second phase, for the disappointment of the Norwegians at the failure of two Territorial brigades to hold up the Germans was in proportion to their high expectations of British prowess. The failures of April 21-23 were followed by a much stouter defence of the Gudbrandsdal by a brigade of British Regulars from France; but the Norwegian troops, withdrawn from the line to recuperate behind the British, had no direct knowledge of these actions, except that the enemy was still gaining ground. It was also known to the Norwegians that a second brigade of British Regulars, which had arrived in the far north on the morrow of the battle in which the *Warspite* crushed the last vestiges of naval resistance at Narvik, found the hoped-for immediate assault on the iron-ore port too problematic to be attempted.

In all areas, but particularly of course in the far north, British troops were terribly handicapped by their complete ignorance of any technique of fighting in snow—a matter which was not even mentioned in Field Service Regulations. The Norwegians might perhaps have anticipated this: but they could not have anticipated the deficiency which dominated the third phase of the campaign, namely a hopeless inferiority to the Germans in air power. The one squadron of obsolescent fighters, which the R.A.F. tried to operate from a frozen lake at the head of the Gudbrandsdal, was eliminated within twenty-four hours; the Allied supply of anti-aircraft artillery was also utterly inadequate. This factor had already added to the German advantages on the battlefield; but its chief effects were to cause the cancellation of an intended forcing of the entrance to the long Trondheim fiord for a seaborne assault on the city, and then the abandonment of the pincer movement against it from remoter positions north and south. The base at Namsos was heavily bombed immediately after the arrival of a French brigade, which never saw action there. Those at Aandalsnes and Molde, which supplied the troops in the Gudbrandsdal, began to go up in flames at the very moment when the first Regulars were beginning to hope that, given reinforcements and artillery, they would be able to bring the enemy to a final halt in the upper parts of the valley. The decision to evacuate central Norway was taken by the British government (which controlled inter-Allied operations in Norway) on April 26. This was a fortnight after they had undertaken to recapture Trondheim as an alternative seat for the Norwegian government, ten days after the landing of the first troops to make good their offer. The Norwegian forces which had co-operated with the Allies had had small losses, but were too bitterly disappointed to wish to continue the campaign by a transfer northwards. They were quickly demobilized and local armistices signed. Five towns in central Norway having been reduced to ashes because they harboured (or were believed to harbour) Allied troops, it was not altogether easy for Norwegians to share without reserve in the rejoicings of the B.B.C. when they made good their own escape from the power of the *Luftwaffe* at the cost of two destroyers sunk at sea with about 100 men.

There remained the siege of Narvik, where 2,000 German-Austrian mountain troops and about the same number of naval ratings from the sunk destroyers faced two brigades of Norwegians, who were used to the terrain, and three brigades of British, French, and Polish troops, who were not. The British command may have been dilatory; it was certainly very slow to establish close relations with the Norwegians, who battled their way forward through the wilderness of high mountains along the Swedish frontier, engaging the whole attention of two of the three German infantry battalions. While the

Allies made slow progress from their base, which was seventy miles from Narvik by the passage through the Leads, the Germans advanced so rapidly from the Namsos area to relieve the siege that in the end the whole of the British brigade was sent to reinforce the Norwegians and the British independent companies (an antecedent of the commandos) who were falling back before them. They failed to hold the Germans, but meanwhile the establishment of a British fighter force provided air cover at long last for the final assault on Narvik, which fell to two French and one Norwegian battalion on the evening of May 28.

The Germans had suffered their first defeat in Europe. But, since the opening of their great offensive on the western front on May 10, it had become increasingly apparent that the campaign in North Norway was only a sideshow: France needed her soldiers, Britain her ships, for more urgent purposes of defence. The logic of the situation was inescapable, but for the Norwegians unspeakably bitter. There was not even time for them to force the surrender of the Germans whom they had driven back against the Swedish frontier. The British brigade began to be withdrawn from Bodö—another base destroyed by the *Luftwaffe* to the great loss of its inhabitants—on the day after the recapture of Narvik, and by the morning of June 8 the Allied evacuation from North Norway was complete. General Ruge stayed to organize demobilization and an armistice for his troops. The king and government after anguished consideration went with the Allies. The assets they still disposed of were the following: a legally (but not practically) inassailable claim to exercise sovereign power on behalf of the land they left conquered behind them; a large merchant fleet, placed under requisition since April 22 and administered through a shipping mission in London; the gold reserve from the Bank of Norway; the relics of a small navy; and a handful of army officers and airmen. The first news which greeted them on their arrival in Britain was that Italy had found it expedient to enter the war on the other side, and that the French were abandoning their capital to the enemy. It required much faith to believe that the new path on which Norway had entered with the abandonment of her age-long neutrality could be a path which led on to fortune.

In the tragic summer and autumn of 1940, when the Germans seemed to have all Europe at their mercy, it looked for a time as though they might succeed in driving a wedge between the Norwegian people in general and these few representatives overseas. At an early stage in the campaign in Norway a small Administrative Council had been set up under the authority of the Supreme Court: this replaced Quisling's usurped powers and dealt with the Germans on day-to-day matters in the area subject to military occupation. When the campaign was over, the German Reich Commissar, who was a keen Party man and had the confidence of Hitler, brought every pressure to bear upon the Council and the politicians to declare that the king and his ministers could not exercise their constitutional functions from exile, and to agree to their replacement by a Council of State, chosen initially by the party groups in the Storting. The king and government protested by broadcast statements, which referred to the plenary powers granted them in constitutional form on April 9. Nevertheless, in the second week of September the Party groups voted by a majority of 75-55 that the Royal House had ceased to reign for the duration of the war and agreed that the members of the new Council of State should fill vacancies at their own discretion, as desired by the Germans. But at the last moment new difficulties arose, from German pressure to put a Norwegian Nazi into the key position of minister of justice. The Reich Commissar lost patience, and on September 25 replaced the Administrative Council by a provisional ministry of Quisling's supporters. At the same time the proclamation of a ban on all other political parties made it clear that the Germans had given up hope of basing the occupation upon a show of legality and a show of popular support.

Henceforth there were four powers in Norway. The Reich Commissar, with the often reluctant support of the German army, organized economic exploitation, pro-German propaganda, courts of injustice, and all the machinery of the police state. Quisling, who was formally declared Minister President on February 1, 1942, was all the time engaged in building up his imitation of the German Nazi Party, with *hirdmenn* in place of Hitler's original Brownshirts, much talk about the planning of a New Order for Europe (which ensnared a few idealists), and good jobs in the Quisling-controlled administration to fetch in the social misfit, the unashamed careerist, the greedy speculator, and the thug, who in every country rise to the surface in troubled times. Thirdly, there was the great mass of people who, having families to feed and employment they might lose, busied themselves over their everyday affairs, avoiding collaboration with the Germans, as far as circumstances allowed, and shunning contamination by the quislings. Lastly, the leaven which leaveneth the whole lump — soldiers who when the campaign in Norway ended hid their weapons in readiness for a better day; friends of Britain, who could not sever the ties of a lifetime and consoled themselves that the British always lose every battle except the last; champions of the free and independent realm proclaimed in the Norwegian constitution, who would die for a matter of principle.

The government in exile showed great discretion in not attempting to direct from outside the slow growth of the spirit of resistance inside the country. Instead, they did their best to develop the resources left at their immediate disposal. In the mercantile marine they possessed a floating empire, of which only one-fifth had fallen into German hands as a result of the invasion. It was a fast fleet (sixty-nine per cent diesel-engined) and included 2,000,000 tons of tankers, which in the critical autumn of 1941 carried no less than forty per cent of the British oil supply. At that time an Anglo-Norwegian committee was set up to forestall any difficulties in interpreting an agreement, by which the Norwegian government bound itself to give absolute priority to needs of war transportation. High freights enabled them — unlike certain other exiled governments — to be fully self-supporting. Heavy sacrifices, amounting in the end to over half the fleet, enabled them also to hold their heads high, as representing a country which had not been knocked out of the war. The armed forces were necessarily a smaller affair. About 1,000 men, recruited largely from the Antarctic whalers, began training at Dumfries in August 1940. This was the nucleus of a brigade, which prepared strenuously for the long-delayed reconquest of their native land. Meanwhile, the Norwegian navy was able to purchase replenishments, so that, in spite of losses on convoy service and in the invasion of France, it ended the war having the same strength as when it began. The Royal Norwegian Air Force, on the other hand, was a new creation in exile, with pilots trained at 'Little Norway' in Toronto to operate from the coasts of Britain and Iceland. Two fighter squadrons and two of submarine-hunting seaplanes established a tradition: the former were officially described as 'second to none in Fighter Command'. The loss of life was almost exactly one-third of the 750 picked young men engaged.

The government also had a part to play in international relations. In doing so, it was helped by the fact that Conservative, Liberal and Agrarian members were added to the Labour Cabinet in London, and the foreign office was taken over by a lawyer, Trygve Lie, with an experience of long drawn out industrial negotiations which he quickly learnt to apply in other spheres. To begin with, Norway was most valuable to the Allied cause as an ideal subject for Roosevelt's propaganda against American isolationism. The Middle West, which was the most isolationist section of the Union, contained the largest Scandinavian element in its population. It was not easy for them to resist appeals from these victims of Hitler's aggression—a democratic, peace-loving, united, bourgeois people such as Americans instinctively admired. From this it was an easy step to the idea of an Atlantic alliance—'The Atlantic does not divide us, on the contrary it unites us'—of which Lie made himself the spokesman as early as December 1940. As the war unfolded, the idea underwent two modifications, both of them important for Norway after the war. On the one hand, Lie was quick to set his Atlantic alliance within the framework of a new 'community of nations'—to quote the title of an article he contributed to *The Times* (November 14, 1941)—in which both Soviet Russia and China must find a place. On the other hand, the government in exile felt free to treat with polite frigidity proposals for a new Scandinavian union which began to be made in influential circles in Sweden in 1942. Their high-mindedness appealed to Sir Stafford Cripps, who was unaware of their dangerous relationship to Polish schemes for the establishment of a central zone, perhaps including the Baltic States, for the purpose of excluding Soviet influence from post-war Germany. The Norwegian government, however, could not help but be influenced by the attitude of unbenevolent neutrality which the Swedish authorities adopted towards them in order to placate a seemingly invincible Germany. After the death of the Norwegian minister in October 1940 the Swedes refused for three years to recognize an official successor in Stockholm; for nearly as long a period they allowed German troops of occupation to pass freely to and from North Norway over their railways; and the 50,000 refugees who flooded across the frontier from Norway, though everywhere befriended by the Swedish people, were subjected by the authorities to very strict control. In 1943, when the Germans were beginning to lose the war, a complete change set in, as a result of which Norway was able eventually to build up a trained force of 12,770 'police troops' from among the refugees in Sweden—nearly equal in number to the manpower of all the three Norwegian fighting services in Britain. In the last weeks of the war, too, the Swedes made a notable contribution to the idea of Scandinavian solidarity, when Count Fulke Bernadotte secured the release of Norwegian and Danish political prisoners from concentration camps in Germany. But Norway had gained prestige during the war and Sweden had lost it; king Haakon is said to have expressed the change of relationship very well—'No more talk about the big brother'.

Meanwhile, in Norway itself the position had changed with increasing rapidity, as more and more people felt the twin pressures of economic exploitation and political subjugation. As to the former, post-war calculations show that about forty per cent of the entire economic activity of the nation was diverted to German war purposes; also that the cost per head of being occupied was for the Norwegian thirty per cent heavier than for the Belgian, 300 per cent heavier than for the Dane. As to the latter pressure, comparisons are invidious, but it seems likely that the Norwegians were more naively surprised than peoples with a more tragic history at the completeness of the extinction of their liberties. Certainly, they had special advantages when they awoke to their situation, in the existence of the long neutral frontier to Sweden and the more dangerous but tempting passage to and from the Shetlands, which meant that they were never completely cut off from the free world. Nor should we ignore the strength of the traditional Norwegian distaste for regimentation and for any suggestion of an authoritarian attitude, even on the part of leaders they respected.

It is characteristic of the broad cultural front, on which passive resistance developed, that it began in the later months of 1940 with the popular sports organizations—and the Supreme Court. The sportsmen maintained a boycott of events in which Germans took part and of the whole programme of football fixtures, athletic competitions, etc, arranged by Norwegian Nazi authorities. In December the judges of the Supreme Court, which was the only independent constitutional body remaining in the country, resigned office rather than accept the validity of Nazi administrative orders. In the New

Year the struggle against nazification was taken up by the Church, with the result that its bishops were soon under house-arrest. The struggle then transferred itself to the schools, where resistance to the intrusion of Nazi teaching culminated in March 1942, when 1,100 teachers were arrested and 500 of them deported to forced labour in Finnmark. There followed a similar ideological battle in the university: students as well as teachers were sent to Germany, and eventually all higher instruction came practically to an end.

The events which we have described effectively prevented Quisling and his supporters from getting a hold upon the more thoughtless elements of the population, as they might have done. But they did not directly impede the German war effort. From that point of view the attitude of the trade union leaders, which naturally became firmer after the entry of Russia into the war, was more crucial. In September 1941, when a strike about milk deliveries to work-places provided the excuse, the Germans proclaimed a state of emergency in the Oslo area, under which they immediately executed two trade union leaders and imposed savage prison sentences upon a dozen others. Direct opposition in the economic field was thus shown to be easily crushable; it also presented enormous difficulties in attempting to distinguish those parts of Norwegian production which directly served German interests from those which could only be impeded at serious cost to Norway. It is therefore right to see the culmination of the civil resistance movement in Norway in the struggle to stop about 70,000 young men from being called up in 1944 for a Nazi labour service organization, which might have brought its victims either into the German army or into German industry—both by that time desperately in need of recruits. Instead, they took to the woods, where supplies were somehow organized for them; thousands made their way across the frontier to join the police troops in Sweden; only a few hundred were ever set to work.

The Home Front had as its civil leader the Chief Justice of the former Supreme Court, supported by the bishop of Oslo, the rector of the university, some leading businessmen and civil servants, and representatives of Labour, including the post-war prime minister. From the autumn of 1941 they had their own spokesman in the cabinet in London. But they would be the first to acknowledge the importance of the military organization, 'Milorg', which grew up in loose relationship with them. From small beginnings in the period of intense depression after the abandonment of the Allied campaign in Norway, and in face of numerous setbacks, when bad luck, inexperience, or indiscretion betrayed their units into enemy hands, Milorg likewise came to receive official recognition in London, both by the Norwegian government and by the British and, later, American authorities.

Military activity in occupied Norway was of three kinds. In 1941 (and for one strictly limited purpose in January 1943) the British launched commando raids on outlying areas. Industrial plants which worked for the enemy were destroyed, prisoners taken, and nearly 700 Norwegian volunteers brought back by the fleet to Britain. But the main object was a war of nerves, and the Germans retaliated with such cruelty towards the remaining population of the raided areas that the Norwegian government, some of whose few troops had participated, was anxious for such raids to be discontinued. Secondly, there were sabotage ventures by Norwegians trained in Britain, of which the two raids on the vital objective of the heavy water supply at Rjukan are the best-known example. The 'Linge Company' (Norwegian Independent Company No 1) of 530 men, of whom fifty-five lost their lives, was the main force used in this way, and Max Manus, who specialized in attaching limpet mines to enemy shipping under their very nose in Oslo harbour, was its best-known member. Nevertheless it was the third activity, that for which Milorg was primarily responsible, which mattered most to the future of Norway. Milorg, it is true, also played a large part in sabotage work, such as the interruption of communications to stop German reinforcements moving southwards in the last part of the war. But sabotage was the concern of the few; Milorg's main business was to raise a Home Army.

In a request for the maximum of help, despatched to London about Christmas 1942, the case is stated as follows:

> The Council of Milorg claims that the desire to play an active part is evidence of a valuable national instinct, which must not be stifled, and that our authorities in the U.K. ought to do everything in their power to equip the volunteers at home, so that their effort shall not be in vain. . . . The Council is of course aware of the importance it has for the future that the country should preserve its leading men, but it is also important for the future that the people should be able to find strength and self-respect in the knowledge

that liberation was not merely a gift from others, but also the result of our own efforts. . . .Conclusion. . . . A rising of Norwegian volunteers behind the enemy's lines has a national, besides its purely military, importance.[1]

Churchill always favoured an attack on the Germans in Norway, whether as a main operation or as a diversion; but the greater immediate importance of other fronts prevented the sending of military supplies in any quantity until 1944. Meanwhile, the Norwegians did what they could on their own account: they even improvised the manufacture of sten-gun parts in sixteen separate workshops, ready for assembly in a seventeenth establishment where, in case of discovery, they were all stamped 'made in England'. But during the last winter of the war, when it seemed as likely as not that the last desperate stand of the enemy would be made in a Norwegian 'redoubt', more arms were sent across. Norwegians then trained feverishly, in large numbers, and at great risk: in two instances their bases out in the wilds were discovered and attacked by the enemy in force. Nevertheless, we must recognize that the eventual surrender of the 350,000 German troops in Norway without showing fight was a crowning mercy for the whole country. For the Milorg army, counting the police troops trained in Sweden, would have been outnumbered by about seven to one, and the promptest Allied help could not have prevented the infliction of almost irreparable loss.

As it was, the only Norwegian troops who took part in operations in Norway, other than the disarming of the enemy after his surrender, were a small party that came in with the Russians from the north-east in November 1944, to make what headway they could across the area of ruthless devastation which the Germans interposed between themselves and their pursuers in Finnmark and Troms. There were 700 persons rescued by the British Navy from one island, Söröya, of whom some fifty had braved the arctic winter months huddled under an upturned fishing boat. But although Milorg never had the chance to go into full-scale action, it had been the backbone of a resistance which left devastated areas and heroic memories in many Norwegian homes. Apart from the 630 Jewish residents, who fell as victims to Hitler's feud against their race, the Norwegian

[1] *Norges Krig*, edited by Professor Sverre Steen and others, 3 vols., Oslo, 1947, Vol. I, p. 780.

fight against the occupation and its native minions had cost nearly 1,500 lives. Half of these were cases of deportees who never returned from German concentration camps, but 366 Norwegian citizens were officially declared executed, 162 were killed while trying to escape arrest, 130 died in prison in Norway, forty-three committed suicide while in enemy hands, and thirty-eight men and one woman are known to have been tortured to death.

King Haakon landed at the quay in Oslo, deeply moved by his reception, on the fifth anniversary of his reluctant departure from his country's soil. His popularity with all classes of his subjects had mounted during the later years of the war, and was a national asset which did not disappear with the final return to Norway. His ministers, by agreement made in advance with the Home Front leaders, resigned office at once in favour of a new coalition government, and when an election gave Labour an absolute majority of one in the new Storting, the new Labour government which was formed —and which was destined to hold office for a record period—contained no more than two or three of the men who had been in power on the fateful April 9, 1940. The Norwegians are great worshippers of law and system in their public business. No country was more resolute in bringing to book all who had joined the Nazi Party or in any way collaborated willingly or profitably with the German invaders. Yet no country was more civilized in the penalties it applied: there were only a handful of capital sentences, and Quisling himself was twice examined by medical experts to see whether a plea of insanity could be established.[1] At the same time, there was an exhaustive parliamentary inquiry into the political and military responsibility for the unpreparedness and ineffectiveness of Norwegian defence against the German invasion: every single officer of the Norwegian army was required to account for his actions or inaction at the moment of crisis. This in turn led to an eager canvassing of the motives and doings of the Allies, for it somehow made the failure to keep out the Germans seem less reprehensible, if the alternative had been an invasion by the other side. The general public, however, preferred the evidence of their own eyes, and associated their liberation

---

[1] By October 1948, 89,406 cases had already been brought to trial, resulting in 48,212 convictions (12,000 persons imprisoned, 38 executed)—O. Hölaas: *The World of the Norseman*, London, December 1949, Chapter 3.

above all with the persistence of the British war effort. British troops, stationed in Norway pending the disarming and repatriation of the overwhelmingly large but fortunately highly submissive enemy garrison, received a hospitality which left a permanent mark on mutual relations.

The last British detachment left in December 1945, and the government was then free to devote its entire attention to tasks of reconstruction. The Germans had drained away the economic resources of the country to the uttermost in support of their own war effort. They had 'paid their way' by drawing a sum of £565,000,000 as credit from the Bank of Norway, bequeathing thereby a terrible problem of inflation. Their 'scorched earth' policy had left Finnmark, the northernmost and least accessible county, in utter ruin; the half-dozen towns farther south, which had been largely burnt in 1940, likewise still awaited rebuilding. Moreover, the loss of fifty per cent of the mercantile marine—in the case of the whaling fleet, seventy per cent—meant a particularly heavy handicap, as this was Norway's chief means of earning foreign assets. But all parties supported the Labour government in an austerity policy, which directed the maximum proportion of the nation's total economic effort towards reconstruction work by restricting consumption. In the three years 1946-8 the Norwegian was rationed more severely than the citizens of other west European countries; prices were kept stable; there was full employment and no time lost through industrial disputes. By July 1947, when the initiation of the Marshall Plan for American aid to Europe caused Norway to think in terms of long-range development, such progress had been made that the existing reserves of foreign exchange were equal to one-half of the value of all the American economic assistance, which was to be received during the next five years under the Marshall Plan. In so far as it is possible to distinguish reconstruction from new development, it might be said that by 1949 Norway had completed the former task, which had originally been estimated to take five years. Finnmark had been largely restored, though at the cost of delays in all other building work; the export industries were flourishing; the mercantile marine had reached its pre-war tonnage; ten floating factories had been available for the Antarctic whaling season of 1948-9.

The Labour majority rose from one to ten at the 1949 election, when its opponents claimed that the existing scheme of proportional representation gave an unfair advantage to the largest party: Labour had in fact polled less than forty-six per cent of votes. Before the next election, therefore, the system was changed for a new method of computation, and at the same time the ancient constitutional rule was abolished, under which the towns elected one-third of the members and the country areas two-thirds in wholly distinct constituencies. But, as Labour still secured an absolute majority of two, it seems clear that their mandate was not merely to restore a war-battered economy, but to reshape it according to their interpretation of socialist principles.

Unlike the Attlee ministry in the United Kingdom, the Norwegian Labour government set no store by nationalization as a dogma: this appears surprising at first sight in a country which has celebrated (in 1954) the centenary of its first nationalized railway. A project for nationalizing the mining industry, for example, in which the State already had a large holding of shares, was unanimously rejected by a parliamentary committee in 1953; and apart from some new power stations (where national ownership likewise has a long history) a single steel mill and an (ex-German) aluminium works were the only important post-war ventures by the State. Instead, the policy was to encourage private initiative on the part of the entrepeneur as well as of the worker, provided that individual enterprise fitted into the general scheme of economic development designed by the state. The controlling instrument was a National Budget, kept quite distinct from the ordinary fiscal Budget, in which the government annually reviewed the developments of the preceding twelve months and, in the light of a long-term plan, showed what ends it desired to achieve in the next twelve-month period. This covered private as much as public economic activity: a former finance minister has indeed termed it 'a programme for the management of "Norway Ltd" '.[1] Import controls and price controls had in fact given the government the whip-hand over private industry, and advocates of a freer economy complained bitterly that the National Budget was so contrived as to make it hard to distinguish programme from mere prophecy. Nevertheless, it may be claimed that the ultimate interest

[1] Quoted, by kind permission, from the unpublished lectures of Mr Erik Brofoss, governor of the Bank of Norway, for the American Summer School at Oslo University, 1956. The author's statements regarding leading economic and social trends are derived mainly from the same source.

of all concerned in Norway's future prosperity was well served by the diversion of the largest possible share of present earnings to long-term developments. These took twenty-eight per cent in Norway, as compared with twelve in the United Kingdom and twenty-two in a young country like Canada. It is also indicative of a prudent handling of the national finances that foreign debt was reduced to a smaller burden in relation to either exports or total national wealth than it had been before the Germans brought ruin to the land.

In matters of purely internal policy, Nygaardsvold's successors continued the social trend of the 'thirties. A fiscal Budget of three times pre-war dimensions was based on a scale of taxation which caused large incomes and family accumulations of wealth to shrink even faster than in Britain. Because social distinctions were always less marked in Norway, the accompanying move towards a classless society made faster progress. A general levelling-up was achieved through the introduction, immediately after the war, of children's allowances for every child except the first, and the extension of paid holidays for wage earners to a length of three weeks a year. Special legislative help was accorded for two particularly arduous types of labour, in the form of free family pensions, payable at an earlier age than the usual, for seamen and for forest workers. This was later extended in a modified form to all persons in state employment. But serious poverty in modern Norway is a matter of geography rather than occupation — occurring chiefly in those districts where the soil yields the poorest return, where the isolated fishermen have only recently learnt to combine effectively for the protection of their interests, and where manufacturing industry has never offered an alternative. Perhaps the most interesting new activity of the state was therefore the introduction of a ten-year plan for North Norway (in 1951) and a four-year plan for the coastal districts north and south of Trondheim (in 1955). The final results cannot yet be seen: but the intention was to provide better communications and electricity supplies; to offer newly broken ground to the farmers and processing facilities to the fishermen; and to encourage private industry to follow the state steel mill into the underdeveloped areas.

But in the last analysis, the value of 'fair shares for all' depends upon what there is to be divided. When the post-war government submitted its long-term programme to the Storting in 1953, it pointed to 'definite limitations that nature herself has set for further expansion in many fields'. Native timber could not wholly supply the existing needs of the paper and pulp industries. A decline was predicted for the cod fisheries; whale catching had had to be restricted by international agreement, or the antarctic whale would quickly have become extinct. There were known limits to the copper pyrites and iron ore mining. Even the agricultural development, which modern machinery makes possible and which has obvious attractions for a small people in an unsafe world, seemed a discouraging waste of effort when calculation showed that across the frontier in Sweden nature yielded almost twice as much food for every man engaged in its production. There was also a general handicap to the development of new industries in the smallness of the domestic market on which to launch their products. Thus the chances of further progress were seen to depend mainly upon the exploitation of Norway's two great assets—the mercantile marine and the hydroelectric facilities.

In 1956 the fleet was the third largest in the world, with a tonnage sixty per cent in excess of the pre-war figure. The output of electric power was more than double what it had been in 1945, but only one-fifth of the estimated potential for the country. In both cases there were plans for continued growth, but they were subject to two forms of external restriction. The electro-metallurgical industries and the carrying trade are alike in this respect: they both demand a level of expenditure on new capital equipment beyond what a small country can provide from its own resources. Each member of the crew of a modern tanker may employ the equivalent of £50,000 of capital; a worker in an aluminium plant makes daily use of what his lifetime's wages would not buy. Thus Norway needs foreign capital for growth, just as America did in the century before the first world war. She is also tremendously dependent upon the international division of labour, which for instance brings alumina from Canada for economical processing and conditions the very existence of a mercantile marine, four-fifths of which trades between foreign ports. Norway, in other words, has a mounting interest in the growth of international order and confidence as the basis of her economic well-being.

The war has also driven Norway's political interests in the same direction. Since 1940 she has again had a common frontier with

Soviet Russia in the far north, and Trygve Lie, the wartime foreign minister, modestly attributed his selection as the first secretary-general of the United Nations Organization to the geographical position of his country, poised between east and west. The events of the war—the battles of the arctic convoys, the fact that Norway's liberation began from the north-east, the basing of Germany's last capital ship upon the northern fiords—had also indicated for that far northern area a new importance, which was destined to grow still more rapidly as peacetime developments in long-distance aircraft brought into prominence the short inter-continental routes over the Pole. Yet for the first three years it still seemed possible for Norway to regain her traditional status of neutrality. Her government in exile had actively promoted the foundation of the United Nations, where Lie might double the role of Nansen in the League. Scandinavianism likewise began to recover strength, for the gallant struggle of the Danish resistance movement in the later part of the war aroused a sympathy and admiration for the Danes which had never existed in the whole of earlier Norwegian history. Feeling towards the Swedes was less enthusiastic, but their neutrality (as we have seen) had been increasingly benevolent and post-war gifts to aid Norwegian reconstruction helped to obliterate bitter memories. Norway contributed a brigade of 4,000 men to the British zone of occupation in Germany: but the creation of a general condition of military efficiency, so that a second 'April 9' would be unthinkable, which had been eagerly planned for during the war, moved slowly, was very costly, and might be deemed unnecessary. Germany was down and out. As for Russia, the apprehensions of the Americans and British were not readily shared by a people with lively memories of the Russian contribution to their liberation and of the part which native Communists had played in the resistance movement: the record number of eleven Communists were returned to the first post-war Storting.

A decisive shock came in the early months of 1948, when the Communist *coup* in Czechoslovakia was followed up by Russian insistence on the signature of a military alliance by the Finns. The Norwegian foreign minister was then forced to recognize the danger of the situation:

As tension between the great powers grows, it becomes increasingly necessary for Norway to clarify her position. There can be

R

no shadow of doubt that geographically, economically, and culturally we are a part of Western Europe, and we intend to continue our national existence as a western democracy.[1]

But there were still two possibilities, and in January 1949 Sweden struck a final blow for the cause of Scandinavian unity and neutrality by offering to Norway and Denmark a ten-year military alliance, binding its members not to ally themselves militarily with any other power. Norway would not agree to cut herself off from American supplies of arms, which the Americans made clear would only be available to signatories of the North Atlantic treaty which they were then canvassing. The upshot was that Norway carried Denmark with her into the new alliance, formed at Washington on April 4, 1949. Tension on the Russo-Norwegian frontier was for a few months acute, and the Russians were only to a limited extent placated by Norwegian assurances that in peacetime no foreign power would be allowed the use of bases on Norwegian soil, on the mainland or even on Spitsbergen. By 1956 the feeling of acute crisis in northern Europe had abated; but Norway's adhesion to NATO had not lost either its precautionary value or its importance as a turning-point in her international relations.

On the one hand, the Norwegians had necessarily become defence-minded. Rearmament was made a top priority, which affected the whole structure of national expenditure. Although about £150,000,000 worth of equipment was provided free from American sources, and other items—such as the building of new airfields—were covered by common NATO funds, Norway herself had in the peak three years 1952-5 to treble her pre-NATO rate of military expenditure, and it remained at a figure well above double. Apart from the continuance of universal military training at a NATO level of efficiency, when otherwise there might have been some relaxation towards pre-war standards, there was an increase of fifty per cent in the permanent cadres. North Norway, in particular, was now thought of in terms of its relation to atomic warfare rather than as an outlying area so thinly populated that its loss could be accepted at a pinch. On the other hand, the alliance intensified and perpetuated the effect of the war in fostering the general interest in the American and the British ways of life. To identify this with trade

[1] Mr Halvard Lange, speaking in Oslo, April 19, 1948.

relations would be to take too narrow a view : some sharp disagreements in international affairs did not seriously impair the growing influence of the English language and of American and British institutions.

❀

The era which followed post-war reconstruction does not lend itself to a narrative account, for in Norway—as elsewhere in Scandinavia—the national life pursued an uneventful though enviable course. Public opinion firmly supported UN, encouraged inter-Scandinavian links, welcomed the call to help underdeveloped nations, and (with some exceptions) accepted NATO obligations as a necessary insurance. Domestic affairs, too, lacked any obvious landmark, except for the death in 1957 of King Haakon, long the doyen of European monarchs, and his son's accession as Olav V. The Labour Government continued in office almost without interruption for two decades; and even when the quadrennial election of 1965 replaced it by a coalition of the four opposition parties under Mr Per Borten, there was no dramatic change of course.

Under the established regime of state planning and control the economy showed a high level of production, consumption, and investment. By 1960 the mercantile marine was already twice its pre-war size; by 1965 one-third of the huge hydro-electric potential of the country had been brought into use; the export trades flourished, with metal products and ores now taking first place; and in default of admission to the Common Market, commerce derived some new stimulus from EFTA. The gross national product rose to two and half times what it was before the war, and despite grave inflation and a heavy deficit in foreign payments the Krone successfully avoided devaluation in November 1967.

Apart from a chronic shortage of housing—partly due to a population growth of nearly 20 per cent in twenty years—the Norway of 1968 presented the general picture of a rapidly rising standard of life among the masses, to be crowned by a generously framed People's Pension. As the most egalitarian of the social democracies of western Europe, the new Norway was applauding the democratic choice of bride made by Crown Prince Harald, himself a member of the generation which had grown up among the phenomenal developments of the years since the liberation.

CHRONOLOGICAL TABLE OF
MAIN EVENTS

EVENTS IN NORWAY

c. 880-c. 940 Reign of Harald Fairhair (dates very uncertain)
c. 900 Battle of Hafrsfiord (date very uncertain)
c. 945 Deposition of Eric Bloodaxe
995-1000 Reign of Olaf I (Tryggveson)

1015-28 Reign of Olaf II (the Saint)
1030 (July 29) Olaf's death at Stiklestad

1066-93 Reign of Olaf III (the Peaceful)

1130-1240 Period of (intermittent) civil war
1152 Archbishopric of Trondheim established by Nicholas
    Breakspear
1177-1202 Reign of Sverre
1184 Sverre's final victory over Magnus V (Erlingsson) at Fimreite
1217-63 Reign of Haakon IV (Haakonsson or The Old)

1277 Concordat of Tönsberg

1319 First dynastic union (with Sweden)
1349 The Black Death.
1387 Death of Olaf IV

1450 Oldenburg dynasty established

NORWAY AND THE WORLD

793 First accurately-dated Viking raid, on Lindisfarne
853-71 Conquests of Olaf (the White) in Ireland
c. 874 Settlement of Iceland begun
930 *Alting* established in Iceland
c. 947-8, c. 952-4 Eric Bloodaxe king of York
984 Settlement of Greenland
1000 Leif Ericsson visited 'Vinland'
1000 Battle of Svolder
1014 Battle of Clontarf
1016-35 Reign of Canute the Great
1043 Magnus I's victory over the Wends at Lyrskog Heath
1066 Harald Hardrada killed at Stamford Bridge
1098-1103 Magnus III (Bareleg)'s expeditions to Scotland, Wales and Ireland
1107-1111 Sigurd I's expedition to the Holy Land

1180-83 Archbishop Eystein in England

1217 Anglo-Norwegian commercial treaty
1263 (October 2) Battle of Largs
1266 Treaty of Perth, ceding the Hebrides and Man to Scotland
1290 (September) Margaret, the Maid of Norway, died in the Orkneys
1375-1412 Queen Margaret's domination of the North

1397 The Union of Kalmar
1406 Philippa, daughter of Henry IV of England, married to king Eric
1468 Orkneys and (1469) Shetlands mortgaged to the Scottish Crown
1490 Henry VII's trade treaty with Denmark-Norway

EVENTS IN NORWAY

1506-11 Duke Christian (later Christian II) viceroy in Norway
1531-2 Christian II's expedition to Norway
1536 Triumph of Christian III over the Roman Catholic Church and the Norwegian state
1559 Power of the Hanseatic Factory in Bergen finally overthrown
1588-1648 Reign of Christian IV
1604 Christian IV's legal code
1612 Scottish mercenaries under Colonel Sinclair ambushed by peasants in Gudbrandsdal
1642-51 Hannibal Sehested Statholder of Norway
1660 Establishment of absolutist, hereditary monarchy
1664-99 Gyldenlöve Statholder of Norway
1665 Anglo-Dutch naval battle at Bergen
1687 Legal code of Christian V published

1716 Tordenskjold's victory at Dynekilen
1718 (December 11) Charles XII of Sweden killed at Halden
1741 The Conventicle Ordinance
1760 The Trondheim Society founded
1766-1808 Reign of Christian VII
1796-1804 Religious revival led by Hauge
1797 Low tariff introduced

1807-14 The Hunger Years

1814 (May 17) Free constitution established at Eidsvoll
(August 14) Convention of Moss
(November 4) Union with Sweden accepted
1818-44 Reign of Charles XIV John (Bernadotte)
1833 First Peasant majority in the Storting
1837 Local self-government re-introduced
1844-59 Reign of Oscar I
1845 Death of Wergeland
1848 Aasen's *Grammar of Popular Norwegian* published
1848-50 Thrane's socialist movement developed
1859-72 Reign of Charles XV
1871 Commencement of annual sessions of the Storting
1872-1905 Reign of Oscar II
1884 Ministers made responsible to the Storting

NORWAY AND THE WORLD

1517 Start of the Lutheran Reformation at Wittenberg
1530 Lutheran preaching authorized in Denmark

1563-70 The Seven Years War of the North

1618-48 The Thirty Years War
1626 Christian IV defeated by Tilly at Lutter

1666 Fire of London

1700-21 The Great Northern War
1706-8 Holberg in England
1721 Hans Egede's mission to Greenland
1756-63 The Seven Years War
1770 (Sept.)-1772 (Jan.) Struensee in power
1772 The Norwegian Society in Copenhagen founded
1780-2 First Armed Neutrality of the North
1792-1814 French Revolutionary and Napoleonic Wars
1800 Second Armed Neutrality of the North
1801 Battle of Copenhagen
1807 Surrender of the Danish-Norwegian fleet after bombardment of Copenhagen
1814 (January 14) Treaty of Kiel
1821 Cleng Peerson's first visit to America
1825 (July 5) *Restauration,* first emigrant ship, sailed from Stavanger
1830 July Revolution in France
1831 Wergeland's visit to England and France
1838 Thrane in France and England
1848 The Year of Revolutions
1848-9 War in Schleswig-Holstein
1849 Repeal of the Navigation Laws in Britain
1854-6 Crimean War
1862 Homestead Act (land for settlers in U.S.A. at 1.25 dollars an acre)
1864 Danes lose Schleswig-Holstein
1880 Björnson's visit to America

EVENTS IN NORWAY

1895 Union crisis: compromise imposed by Sweden
1898 Manhood suffrage (at 25)
1905 (June 7) Union with Sweden declared to be dissolved
(November 18) Prince Charles of Denmark elected king, as
Haakon VII
1906 Death of Ibsen
1909 Concession Laws
1910 Death of Björnson
1913 Universal suffrage
1915 Completion of Castberg's social reforms
1925 Annexation of Spitsbergen legally effected
1930 Death of Nansen
1935 Labour Government
1940 (April 9-June 9) Campaign against the German invasion
1945 (June 7) Return of King Haakon to Norway

1949 Post-war reconstruction approximately completed
1951 Permanent linguistic commission appointed
1952 End of food rationing (sugar, coffee)
1953 Permanent price control law passed

1955 State steel works at Mo commenced production
1956 Ordination of women priests authorized
1957 (September 21) death of Haakon VII; accession of Olav V
1958 Short-term economic recession
1959 45-hour working week established
1960 Boiling heavy-water reactor, first in world, at Halden
1961 Unanimous Storting resolution against peacetime stationing of
nuclear weapons in Norway
1962 Nordland Railway opened to Bodö
Mining disaster at King's Bay, Spitsbergen
1963 One-month anti-socialist Coalition Government under Lyng
1964 Four-year Plan for 20 per cent increase of GNP
1965 Legal annual holidays extended to four weeks
Anti-socialist Coalition Government under Borten
1966 English made an obligatory subject in primary schools
1967 Contributory 'People's Pension' scheme introduced
1968 Working week reduced to 42 hours

NORWAY AND THE WORLD

1893-6 Voyage of the *Fram*

1911 (December 15) Amundsen arrives first at the South Pole

1914-18 First World War

1930 (December) Oslo Convention signed
1933 East Greenland dispute adjudicated in favour of Denmark

1939-45 Second World War
1940-45 King and Government resident in Britain
1949 (April 4) NATO treaty signed in Washington
1951 SHAPE regional command for Northern Europe set up
1952 Norwegian technical aid to India begun
1953 Nordic Council set up to promote Scandinavian co-operation
1954 Trans-Arctic air route to Los Angeles introduced

1957 Tourists entering Norway first exceeded 1,000,000

1959 Treaty of Stockholm signed for the establishment of EFTA
1960 Norwegian *per caput* contribution to World Refugee Year the largest of any nation participating
1962 Helsinki Convention further defining co-operation among Scandinavian countries
Norwegian Agency for International Development started
1964 Stand-by force of 1250 men set up for UN service
Application to join EEC (renewed from 1962)
1965 Spitsbergen telemetry station set up after Russian protest

1967 Exchange value of Krone unaffected by devaluation of pound

BIBLIOGRAPHY

❀

I GENERAL HISTORIES

H. H. Boyesen: *A History of Norway*, London, 1900 (chiefly the saga stories; a pioneer work first published in America in 1886)

K. Gjerset: *History of the Norwegian People*, 2 vols. New York, 1915 (a standard history, but the 19th century is treated with disproportionate brevity)

G. M. Gathorne-Hardy: *Norway*, London, 1925 (places the history of the country in relation to the modern world; enriched with translations of Norwegian poetry)

W. Keilhau: *Norway in World History*, London, 1944 (a short book by a prominent Norwegian economic and social historian)

H. Koht and S. Skard: *The Voice of Norway*, London and New York, 1944 (a wartime study of the growth of law and liberty)

K. Larsen: *A History of Norway*, New York, 1948 (a history of the civilization of the country in all main aspects, based on modern Norwegian studies)

F. N. Stagg: *North Norway, The Heart of Norway, West Norway and its Fjords, East Norway and its Frontier*, London, 1952-6 (illustrated regional studies, laying emphasis on the dramatic and picturesque features of local history)

II ARCHAEOLOGY AND THE VIKING AGE;
SETTLEMENT OVERSEAS

H. Shetelig and H. Falk: *Scandinavian Archaeology*, Oxford, 1937 (expertly translated work of a leading archaeologist and philologist)

G. Turville-Petre: *The Heroic Age of Scandinavia*, London, 1951 (a study of the period ending A.D. 1030, based on a re-examination of source literature)

M. Olsen: *Farms and Fanes of Ancient Norway*, Oslo, 1928 (the fundamental work on place-names)

F. Nansen: *In Northern Mists*, 2 vols. London, 1911 (Arctic exploration in early times)

The Cambridge Medieval History, Volume III, Cambridge, 1924 (chapter on the Vikings by A. Mawer, with bibliography)

T. D. Kendrick: *A History of the Vikings*, London, 1930 (full factual account)

A. Mawer: *The Vikings*, Cambridge, 1913 (a short general study)

A. Olrik: *Viking Civilization*, London, 1930 (a general work by a Danish expert)

M. W. Williams: *Social Scandinavia in the Viking Age*, New York, 1920 (with useful bibliography)

A. W. Brögger and H. Shetelig: *The Viking Ships*, Oslo, 1951 (a profusely illustrated, expert examination)

H. A. Bellows: *The Poetic Edda*, New York, 1923

D. E. Martin Clarke: *The Havamal*, Cambridge, 1923

A. G. Brodeur: *The Prose Edda*, New York, 1916

H. Shetelig (editor): *The Viking Enterprises in Great Britain and Ireland*, 3 parts. Oslo, 1940 (the most up-to-date general investigation)

W. G. Collingwood: *Scandinavian Britain*, London, 1908 (a popular account)

B. G. Charles: *Old Norse Relations with Wales*, Cardiff, 1934

A. O. Anderson: *Early Sources of Scottish History, 500-1286*, 2 vols. Edinburgh, 1922 (all relevant material from Norwegian sources)

A. W. Brögger: *Ancient Emigrants, A History of the Norse Settlements of Scotland*, Oxford, 1929 (an authoritative Norwegian study)

A. B. Taylor: *The Orkneyinga Saga*, Edinburgh, 1938 (translation, with introduction and full notes)

H. Marwick: *Orkney*, London, 1951 (an illustrated popular account, which gives considerable space to the Norse period)

A. Bugge: *Contributions to the History of the Norsemen in Ireland*, 3 vols. Christiania, 1900 (the work of a leading Norwegian historian)

A. Walsh: *Scandinavian Relations with Ireland during the Viking Period*, Dublin, 1922

K. Gjerset: *History of Iceland*, New York, 1925

P. Norlund: *Viking Settlers in Greenland*, Cambridge, 1936

G. M. Gathorne-Hardy: *The Norse Discoverers of America*, Oxford, 1921

H. Hermannsson: *The Problem of Wineland*, Ithaca, New York, 1936 (by an expert in Icelandic)

III   THE MIDDLE AGES

The Cambridge Medieval History, Vols. VI-VIII, Cambridge, 1929-36 (chapters by H. Koht on the Scandinavian kingdoms up to 1300 and from 1300 to 1500; chapter by A. Weiner on the Hansa; bibliographies)

T. B. Willson: *History of the Church and State in Norway*, London, 1903 (covers the 10th-16th centuries, with emphasis on English associations)

S. Undset: *Saga of Saints*, London, 1935 (religious history down to 1285, from a Roman Catholic standpoint)

G. M. Gathorne-Hardy: *A Royal Impostor: King Sverre of Norway*, Oslo and Oxford, 1956,7 (a full modern study)

J. A. Gade: *Hanseatic Control of Norwegian Commerce during the Later Middle Ages*, London, 1951 (a thesis making extensive use of Norwegian authorities)

H. Koht: *The Old Norse Sagas*, London, 1931 (lectures delivered at the Lowell Institute, Boston; bibliography)

W. P. Ker: *Early Historians of Norway* (reprinted in *Collected Essays*, 2 vols., London, 1925)

W. P. Ker: *Epic and Romance*, 2nd edition, London, 1908 (chapter III, Section VII)

H. G. Leach: *Angevin Britain and Scandinavia*, London, 1921 (a study of their literary relationships)

L. M. Larson: *The Earliest Norwegian Laws*, New York, 1935 (the older law of the Gulating and Frostating, with introduction, glossary, and bibliography)

E. Monsen and A. H. Smith: *Heimskringla*, Cambridge, 1932 (useful introduction; reproduces many of the famous illustrations drawn for the Norwegian edition of 1899)

J. Sephton: *The Saga of King Sverri*, London, 1899

G. W. Dasent: *The Saga of Hacon*, London, 1894 (Rolls Series, Icelandic Sagas, Vol. IV)

L. M. Larson: *The King's Mirror*, New York, 1917

IV   MODERN HISTORY (UP TO 1914)

R. N. Bain: *Scandinavia: A Political History from 1513 to 1900*, Cambridge, 1905 (contains no separate chapters on Norway)

B. J. Hovde: *The Scandinavian Countries 1720-1865. The Rise of the Middle Classes*, 2 vols. Boston, Mass., 1943 (a full treatment of economic and social development, keeping the countries distinct, with extensive source-references)

T. Jorgenson: *Norway's Relation to Scandinavian Unionism, 1815-1871*, Northfield, Minnesota, 1935 (the nearest approach to a political history of the period; full bibliography)

O. J. Falnes: *National Romanticism in Norway*, New York, 1933

The Cambridge Modern History, Volume XII, Cambridge, 1910 (section of chapter by L. Stavenow on Norway and the dissolution of the union)

P. Drachmann: *The Industrial Development and Commercial Policies of the Three Scandinavian Countries*, Oxford, 1915 (brief statistical account from about 1800)

B. A. Nissen: *Political Parties in Norway*, Oslo, 1949 (duplicated translation made for the American Summer School; outlines both history and ideology)

T. H. Michell: *History of the Scottish Expedition to Norway in 1612*, London, 1886

Petter Dass: *The Trumpet of Nordland*, Northfield, Minnesota, 1954 (a spirited verse translation by T. Jorgenson, with other literary specimens; illustrated)

E. Seaton: *Literary Relations of England and Scandinavia in the Seventeenth Century*, Oxford, 1935 (shows the comparative unimportance of Norwegian literature in this period)

H. N. Hauge: *Autobiographical Writings*, Minneapolis, 1954 (the first English translation)

D. P. Barton: *Bernadotte: Prince and King*, London, 1925 (a popular biography for the years 1810-44)

B. J. Hovde: *Diplomatic Relations of the United States with Sweden and Norway 1814-1905*, Iowa, 1921 (covers chiefly the period 1814-65, from American materials)

T. C. Blegen: *The Norwegian Migration to America, 1825-60*, Northfield, Minnesota, 1931

G. M. Gathorne-Hardy: *Bodösaken*, Oslo, 1926 (British official correspondence on the Bodö Case)

P. Knaplund: *British Views on Norwegian-Swedish Problems 1880-1895*, Oslo, 1952 (diplomatic reports)

H. Larson: *Björnstjerna Björnson*, New York, 1944

H. Koht: *Life of Ibsen*, 2 vols. New York, 1931 (the Norwegian original has since been revised)

C. B. Burchardt: *Norwegian Life and Literature*, London, 1920 (a study of travel books, criticism of Ibsen, and other material illustrating the growth of English interest)

A. J. Martin and F. Wulfsberg (editors): *Across the North Sea*, Oslo, 1955 (five essays on Anglo-Norwegian relations, chiefly in the 19th century)

F. Nansen: *The Voyage of the Fram*, London, 1897

J. Sorensen: *The Saga of Fridtjof Nansen*, New York, 1932 (the least unsatisfactory of the biographies)

Norway — Official Publication for the Paris Exhibition, Christiania, 1900 (reissued in 1905)

V   CONTEMPORARY HISTORY (SINCE 1914)

W. Keilhau: *Norway and the World War*, New Haven, 1930 (an abridgement of a longer work in Norwegian; published as part of E. F. Heckscher and others: *Sweden, Norway, Denmark, and Iceland in the World War*)

P. G. Vigness: *The Neutrality of Norway in the World War*, Stanford, 1932

M. W. W. P. Consett: *The Triumph of Unarmed Forces, 1914-18*, London, 1923 (the working of the Allied blockade in the Scandinavian countries described by one of its organizers)

S. S. Jones: *The Scandinavian States and the League of Nations*, New York, 1939

C. A. Clausen: *Nansen's Work as High Commissioner*, Urbana, 1932

K. Berlin: *Denmark's Right to Greenland*, London, 1932

O. J. Falnes: *Norway and the Nobel Peace Prize*, New York, 1938

Handbook of Norway and Sweden, London, 1918 (publication of the Naval Intelligence Division of the Admiralty, reissued in 1920)

O. B. Grimley: *The New Norway*, Oslo, 1937 (by an American long resident in the country)

A. Rothery: *Norway Changing and Changeless*, London, 1939 (a popular account)

F. J. Harriman: *Mission to the North*, London, 1941 (experiences of the American minister in Oslo)

M. Curtis (editor): *Norway and the War, September 1939-December 1940*, London, 1941 (documents on neutrality, the *Altmark* affair, invasion, and occupation)

H. Koht: *Norway Neutral and Invaded*, London, 1941 (account by the then foreign minister)

T. Broch: *The Mountains Wait*, London, 1943 (Narvik before and during the siege, described by the then mayor)

O. Nansen: *Day After Day*, O. R. Olsen: *Two Eggs On My Plate*, M.

Manus: *Underwater Saboteur*, and D. Howarth: *We Die Alone* (London, 1949, 52, 53, 55) are representative of a large literature of individual war experiences

C. Buckley: *Norway — The Commandos — Dieppe*, London, 1952

T. K. Derry: *The Campaign in Norway*, London, 1952 (bibliography)

J. Worm-Müller: *Norway Revolts Against the Nazis*, London, 1941 (the first year of German occupation seen through the eyes of a historian and Liberal politician)

W. Warbey: *Look To Norway*, London, 1945 (an English politician's account of the Resistance movement)

R. Kenney: *The Northern Tangle: Scandinavia and the Post-War World*, London, 1946

W. Warbey and others: *Modern Norway. A Study in Social Democracy*, London, 1950 (by members of the Fabian Society, who examined the activities of the Labour Government in the spring of 1948)

G. M. Gathorne-Hardy and others: *The Scandinavian States and Finland: A Political and Economic Survey*, London, 1951 (a survey of post-war conditions, undertaken for the Royal Institute of International Affairs)

A. Martin: *Norwegian Life and Landscape*, London, 1952 (an acute study of Norway as 'a country in transition')

F. Castberg: *The Norwegian Way of Life*, London, 1954 (a partly historical study by a professor of law, undertaken for UNESCO)

O. B. Grimley: *Co-operatives in Norway*, Oslo, 1950

The Trade Union Movement in Norway, 2nd edition, Oslo, 1955 (partly historical; published by the Trade Union Federation)

VI PERIODICAL LITERATURE

The Saga-Book of the Viking Society (Club) for Northern Research, London, 1895 —

Publications of the Society for the Advancement of Scandinavian Study, Urbana, Illinois, 1911 —

The American-Scandinavian Review, New York, 1913 —

The Norseman: An Independent Literary and Political Review, London, 1943 —

Norsk Historisk Tidsskrift, Vol. 27 —, Oslo, 1927 — (Norwegian historical journal: volumes with English summaries)

Viking, Oslo, 1937 — (journal of Norwegian archaeology, with English summaries)

VII   BIBLIOGRAPHIES

Norges Historie: Bibliografi, Oslo, 1926— (annual list of books and articles on Norwegian history. In the latest issue, for 1952, 32 out of 475 items reported are in English; English summaries are also noted)

S. Skard: *Norwegian Culture: A List of Books and Periodicals*, photostat, Library of Congress, Washington, D.C., 1946 (contains a small proportion of items in English and is graded to show comparative importance)

A. Bjorn: *Bibliographie des Sciences Préhistoriques en Norvège 1900-1935*, Oslo, 1936 (refers to twenty-four articles in English, and notices others with English summaries)

H. Hermannsson: *Bibliography of the Sagas of the Kings of Norway*, Ithaca, New York, 1910; Supplement, 1937 (lists translations and commentaries in various languages)

F. Lindberg and J. I. Kolehmainen: *The Scandinavian Countries in International Affairs*, University of Minnesota, 1953 (lists books on foreign affairs 1800-1952, especially in English, French, and German)

F. Isachsen: *Bibliographie d'Histoire Coloniale (1900-1930): Norvège*, Paris, 1932 (works on Spitsbergen and Norwegian Arctic interests)

S. Skard: *Böker om Norges Kamp*, Washington, D.C., 1945 (books and pamphlets in some way connected with the war, printed outside Norway after April 9, 1940)

INDEX

Aaland Islands, 154
Aall, Jacob (1773-1844), 121, 127
Aandalsnes, 243
Aasa, Queen, 34
Aasen, Ivar Andreas (1813-96),
170-1
Absalon, Pedersson (Beyer) (1528-
75), 93, 95-6
Adam of Bremen, 44
Administrative Council (1940), 245
Aelfgifu, 43-5, 47
Agrarian Party, 227, 229-31, 247
Agriculture, 9-12, 16-18, 41, 72, 110,
115, 121
after 1814, 142, 150, 160, 176, 181,
206, 230-3, 256
Air Force, 246, 258
Akershus, 65, 73, 83, 86-7, 97, 106,
118, 124, 204
Albert (Albrecht of Mecklenburg),
King of Sweden, 67, 74
Albert (Albrecht), Duke of Meck-
lenburg, 74
Alfred the Great, 33
Alting, 32
Altmark, 238-9
Aluminium, 207, 256
American influence, 132, 134, 183,
221, 236, 258; see United States
Amtmann, 101
Amundsen, Roald Engelbregt Grav-
ning (1872-1928), 213
Anglo-Saxon Chronicle, 22, 43
Anker, Carsten Tank (1747-1824),
121, 129, 131, 136, 138
Archaeology, 10-11, 13-17, 24-6, 28-
30, 33-4
Arendal, 13, 121
Armed Neutrality of the North,
119, 121
Army, Organization of, 97, 109
after 1814, 133, 139, 157, 189, 199,
202, 215, 234, 241, 246, 258. See
also Rifle Clubs

Asbjörnsen, Peter Christen (1812-
85), 166-7, 170
Athelstan, 36
Aud the Deepminded, 31

Baahus, Baahuslen, 65, 83, 93, 99,
106-7
Bailiffs, 82, 89, 94, 103, 111, 118, 124
Bank of Norway, 140-1, 164, 230,
244, 253
Banks, 115, 117, 126, 129, 216, 228
Berg, Olav Paal (b.1873), 179, 249
Bergen, Mediaeval, 48-9, 52, 55, 58-
61, 66, 76-9, 81
16th-18th centuries, 83, 85, 87,
92-3, 102, 105, 109, 112-13, 117,
119, 122-3
since 1814, 138, 141, 159-60, 169,
181, 199, 240
Bernadotte (King Charles XIV
John), 125, 127-30, 132, 135-9,
142, 144-7, 149, 151, 154-5
Bible, 91, 123
Birchlegs, 56-8
Birkeland, Kristian Olaf Bernhard
(1867-1917), 207
Björnson, Björnstjerne Martinius
(1832-1910), 150, 162, 169-71,
183, 186-8, 190, 192, 196, 199,
204, 213
Black Death, 70-3, 75
Blanche of Namur, 69
Blücher, 240
Bodö, 145, 233, 244
Bodö Case, 138, 145-6
Bonde, 17, 45; see Peasants
Borgarting, 41
Boston, 61
Boström, E. G., 198
Bouvet Island, 224
Bremen, 42, 47, 53
British Opinion and Influence, 113,
120, 136, 149, 176, 179, 201,

208-10, 212-13, 219, 220, 223, 236, 246, 252, 258
Brofoss, Erik (b.1908), 254
Bull, Ole Bornemann (1810-80), 150, 165, 169
Bygd, 11

Caithness, 27, 51
Canning Industry, 180, 211, 217
Canute, 21, 42-3, 45, 50
Capital, Scarcity and Provision of, 61, 79, 92, 110, 111, 114-15, 122
  since 1814, 140, 159, 161, 181, 183, 207, 222, 253, 256
Carlingford, Battle of, 29
Caroline Matilda, Queen, 116-17, 119
Cassiodorus, 17
Castberg, Johan (1863-1926), 209-11, 218, 231
Castlereagh, 136, 145
Celtic Influences, 16, 25, 28, 31
Charlemagne, 21, 24, 38, 45
Charles V, Emperor, 83, 86, 87
Charles XII of Sweden, 105-7, 225, 235
Charles XIV John, see Bernadotte
Charles XV, 154-8, 175
Charles, Prince, see Haakon
Christian I, 81-2
Christian II, 83-4, 86-7
Christian III, 86-8, 90-4
Christian IV, 94-8
Christian V, 100, 102-5, 111
Christian VI, 116
Christian VII, 116-17, 125
Christian IX of Denmark, 157
Christian August, of Augustenburg, 128
Christian Frederick, Prince and King (Christian VIII of Denmark), 129, 131-8, 144, 152
Christiania, see Oslo
Christianity, see Religion
Christie, Wilhelm Frimann Koren (1778-1849), 138, 141
Christopher of Bavaria, 76
Churches, 48
Climate, 11, 15, 26, 72, 110
Clontarf, Battle of, 37
'Coggs', 78

Colbjörnsen, Christian (1749-1814), 118-19, 129, 135
Collett, Jacobine Camilla (1813-95), 184
Collett, John (1758-1810), 121
Commerce, see Trade
Communist Party, 230, 257
Concession Laws, 208-9, 222
Conservative Party, 177, 190-3, 195, 197, 200, 205, 211, 225-7, 247
Constitution of 1814, 132-5
  development and amendment, 138, 144-8, 150, 173, 177-80, 194
Consular Service, 147, 196-8, 200
Conventicle Ordinance, 112, 124, 148
Co-operative Movement, 165, 232-3, 255
Copenhagen, 83, 87, 95, 99, 105, 109, 111, 113, 116, 120-1, 125, 153, 201
Copper Mining, 96, 120, 219, 256
Corn, Importation of, 49, 61, 66, 73, 78-9, 92, 109, 115, 117-18, 126, 154, 181, 221, 229
Coronations, 55, 57, 82, 83, 142
Cottars, 111, 120, 124, 142, 165, 181, 183, 206, 210
Council, Privy, 62, 69, 75, 76, 83-9
Crimean War, 154, 161
Croziermen, 58-9
Crusades, 51, 54

Dahl, John Christian Clausen (1788-1857), 150
Danegeld, 25, 39-40
Dass, Peter (1647-1707), 112
Denmark, Relations with, 14, 20
  in Viking period, 23, 29, 35, 38-40, 42-5
  mediaeval, 50, 54-5, 57, 66
  since 1814, 130, 134-6, 144, 153-7, 203, 216, 226, 257
Denmark, Union with: establishment, 68-70, 73-7, 81-8
  absolutist period, 100-4, 116-18, 122
  trade relations, 92, 96, 104, 109-110, 122
  foreign policy, 93-4, 97-102, 105-9, 125-9
Douglas, Count, 197-8, 202

Drammen, 164-5, 215
Dublin, 29, 30, 37, 40, 51
Dynekilen, Battle of, 106-7

Edda, Poetic, 32
Edda, Prose, 62
Education, 91, 112, 115-16, 123, 148,
    163, 187, 190, 249
Egede, Hans Poulsen (1686-1758),
    109
Eidsivating, 39
Eidsvoll, 131-2, 141, 149, 159
Einar, Earl of Orkney, 27
Electoral System, 131, 134, 148, 180,
    189, 205, 227, 254
Emigration, 19, 26, 32, 43, 104, 165-
    6, 182-4, 186, 213-14, 228
England, Relations with, in Viking
    period, 22-5, 30, 33, 36, 37-43
    mediaeval, 49-52, 56-8, 61, 63,
    65-6, 78, 83-4
    16th-17th centuries, 91-2, 96, 98,
    101-2, 104-6
    see also United Kingdom, British
    Opinion, Scotland
Eric I Bloodaxe (c.895-954), 38-9
Eric II Priest-hater (1268-99), 64-5
Eric, Duke, of Sweden, 66, 69
Eric of Pomerania, 74-6, 81
Eric the Red, 37, 226
Erling Skakke (c.1115-79), 54, 56
Ethelred the Unready, 25, 39-41
Euphemia, Queen, 65
Eystein, Archbishop (d.1188), 54-7

Factories, 104, 150, 160, 206, 209-11
Faeroes, 26, 31, 40, 53, 56, 60, 129
Feminist Movement, 184, 205
Fimreite, Battle of, 56
Finland, 33, 127-8, 139, 154-5, 195,
    237-8, 257
Finnmark, 11-13, 85, 96, 109, 115,
    154, 251, 253
Fisheries, early history, 10-11, 49,
    78, 80
    since 1814, 141, 160, 180, 208,
    218-21, 228, 233, 255
Flag, History of, 147, 151, 178, 187,
    198
Fogder, 82; see Bailiffs
Fram, 199, 213

France, Relations with, in Viking
    period, 31, 34
    mediaeval, 65, 68
    modern, 119, 125, 129, 132, 134
    after 1830, 146, 149, 155, 157, 159
    241, 243-4
    see also French Revolutions
Franchise, see Electoral System
Frederick I, 84-6
Frederick IV, 105-6
Frederick V, 116
Frederick VI, 117, 125, 128-9
Frederick VII of Denmark, 152-3,
    155
Fredrikstad, 137
Free Trade, 115, 117-18, 147, 158,
    180, 229
French Revolutions, Influence of,
    119, 132, 146, 175
Frey, 18
Friars, 64, 80
Frisians, 25, 26
Frostating, 39, 54
Fulford, Battle of, 50
Fundamentalism, 185, 190-1
Fylke, 18, 47

Garborg, Arne (1851-1924), 190
German Influence, 46, 54, 75, 115,
    128, 196, 217; see also Hanse
Germany, Relations with, 61, 153,
    173-4, 186, 197, 215
    since 1914, 216-21, 235, 237-52,
    257
Godthaab, 109
Gokstad ship, 33-4
Gotland, 76, 81
Great Northern War, 105-8
Greenland, 32, 37, 40, 53, 60-1, 72,
    96, 109, 129, 188, 199, 226, 233
Grieg, Edvard Hagerup (1843-1907),
    167, 185
Griffenfeld, Count, 100, 102
Grimkell, Bishop, 42-4, 47
Gudbrandsdal, 98, 187, 241-3
Gulating, 36, 39
Gyldenlöve, Ulrik Frederik, 102-3

Haakon I the Good (c.920-c.960),
    36, 38-9
Haakon III Sverreson (d.1204), 59
Haakon IV Haakonsson (1204-63),

59-63, 170
Haakon V Magnusson (1270-1319), 65-8
Haakon VI Magnusson (1340-80), 69-70, 73-4
Haakon VII, King (b.1872), 201-5, 240, 244, 248, 252
Hafrsfiord, Battle of, 35-6
Halden, 99, 106-7, 118, 137, 199, 203
Halfdan the Black, 34, 63
Hallvard, Saint (c.1020-c.1043), 49
Hamar, 53, 82, 93
Hambro, Carl Joachim (b.1885), 225, 235
Hamburg, 140
Hammarskjöld, Hjalmar, 217
Hammerfest, 126, 206
Hamsun, Knut (1859-1952), 213
Hans, King, 82
Hanse, Hanseatic League, 66, 74, 76-84, 85-6, 92-3
Harald I Fairhair (c.860-c.940), 35-6, 38, 48
Harald III Hardrada (1015-66), 45, 50
Harald IV Gilchrist (c.1103-c.1136), 52
Harthacnut, 50
Hauge, Hans Nielsen (1771-1824), 122-4
Haugeanism, 122-4, 163, 183, 185, 187, 190
Havamal, 32
Hebrides, 28, 51, 53, 63
Hedeby, 33
Hegra, 241
Heimskringla, 36, 42, 50, 62
Herjedal, 98-9
Hirdmann, 62, 245
Historia Norvegiae, 17, 169
Historical Literature, 58, 62-3, 113, 115, 167-9, 188-9
Hitler, Adolf, 226, 235, 237-9, 245
Holberg, Ludvig, Baron (1684-1754), 112-4
Holland, see Netherlands
Holstein, 81, 104, 129, 155
Horder, 16, 22
Hull, 61
Husmenn, 120; see Cottars
Hydro-electricity, 206-8, 210, 222, 228, 256

Ibsen, Henrik Johan (1828-1906), 82, 158, 169-71, 184-5, 189, 198, 213
Ibsen, Sigurd (1859-1930), 196, 198-9, 204
Iceland, Settlement of, 18, 31-2, 36
conversion, 40, 53
after annexation, 60, 70, 71, 83-4, 115, 129
Ihlen, Nils Claus (1855-1925), 217, 219, 221
Impeachments, 133, 179
Inge I Hunchback (1135-61), 52-3, 56
Inge II Baardsson (1185-1217), 59
Ireland: in Viking period, 25, 28-31, 37, 38, 40, 51
mediaeval, 63
comparison with, 142
modern, 149
Iron, Iron Industry, 10
primitive, 16, 24
modern, 96, 121, 143, 161, 256
Isabella Bruce, Queen, 65

Jaabaek, Sören Pedersen (1814-94), 176, 182
Jan Mayen Island, 223
Jemtland, 60, 98-9
Jews, 149, 251
Jon the Red, Archbishop (d.1282), 64-5
Jostedal, 71
Jury System, 177, 189

Kalmar, Union of, 75
Karl, see Charles
Karlstad, Conventions of, 202-4, 210
Kiel, Treaty of, 129-31, 139, 144
Kielland, Alexander Lange (1849-1906), 190-1
King's Lynn, 61, 66, 81
King's Mirror, The, 62
Kirkenes, 13
Knudsen, Aanon Gunerius (Gunnar) (1848-1928), 204-5, 217, 226-7
Knut Alvsson (c.1455-1502), 82
Koht, Halfdan (b.1873), 234-5, 240
Kongsberg, 96, 141
Kongsvinger, 137, 199, 203
Kristiansand, 13, 97, 137, 240

Labour Movement, Party, 165-6, 190, 201, 208, 211-12, 223, 227, 229-35, 249, 252-5
Lade, 18, 35, 40
Lade, Earls of, 35-6, 38-40, 43
Lagting, 45, 46
after 1814, 133, 179
Lake District of England, Settlement in, 30
Landsmaal, see Language
Lange, Christian Louis (1869-1938), 225
Lange, Halvard Marithey (b.1902), 258
Language, Development of the, 14, 19, 47, 53, 57, 90, 167, 169, 171-2, 190, 205, 227
Lapps, 13, 15, 33, 96, 109, 203
Largs, Battle of, 63
Latin, Use of, 47, 80-1, 95, 113, 163
Law, Legal System, primitive, 18
mediaeval, 39, 45-7, 63-4
17th century, 95, 103
modern, 147, 160, 162
Leads, The, 11-14, 19, 102, 126, 218, 221, 238, 242
League of Nations, 224-5, 234-5, 237
Left, see Liberal
Leidang, 39, 58, 78
Leprosy, 142, 188
Lex Regia, 100-2, 132
Liberal Party, 173, 177-80, 189-93, 205, 227-31, 247
Lie, Trygve Halvdan (b.1896), 247, 257
Linge Company, 250
Liquor Laws, 143, 162-3, 205, 227-8
Literature, Mediaeval, 62, 65
16th-18th centuries, 95, 112-14, 120
19-20th centuries, 148-50, 166-72, 184-8, 213, 235
Local self-government (1837), 148
Lofoten Islands, 13, 49, 61, 109, 145
Lofthus, Christian Jensen (1750-97), 118-19
London, Viking Attacks, 37, 40, 41
trade relations, 49, 77, 104, 120-1, 160-1, 202
Long Serpent, The, 40
Lübeck, 77, 86, 92, 139
Lumber Trade, see Timber

Lund, 53, 57
Lunge, Vincens (1486/7-1536), 85-7, 90, 92
Lyrskog Heath, Battle of, 50

Maere, 18, 38
Magic, see Religion
Magnus I the Good (1024-47), 45, 46, 50
Magnus III Bareleg (1073-1103), 51
Magnus IV the Blind (c.1115-39), 52
Magnus V Erlingsson (1156-84), 54-6
Magnus VI Law-mender (1238-80), 62-4, 95
Magnus VII Eriksson (1316-74), 66-70
Magnus, Erlendsson, Earl and Saint (c.1080-1115), 51
Malmö meeting of kings, 216
Man, Isle of, 28, 51, 53, 63
Manus, Max (b.1914), 250
Margaret, Maid of Norway (1283-90), 65
Margaret, Queen, 69-70, 73-5, 152
Market-place, Battle of the (1829), 146, 149
Maud, Queen, 201, 203, 212
Mercantile Marine, Growth of the, 92, 104-5, 114, 119, 121
after 1814, 140, 160-2, 180-1, 196, 207, 215, 218, 222, 227, 231, 237, 246, 253, 256
Methodism, 122, 183
Michelsen, Peter Christian Hersleb Kjerschow (1857-1925), 199-205, 209
Middle Class, Growth of, 89, 92-3, 104, 121, 140, 152, 166, 222, 228-9
'Milorg', 249-51
Mining, 10, 96, 208, 254
Ministers, Position of, 133-4, 144, 152, 156, 175, 177-80, 240
Moe, Jörgen Engebretsen (1813-82), 166-7, 170
Molde, 243
Monarchy, Origin and Growth, 36, 44-5, 52, 54-5, 57-9, 65, 74
in 20th century, 201, 203-5, 252
Monasteries, 48, 52, 64, 71, 81, 85, 90
Moors, 30-31, 51
Morier, John Philip, 137

Moss, 106
    Convention of, 137-8
Moster, 42
Mowinckel, Johan Ludwig (1870-1943), 220, 231
Munch, Edvard (1863-1944), 213
Munch, Peter Andreas (1810-63), 167-9

Namsos, 242-3
Nansen, Fridtjof (1861-1930), 187-8, 199-201, 203, 221, 224-6
Nansen, Hans, 100
Narvik, 13, 159, 203, 238, 240-4
National Budget, 254
NATO, 258
Navigation Acts (British), 104, 114, 140, 161
Navy, Organization of, 38-9, 97, 109, 126, 199, 215, 216, 221, 241, 244, 246
Naze Kings, 18
Nazi Party (Norwegian), 231, 245, 248-9, 252
Netherlands, Relations with the, 78, 84, 91-2, 97, 101-2, 104-6
Newspapers and Periodicals, 119, 150, 164, 171, 176, 182, 184, 187, 221
Nicholas Arneson, Bishop (c.1145-1225), 57-8
Nicholas Breakspear, Cardinal, 53-4
Nidaros, see Trondheim
Nobel Prizes, 187, 225, 236
Nobility, 57-8, 69, 75, 82, 85, 89, 94
    abolition, 143-4
Nordic 'Race', 14, 20, 168
Nordland, 12, 49, 112
Normandy, 27, 31, 41, 45
Norsk Hydro, 207, 222, 229
North Norway, 12, 33, 35, 40, 43, 69, 79, 96, 109, 112, 123, 126
    since 1814, 142, 143, 207, 211, 223, 237-7, 247, 255, 258
Northern Council, 259
Northumbria, 30, 36, 37, 39, 50
Norwegian-Americans, 19, 182-4, 214, 247
November Treaty (1855), 154, 214
Nygaardsvold, Johan (1879-1952), 230-1, 234

Odal Tenure, 17, 27, 103, 120, 133
Odelsting, 133, 179
Odin, 18, 23, 24, 32
Official Class, 58, 61-2, 71
    in Danish period, 75, 91, 101, 115-16, 118, 124
    after 1814, 132, 143, 147-8, 152, 174, 177-9, 190, 195
Ohthere, 33
Olaf I Tryggveson (968-1000), 39-40, 42
Olaf II Saint (995-1030), 41-4
Olaf III the Peaceful (c.1050-1093), 47, 49
Olaf IV Haakonsson (1370-87), 70, 74
Olaf V, King (b. 1903), 203, 259
Olaf, Crown Prince (b.1903), 203
Olaf Engelbriktsson, Archbishop (c.1480-1538), 85-7
Olaf the White, 29-31, 35
Old Norse, 32, 90, 169, 170-1
Öreting, 18, 46
Orkney Islands, 27-8, 36, 51, 58, 60, 63, 65, 75, 82
Oscar I, 139, 151, 153-5
Oscar II, 175, 178-9, 197, 200-1, 203
Oseberg Ship, 33-4
Oslo, 11, 12
    in middle ages, 48-9, 57-8, 61, 65-6, 70, 76, 82-3, 86-7
    modern, 97, 106, 116, 121
    since 1814, 136-7, 141, 143, 146, 159-60, 169, 197, 206, 208, 236, 240, 242, 249-50
Oslofiord, 12, 35, 41, 241
Oslo Convention (1930), 234

Paris, Matthew, 68
Parties, see Conservative, etc.
Peasant Class, 17, 41, 45, 55, 72, 89, 90, 94, 96, 98, 103, 106, 110-11, 118, 121-2
    after 1814, 131, 133-4, 143, 156, 185-7, 229, 230
Peasant Opposition (in Storting), 147-8, 151-2, 159, 167, 171, 176-7
Peerson, Cleng, 143, 182
Perth, Treaty of (1266), 63
Peter I Island, 224
Philippa, Queen, 75-6
Physical Features, 9-13

Picts, 26, 27, 30
Pietism, 111-12, 116, 122-3
Place-names, 19, 20, 26, 227
Polar Exploration, 199, 213
Polish Troops, 243
Population, 20, 26, 71, 110, 120, 122, 142, 181, 209
Prehistoric Period, 13-21
President of the Storting, 138, 178
Prohibition, see Liquor Laws
Proportional Representation, 205, 227, 254
Pytheas, 15
Quantum Saws, 104
Queen Maud's Land, 224
Quirini, Pietro, 79-81, 115
Quisling, Vidkun Abraham Lauritz Jonssön (1887-1945), 229, 239-40, 242, 245, 252

Radicals, 191, 196-7, 200, 203, 210
Ragnarok, 24, 32
Railways, 10, 159, 233, 254
Religion, pre-Christian, 13, 15, 17-18, 23-4, 28, 47
period of conversion, 38-42
mediaeval church, 46-9, 52-5, 57-9, 64-5
Reformation, 84-7, 90-1, 95, 102
modern, 185, 187, 190-1, 205, 249
see also Pietism, Haugeanism
Republicanism, 149, 186-7, 194, 204-5
Rifle Clubs, Volunteer, 178, 189
Rjukan, 207-8, 250
Roads, 10, 96, 159, 233
Rolf the Ganger (Rollo) (c.870-c̀.930), 27
Rölvaag, Ole Edvart (1876-1931), 183
Roman Empire, Influence of, 16, 30, 48
Röros, 96, 120
Röst, 79-80
Rostock, 66, 85
Ruge, General Otto (b.1882), 241, 244
Runes, 16, 24
Russia, Relations with: in Viking period, 25, 39, 43-5
mediaeval, 60, 65,
16th-18th centuries, 96, 106, 120

since 1800, 127-9, 132, 145, 153-4, 161, 223-4, 234, 237-8, 249, 251, 257-8
Ryger, 16

Sagas, 27, 30-3, 58, 62-3
Sars, Johan Ernst Welhaven (1835-1917), 188-9
Sars, Michael (1805-69), 188
Scandinavianism, 20, 70, 73, 127, 152-8, 169-70, 216, 225-6, 247, 257-9
Scania, 74, 77, 99, 127, 153
Schleswig, 74, 81, 153, 155, 157, 186
Schleswig-Holstein, 109, 122, 125, 153, 157, 164
Schumacher, Peder, see Griffenfeld
Schweigaard, Anton Martin (1808-70), 158-60, 162
Scotland, Relations with: in Viking period, 30, 31, 37
mediaeval, 51, 53, 58, 63, 65, 82
modern, 92, 97, 246
see also United Kingdom
Sehested, Hannibal, 98
Selmer, Christian August (1816-89), 178-9
Seter, 10
Seven Years War of the North (1563-70), 93
Shetland Islands, 21, 26-27, 36, 82, 248
Ships and Shipbuilding, 13, 24, 33-4, 78, 97, 121
after 1814, 160, 180, 227, 246, 253, 256
see also Mercantile Marine
Sigurd I the Crusader, 51-2
Sigvat Thordarson, 41-2
Sinclair Expedition (1612), 97-8
Skalds, 24, 41, 187
Skiringsal, 33, 48
Skule Baardsson, Duke (1188/9-1240), 59, 62, 170
Slaves, 31, 45
Snorre Sturlason, 62; quoted, 35, 42
Social Conditions, prehistoric, 17, 34
mediaeval, 46, 60-1, 70-2, 79-81
early modern, 89-91, 102-4, 110-16, 120-1

19th-20th centuries, 142-3, 164,
  182, 206, 210-11, 231, 253, 255
Social Reforms, Modern, 162-4, 195,
  231-2, 236, 255
Socialism, see Labour Party
Societies: Trondheim Scientific, 115
  for the Welfare of Norway, 128
  for the Limitation of Emigration,
  213
  Norwegian Association, 214
  Northern Society, 225
Sogne Fiord, 34, 71
Söröya, 251
Spain, Relations with, 228
Spitsbergen, 223, 258
Stamford Bridge, Battle of, 45, 50
Stang, Emil (1834-1912), 195, 197
Stang, Frederik (1808-84), 174-5,
  177-8
Statholders, 138, 144, 146-7, 156,
  174-5
Stavanger, 48, 85, 141, 143, 147, 180,
  233
Stavkirker, 48
Steamers, 159, 180-1, 207; see also
  Ships
Stiklestad, Battle of, 43-4
Stockholm, 77, 84, 200
  Norwegian Ministers in, 135, 151,
  154, 175, 192, 198, 200
Storting, Organization of, 133-4,
  177, 200
Struensee, Johann Friederich,
  Count, 117
Sturla Tordsson, 60, 62
Submarine Warfare, Effects of,
  218-22, 242, 246
Suderöerne, see Hebrides
Sundt, Eilert Lund (1817-75), 163-4
Sunniva, Saint, 48
Supreme Court, 126, 134, 179, 245,
  248-9
Sutherland, 27, 51
Svalbard, see Spitsbergen
Sverdrup, Jakob Liv Rosted (1845-
  99), 190
Sverdrup, Johan (1816-92), 173-80,
  183-4, 189-92
Sverre Sigurdsson (c.1150-1202), 56-
  59, 60, 62
Svolder, Battle of, 40
Sweden, Relations with, 12, 13

in early history, 20, 33
  mediaeval, 56, 66, 68-70, 73-6,
  81-2, 84
  1563-1810, 93, 97-9, 102, 105-7,
  126-9
  since 1905, 214, 216-17, 247-8,
  257-8
Sweden, Union with (1814-1905),
  128-30, 135-9, 145-7, 156, 161-2,
  174-5, 192, 194-204
Swithun, Saint, 48

Tankers, 227, 237, 246
Tariff, 105, 115, 145, 147, 158-9, 197
Taxation, 32, 36, 54, 83, 89, 94, 103,
  116-18, 133, 142, 176, 217, 222,
  255
Telegraph and Telephone, 159, 180,
  206
Telemark, 241
Tenant Farmers, 45, 55, 72, 103, 111,
  131
Theatres, 113, 169-70
Thor, 23
Thrane, Marcus Möller (1817-90),
  164-6, 176, 232
Timber Trade, 13, 50, 91-2, 104, 119,
  121, 126
  after 1814, 133, 140, 180, 207
  see also Woodworking Industries
Ting, 18, 26, 27, 39, 42, 63-4, 133, 148
Tithe, 51, 55, 91
Tönsberg, 48, 55, 58, 65, 69, 76
Tönsberg, Concordat of, 64-5
Torbjörn Hornklove, 36
Tordenskjold, Peder Wessel, Baron
  (1691-1720), 107-8
Torgils, 29
Tourists, 120, 173, 185, 212, 235-6
Towns, Growth and Government
  of, 11, 48, 61, 64, 96-7, 103-4,
  114, 118, 121
  since 1814, 133, 141, 148, 158-9,
  164, 236
Trade, Internal, 24, 35, 104, 110,
  114-15, 159-60, 182, 206, 229, 256
Trade, Overseas, 21, 48, 49, 60-1, 66,
  78-9, 80
  16th-18th centuries, 91-4, 104-5,
  109-10, 114-15, 121
  since 1814, 141, 158-60, 180, 217-
  21, 227-8, 231, 234, 237, 256, 259

Trade Unions, 211-12, 229-30, 232
Tranmael, Martin Olsen (b.1879),
    211-12, 223, 230, 234
Troms, 12, 251
Tromsö, 33, 257
Tröndelag, 12, 14, 16, 18, 35, 40, 41,
    43, 56, 91, 99, 129
Trondheim, in early history, 12, 18,
    43-4, 48, 53, 55-6, 59, 61, 64,
    80-2, 86-7
    modern, 91, 98-9, 102, 107, 109,
    115, 119, 122, 131, 141-2, 197,
    240-3
Trondheim Cathedral, 43, 54-5, 57,
    61, 168

Ueland, Ole Gabriel Gabrielson
    (1799-1870), 147-8, 151, 174, 176
Undset, Sigrid (1882-1949), 235
Union, Act of (1814), 139
United Kingdom, Relations with,
    119-21, 125-9
    1814-1905, 135-7, 140, 145, 154,
    157, 160-1, 201-3
    since 1905, 208-9, 214, 217-21, 234,
    236-44, 250-3, 259
United Nations, 257
United States, Relations with, 114,
    132, 134, 143, 182, 214
    since 1914, 221, 247, 253, 258
University, 114, 117, 128, 141, 152-3,
    205, 249
Uplands, 12, 34, 35, 41
Uppsala, 20, 33, 155

Varangians, 23
Vardöhus, 65, 96
Vestfold, 12, 19, 20, 29, 33, 35
Veto, Royal, 134, 144, 148, 151, 156,
    178-9, 197, 200

Viceroys, 83, 89, 98, 102, 129, 154,
    156
Victual Brothers, 77-8
Viking Expeditions, 21-42, 45, 51
Vinje, Aasmund Olavsson (1818-
    70), 171, 174, 190
Vinland, 37
Voluspaa, 32

Waldemar IV, 69-70, 73-4
Waldemar, Prince, 203
Wales, Relations with, 30, 38, 58
    comparison, 90
Walkendorf, Eric, Archbishop, 83-4
Wedel Jarlsberg, Fredrik (Fritz)
    Hartvig Herman (1855-1942),
    201, 203, 223
Wedel Jarlsberg, Johan Caspar
    Herman, Count (1779-1840),
    126-8, 134-5, 138, 147, 175
Welhaven, Johan Sebastian Cam-
    mermayer (1807-73), 149
Wends, 50
Wergeland, Henrik Arnold (1808-
    45), 148-50, 162, 167, 188, 204
Wergeland, Nicolai (1780-1848),
    149
Wessel, Johan Herman (1742-85),
    116
Whaling, 19, 109, 180, 208, 223, 226,
    227, 253, 256
William of Sabina, Cardinal, 60
Woodworking Industries, 180, 207,
    222, 228, 256
World War, First, 216-23
World War, Second, 237-52

Ynglings, 33
York, 37, 39, 44, 50

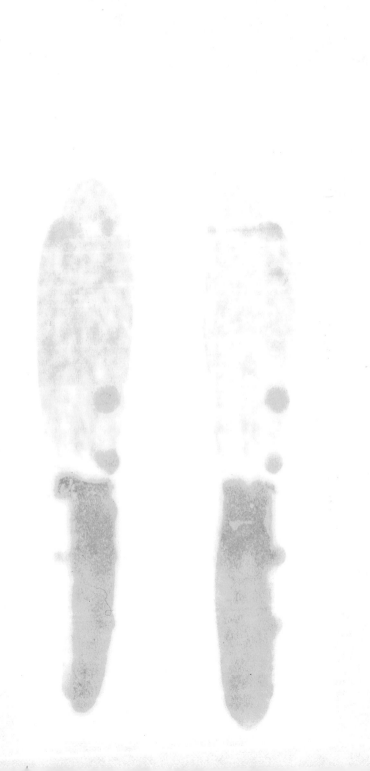

pocket inside

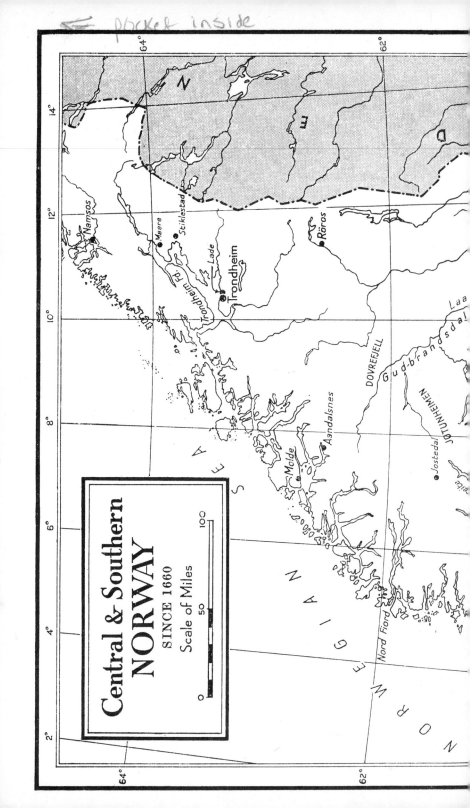

Central & Southern NORWAY

SINCE 1660

Scale of Miles